FOR Dummies™
BESTSELLING BOOK SERIES

Mixed Breeds For Dummies®

Questions to Ask When Adopting a Rescue Dog

Rescue dogs can make excellent pets and companions. When you're considering a rescue dog, be sure to ask the following questions:

- What is the gender of the dog? Has the dog been spayed or neutered?
- How old is the dog?
- What is the breed mix?
- How big is the dog?
- Is the dog housetrained?
- Does the dog live well with other dogs, cats, and/or children?
- Does the dog have any behavioral problems?

- Where is the dog currently living? Indoors or out? Pen, crate, or loose?
- What are you feeding the dog? Does the dog have any food allergies?
- Can I come meet the dog? If you do go to meet the dog, pay close attention to his living conditions and evaluate his temperament (see the "Temperament Testing" section on this Cheat Sheet).

Temperament Testing

When you're considering bringing a dog into your home, you want to test his temperament to see how he'll respond in a variety of situations. Here's how:

1. **Touch the dog all over.**

   Does he flinch when you touch any area of his body? For example, does he put his mouth on you when you touch his toes? Or, does he become a marshmallow and allow you to touch him all over? *Hint:* Marshmallows are sweet.

2. **Roll some toys across the floor. Toss some keys. Drop a book.**

   If the dog is bothered by specific objects or movement, he'll require a lot of patience and encouragement — but he can still be a great all-around dog.

3. **Lift the dog's front end, leaving his hind legs on the floor.**

   If he struggles when you pick him up, he likely has dominant tendencies. A dominant dog may be more challenging to live with than one who is submissive. A dominant dog requires an assertive owner who will take the time to train him and maintain a very scheduled lifestyle, while a submissive dog will tend to naturally fall into his place within your family, though he would likely benefit from training, too.

4. **Give the dog a toy, and then take the toy away.**

   If he grabs the toy from your hands or tries to keep you from taking the toy from him, he may be possessive. If the dog has possessive tendencies, he can be dangerous for young children. Only a very assertive guardian should adopt this dog — someone who will be persistent and fair. A giving dog will be more fun to play with and less likely to injure youngsters or other dogs.

5. **Crouch down and clap your hands.**

   If the dog comes to you readily, he's likely very friendly and social. If not, he may be shy. A dog who is shy will require a quiet home without youngsters. He'll need time to acclimate to new situations, so his guardians need to be patient. An outgoing dog will usually be a better combination with other dogs, people, and especially children.

Mixed Breeds For Dummies®

Cheat Sheet

Gear Up!

Before you bring your mixed-breed dog home, you'll need lots of supplies on hand. Here's a shopping list to take with you to the local pet store or to have near your computer when you shop online:

- **Travel crate:** The crate should be big enough for your dog to turn around, stand, and lie comfortably.

- **Travel bowls:** Travel bowls are made of collapsible canvas with nylon water-proof lining. They fold up and are easy to store.

- **A collar and leash:** Your dog should have a comfortable collar made of cotton or nylon that can be adjusted easily as he grows or fills out. The leash should be sturdy, but not too thick to hold securely in your hand. I suggest a ½-inch-wide, 6-foot-long leather leash.

- **Food:** Make sure you have at least a two-week supply of the food the dog is currently being fed. If you want to switch his food, do so gradually over a period of two weeks, mixing the new food in with the old.

- **Dishes:** If the dog is small, you can use any kind of dish, because he's not likely to destroy it. If you have a medium to large dog, get stainless steel dishes — they can't be destroyed and are easily cleaned. Also keep the bowls the appropriate size for the dog — small dishes for small dogs and big dishes for big dogs.

- **Crate or pen:** You can either get a crate or pen that fits the dog's current size, or buy one that will fit the dog when he's fully grown. If you get a crate for your puppy to grow into, be sure to buy a divider so that he doesn't get too much space too soon. (If he has too much space, he may be prone to peeing or pooping at one end and sleeping at the other.)

- **Bedding:** Choose a bed that's big enough for your dog and that's more likely to be chew-proof. If your dog is not yet housetrained, you can get a waterproof bed, too.

- **A variety of toys:** Stay away from sticks, chips, and anything that can cause allergic reactions. Get your dog hollow toys that can be filled with food, or sturdy toys that your dog isn't likely to chew through. If you want to test your new dog to find out if he'll destroy a plush toy, buy one without strings, plastic parts, or color dyes, and keep an eye on your dog when he plays with the toy.

Online Dog Supplies

Need lots of supplies? Get 'em cheap and delivered to your door. These sites offer discounted supplies, food, and medications, giving you from 10 percent to 50 percent off a similar purchase at a pet-supply store:

- **1-800-PetMeds:** www.petmeds.com
- **J-B Wholesale Pet Supplies, Inc.:** www.jbpet.com
- **Jeffers Pet:** www.jefferspet.com
- **Omaha Vaccine Company:** www.omahavaccine.com
- **PetEdge.com:** www.petedge.com
- **PetFoodDirect.com:** www.petfooddirect.com
- **UPCO:** www.upco.com

Note: Prior to ordering medications from any online pharmacy, check out www.fda.gov/fdac/features/2006/600_pets.html to make sure you're not purchasing counterfeit or expired drugs.

Mixed Breeds

FOR

DUMMIES®

by Miriam Fields-Babineau

Wiley Publishing, Inc.

Mixed Breeds For Dummies®

Published by
Wiley Publishing, Inc.
111 River St.
Hoboken, NJ 07030-5774
www.wiley.com

Copyright © 2007 by Wiley Publishing, Inc., Indianapolis, Indiana

Published simultaneously in Canada

For general information on our other products and services, please contact our Customer Care Department within the U.S. at 800-762-2974, outside the U.S. at 317-572-3993, or fax 317-572-4002.

For technical support, please visit www.wiley.com/techsupport.

Wiley also publishes its books in a variety of electronic formats. Some content that appears in print may not be available in electronic books.

Library of Congress Control Number: 2007925989

ISBN: 978-0-470-12087-3

Manufactured in the United States of America

10 9 8 7 6 5 4 3 2 1

WILEY

About the Author

Miriam Fields-Babineau has been a professional animal trainer since 1978 and has enjoyed exhibiting horses and dogs since childhood. She holds degrees in psychology and zoology from the University of Maryland. She is a member of the Dog Writers' Association and the Cat Writers' Association and is listed in numerous editions of *Who's Who in America*.

Fields-Babineau has been writing professionally since her first article was published in *Canine Chronicle* in 1986. She is the author of 35 books including *Click & Easy: Clicker Training for Dogs; Cat Training in 10 Minutes; Labradoodle: Comprehensive Owner's Guide; The ABCs of Positive Training; Training Your Mixed Breed; Training Your Puppy in 5 Minutes; Raising Dogs the Natural Way; The Perfect Retriever;* and *Multiple Dog Households*. She has also published three short stories (one of which appeared in *Christmas Cats: A Literary Anthology* for Penguin, USA) and two novels: *The Tocharian,* a romantic fantasy-adventure, and *Evil,* a thriller.

She has provided animal actors for media productions since 1983, participating in the filming of commercials, advertisements, TV programs, videos, and feature films.

Fields-Babineau also designed the Comfort Trainer head halter for dogs, the All-in-One Leash, and the Clicker Spoon training tool for cats. Miriam Fields-Babineau currently resides in beautiful Amherst, Virginia, with her husband, Mike; son, Brendon Kyle; four dogs; four cats; and two horses.

Dedication

For my mother, Dr. Rona M. Fields, who instilled in me the desire to succeed regardless of the obstacles.

For my first mixed breed dog, Huxley, who gave her loyalty and love to three growing children.

For my current mixed-breed dog, Princess, who's thrilled to be loved, though she believes that entails sitting in someone's lap — even though she weighs 50 pounds.

To my husband, for his patience, love, and dedication to all I do.

Author's Acknowledgments

Because I've been writing books for 15 years, I've long been aware of the difficulty of bringing them to press and promoting their sale. Both my parents are writers, so you can say it's in my blood. Regardless of whether or not my writing was published, the sheer art and use of my imagination was the reward. However, several of my publishers have made the art more enjoyable. Wiley Publishing is one of them.

I'd like to thank all those at Wiley Publishing who have had the faith in me to produce the book they envisioned, especially Stacy Kennedy, my acquisitions editor, whom I've known for many years. I'd also like to thank my project editor, Elizabeth Kuball, for her endless support, helpful suggestions, and the ability to keep me on my toes and delivering the work in short order, regardless of my hectic schedule.

Thanks also to Jean Krason, DVM, who let me pick her brain while we worked on a West Virginia Lottery television commercial together with her Australian Shepherd, Kaila. During our waiting periods (of which there are many in production work), she helped me learn more about breed-related health issues, as well as general veterinary and first-aid information.

Thanks also, to Nicole Quinn, DVM, my technical editor, for maintaining my accuracy.

Most of all, I want to thank all the mixed-breed dogs I've known and trained, because nobody teaches a trainer more than the animal students she works with.

Publisher's Acknowledgments

We're proud of this book; please send us your comments through our Dummies online registration form located at www.dummies.com/register/.

Some of the people who helped bring this book to market include the following:

Acquisitions, Editorial, and Media Development

Project Editor: Elizabeth Kuball

Acquisitions Editor: Stacy Kennedy

Copy Editor: Elizabeth Kuball

Technical Editor: Nicole Quinn, DVM

Editorial Manager: Michelle Hacker

Consumer Editorial Supervisor and Reprint Editor: Carmen Krikorian

Editorial Assistants: Erin Calligan Mooney, Joe Niesen, Leeann Harney, and David Lutton

Cover Photos: © Legacy Photography

Cartoons: Rich Tennant (www.the5thwave.com)

Composition Services

Project Coordinator: Heather Kolter

Layout and Graphics: Joyce Haughey, Stephanie D. Jumper, Laura Pence, Brent Savage

Illustrator: Barbara Frake

Anniversary Logo Design: Richard Pacifico

Proofreaders: Aptara, Cynthia Fields, Susan Moritz, Christine Pingleton

Indexer: Aptara

Publishing and Editorial for Consumer Dummies

Diane Graves Steele, Vice President and Publisher, Consumer Dummies

Joyce Pepple, Acquisitions Director, Consumer Dummies

Kristin A. Cocks, Product Development Director, Consumer Dummies

Michael Spring, Vice President and Publisher, Travel

Kelly Regan, Editorial Director, Travel

Publishing for Technology Dummies

Andy Cummings, Vice President and Publisher, Dummies Technology/General User

Composition Services

Gerry Fahey, Vice President of Production Services

Debbie Stailey, Director of Composition Services

Contents at a Glance

Table of Contents

Introduction

A mixed-breed dog, as the name implies, is one that's a mix of two or more breeds — as opposed to purebred dogs, which can trace their lineage back to purebred parents and grandparents and on and on. Believe it or not, mixed-breed dogs are more numerous than purebred dogs and, until recently, they were thought of as less-than-ideal pets and companions. But with the new designer-dog hybrid craze, all that has drastically changed. Many people are willing to spend upwards of $2,000 for a mixed-breed dog just because they know the dog's parents were purebreds.

Even though mixed-breed dogs — designer or not — may not have consistent attributes (like size and appearance), they can make *great* companions, often with fewer physical problems than pedigreed dogs.

I should know: I've been training dogs for more than 30 years. Plus, my studies in psychology and zoology have gone a long way toward helping me understand why dogs behave the way they do. I've written and published numerous articles and books about dogs, their behavior, care, breed specifics, and training. I've researched numerous breeds, including their characteristics and behavior. And as a professional trainer, I've worked with many breeds and breed mixes, teaching them to behave and live harmoniously with their human companions as well as other animals.

In this book, I've brought together all the material you need to help you live with and train your mixed-breed dog. **Remember:** A dog doesn't have to have a pedigree to be a good companion. It merely has to have quality care, guidance, consistency, and understanding. *Mixed Breeds For Dummies* will help you develop a great relationship with your mixed-breed dog.

About This Book

Although you'll find all kinds of useful information in each chapter of this book, you don't have to read it all to benefit from it. Each chapter contains all the tools you need to accomplish specific goals.

Though this book declares to be about mixed-breed dogs it's actually about *all* dogs, because mixed-breed dogs are the combinations of many dogs. Although designer dogs are actually hybrids, consisting of the breeding of two purebreds, mixed breeds often contain more than two breeds — sometimes as many as ten, or more, depending on the genetics of the parents. The information in this book pertains to all breeds of dogs, so whether you have a mixed breed or a pure-bred dog, you'll benefit from reading this book.

Also, it's true that I have lots of credentials — from degrees to publications to hands-on experience — but this book isn't about my standing up on a soapbox and lecturing you. I know you're busy, so in this book, I tell you only what you need to know and nothing that you don't.

Conventions Used in This Book

Because dogs are living, breathing, thinking creatures, deserving respect, I don't refer to them as *it* — instead, I use *he* or *she,* even if the dog is neutered or spayed (always a good idea). I also try to alternate the use of *he* and *she,* to keep the peace. Finally, I use just a few conventions you should be aware of:

- ✔ Whenever I define a new term, I put the term in *italics* and define it shortly thereafter (often in parentheses).

- ✔ Any numbered steps that you're supposed to follow appear in **bold.**

- ✔ I put all Web addresses and e-mail addresses in `monofont`. *Note:* When this book was printed, some Web addresses may have needed to break across two lines of text. If that happened, rest assured that I haven't put in any extra characters (such as hyphens) to indicate the break. So, when using one of these Web addresses, just type in exactly what you see in this book, pretending as though the line break doesn't exist.

What You're Not to Read

If you're short on time, you can safely skip the sidebars (text in gray boxes) — the information they contain is interesting but not critical. You can also skip any paragraphs marked by the Technical Stuff icon (see "Icons Used in This Book, later in this Introduction, for more information).

Foolish Assumptions

Because you've picked up this book I assume you're not a dummy. You're either thinking of getting a mixed-breed dog or you already own one. Plus, the fact that you want to find out more about your dog makes you exceptionally intelligent. I make some other assumptions about you:

✔ I assume you have, or are about to get, a mixed-breed dog because you wanted a unique individual to love and live with.

✔ I assume that you want just the facts you need to make certain you accomplish your goals. You don't want all the scientific jargon and terminology explaining the background of each topic.

✔ I assume you have a big heart to take on a dog and give her a happy home.

How This Book Is Organized

I divided *Mixed Breeds For Dummies* into six easy-to-follow parts in which you can either find out more about your dog's background or get into the meat of care, training, or fun activities.

You don't have to read the parts or chapters in any particular order, because each is self-contained. Read the chapters that are of the most interest to you first and if you have the time and desire, read the others.

Part 1: Just the Facts Ma'am

The hidden lives of mixed-breed dogs. This section delves into the dark alleys and vacant buildings; places that dogs meet, breed, and bear their young with very little, if any, human intervention. Also in this section you can read about the designer-dog craze. What constitutes a designer dog and why they are so popular that people are willing to spend thousands of dollars on one?

Each mixed breed is an individual — one of a kind. In order to understand your dog, you have to find out as much as you can about his genetic attributes, which will contribute to his overall behavior and demeanor.

In this part, I also show you where to find a mixed-breed dog and how to temperament-test him so that you can ensure you'll give him a forever home and he'll always be part of your heart. From an animal shelter, to breeder, to foster care, there are many places to find mixed-breed dogs — but you'll need to look around a bit before knowing which dog is right for you. You'll know it's the right dog when you feel your heart say, "Wow! I can't live without that dog!"

Part 11: Living with Your Mixed-Breed Dog

After you choose your dog, you'll need to prepare for her. From her first day in your home, you'll need to give her specific household rules. Also, dogs require a special space for containment. And, for the sake of your dog's safety, you'll need to remove dangerous or loose articles that may be chewed or eaten.

So many pet products are available — how will you know what to buy? Don't worry — in this part, I give you a list of the items you'll need.

This part also explains the importance of proper nutrition, veterinary care, grooming, bathing, and daily checks for injury, parasites, and abnormalities.

Part III: Training 101

One of the first things you have to do with a new dog is housetraining. Chapter 10 tells you how, along with scheduling the relief times, crate training, and guiding your dog to go in a specific area. This chapter also shows you how to teach a small dog how to use an indoor potty zone such as paper or a litter pan. A very special part of this chapter covers how to teach your dog to ring a bell to let you know he has to relieve himself.

Basic training is a must for any dog. This section covers all you need to prepare yourself and your dog for positive reinforcement techniques, so both of you will have fun. From the three steps of training success — lure, click, and reward — to simple commands and distraction proofing. Chapter 11 also explains how to find a professional trainer and the various approaches to dog training.

Some mixed-breed dogs who come from shelters or unhappy backgrounds may have some behavioral issues that you'll have to deal with. Chapter 12 explains how to recognize the symptoms of separation anxiety along with how to help your dog overcome this prevalent problem. I also tell you how to deal with some common behavior problems, such as jumping up, begging, nipping, digging, and chewing.

Part IV: Keeping Your Dog Healthy

I begin this part by telling you how to find a good veterinarian, as well as the ins and outs of neutering/spaying, one of the most important aspects of being responsible for a mixed-breed dog. From regular check-ups to vaccinations and controlling parasites, your veterinarian can help you keep your mixed-breed dog in the pinnacle of health and well-being.

In this part, I also cover first aid — a very important topic. Throughout your dog's life, anything can happen — from injuries to illness, from poisoning to weather-related reactions, such as heat stroke.

As your mixed-breed dog ages, she'll have specific health issues that need to be addressed. Your dog's behavior will also change with age. She'll be slower to respond, because her eyesight and hearing aren't as sharp as when she was younger. In this part, I explain why and how these changes may affect your senior dog.

Sadly, you'll need to know when it's the right time to say good-bye to your old friend. In this part I help you move on from the loss of your dog and help you know when to give love to a new one.

Part V: Having Fun with Your Dog

Dog shows aren't just for purebred dogs. Several mixed-breed dog clubs offer the same opportunities to show off your mixed breed.

One of the most exciting activities I'm involved with is production work. My mixed-breed dog, Princess, has been an actress since she completed her obedience training. Film directors love the unique appearance of mixed-breed dogs. There'll never be a shortage of work for them in TV commercials and feature films. In this part, I tell you how you and your dog can see his name in lights.

If you enjoy outdoor activities, you're bound to find a mixed-breed dog who will love to share them with you. From hiking, camping, and boating to swimming and horseback riding, I know my own mixed breed can't get enough. I'm sure your dog will love it, too.

Knowing what to pack when traveling with your dog is very important. Chapter 17 explains how to prepare for a trip and what to bring with you while traveling. Plus, it discusses what to do if your dog decides to go for a walkabout while you're away from home.

What will you do for your dog when you can't bring him with you? You have many options, and knowing more about them will help you make the right decision for your dog and you. In this part, I fill you in.

Part VI: The Part of Tens

Ah, one of the most fun parts of a *For Dummies* book, The Part of Tens.

Knowing why you absolutely must neuter or spay your dog is a key part of owning one in the first place. In this part, I tell you how spaying/neutering can be helpful to your dog, how it can be helpful to you, and how it can be helpful to your community.

I end the book with a chapter on ten places to find mixed-breed events. There'll be no shortage of activities you can do with your dog.

Icons Used in This Book

Icons are those little eye-catching pictures in the margin of this book. These icons are eye-catching for a reason: They flag important information. Here's what they mean:

The Tip icon helps you solve problems faster or explains an easier way to approach an issue.

The Warning icon prevents you from doing something dangerous to your dog, yourself, or others. Heed this icon!

The Technical Stuff icon precedes interesting information, though not vital to your mixed-breed dog's well-being. Although you really don't need to read the information preceded by a Technical Stuff icon, you won't lose much time doing so, and it may help you understand your dog better.

The Remember icon helps you stay on track in maintaining your dog's health and well-being. This information is so important I may say it twice!

Where to Go from Here

Because this book is written in a modular manner — with each chapter a standalone unit — you don't have to read everything in order. In fact, if you already have a mixed-breed dog, you won't need to read the chapters on where to find a dog, nor will you need the information on making sure the dog is right for you. If you get a designer dog, you might want to find out more about how to train her than solve problems that she likely hasn't developed. Or, if you've had a mixed-breed dog for many years and are curious about the changes he'll be going through as he ages, you may want to skip to the chapter about senior dogs. Use the Table of Contents and Index to find the chapters that appeal to you now, and come back to this book as your needs and interests change.

Regardless of where you begin reading, you're sure to discover new things giving you the inspiration to spend time with your mixed breed and enhance your lives.

Yours is a partnership for life. Have fun together!

Part I

Just the Facts, Ma'am

In this part . . .

What is a mixed-breed dog? Why are mixed-breed dogs often treated poorly in comparison with pure-bred dogs? Why are most of the feral dogs mixed breeds? Why do they overpopulate animal shelters and humane societies? This part answers these questions and more.

Mixed-breed dogs are every bit the best friend that any purebred dog can be. They give their loyalty, love, and companionship. They willingly learn and play with you. Many will guard your home and family. Mixed-breed dogs don't know that they don't have pedigrees. All they know is that they want to make you happy!

Since the mid-1990s, a special brand of mixed-breed dog has become every bit as popular as many purebred dogs. This hybrid, a combination of two purebred dogs, is termed a *designer dog*. Designer dogs come in all shapes, sizes, and colors. Though some have been very nearly standardized — such as the Labradoodle, Puggle, and Cockapoo — many aren't. Hybrid dogs can take on the characteristics of either parent, and unless a breeder has figured out a specific parenting combination, the appearance and temperament of the offspring is rarely a known factor. In this part, I fill you in on why the first designer dogs (the Labradoodle and Cockapoo) were originally bred, as well as the pros and cons of owning a designer dog.

In order to fully understand any dog, you'll need to know more about the breeds that your own mixed-breed dog might contain. Your dog will have genetic ties that affect his appearance, behavior, and trainability. I outline the major breed groups, discuss their specific characteristics, and tell you how they might influence the attributes of a mixed breed.

Finally, if you're in the market for a mixed-breed dog, you need to know where to find one and which questions to ask before you bring the dog home. I cover both in this part.

Chapter 1

Mixing It Up: Introducing the Mixed Breed

In This Chapter

▶ Understanding what makes a dog a mixed breed

▶ Recognizing that size doesn't matter — a dog is a dog

▶ Remembering that your dog — no matter his mix — wants to be your best friend

The offspring of purebred dogs all look alike on the outside, and have similar personalities and temperaments. You can't say that about mixed-breed dogs. No two are exactly alike — even those from the same litter. Although their environment has a lot of impact on their future behavior, they still have specific genetic codes that are difficult to decipher.

Mixed-breed dogs — especially so-called "designer dogs" — have recently experienced a surge in popularity. Though actually hybrids — the offspring of two purebreds — designer dogs are highly prized for their unique characteristics. Designer dogs are very expensive, because they're in short supply and highly desired.

Very small mixed breeds have also become very popular. They're easy to transport, can be carried in a handbag, and offer all the affection and playful antics of their larger cousins. From 3 to 7 pounds, so-called "pocket dogs" are gaining ground, probably fueled by the fact that they're carried by their celebrity owners down the red carpet. Many of the current, popular pocket dogs are hybrids — the mix of two very small purebred dogs.

Most dogs — regardless of their breed or size — merely want to be with their human companions. Your dog looks to you for direction, companionship, food, shelter, and understanding. In return, your dog offers friendship, trust, and love. He'll never grow up and move away, he's there when you need someone to talk to, and he's always ready to join in a game. Your dog doesn't have to be pure-bred to fulfill your needs. After all, your dog doesn't know what purebred is — all he knows is that he wants to be with you.

A Mutt by Any Other Name: Defining Mixed Breeds

A mixed-breed dog is one who has been conceived by two different purebred or mixed-breed dogs. The parentage of many mixed-breed dogs is unknown, because the breeding wasn't planned. Two unsterilized dogs crossed paths when the female was in heat, and the rest is history.

Mixed-breed dogs are alternatively called mutts, mongrels, or Heinz 57 dogs. No matter what they've been called, they aren't the sought-after purebred dog that people pay a lot of money to buy. Mixed breeds aren't recognized by the American Kennel Club (AKC) and cannot compete in AKC-sanctioned shows. They're often frowned upon by purebred dog enthusiasts, who see mixed breeds as a dilution of the breed.

However, in recent years, mixed-breed dogs have become more popular. Not only are there now official clubs and events for mixed-breed dogs, but the AKC has allowed them to participate in its Canine Good Citizen certification tests (see Chapter 19). They're being put to work as service dogs, therapy dogs, and search-and-rescue dogs. They're valued as pets and companions. In some parts of the world, owning a mixed-breed dog is considered chic.

Each mixed-breed dog is unique. Even designer dogs don't meet any specific standard, such as those seen in purebred dogs. There's no guarantee of the adult dog's height, appearance, or temperament. What happens happens.

Although some designer-dog breeders claim that their mixed-breed pups are healthier due to breeding two different breeds together, this isn't always the case. The health of the pups depends on the two individuals who are mixed. Only through careful testing of the parents — such as X-raying hip joints, testing the eyes and heart, testing blood for specific diseases, and temperament testing for overall personality — that a breeder can be somewhat certain that the offspring will be healthy. Although most professional purebred dog breeders do these tests, few designer-dog breeders do so. And you can be sure that the owners of those wandering pets who crossed paths didn't do so either.

A designer dog is a dog whose parents were both purebred dogs, of different breeds. For example, a Golden Doodle has one parent who is a purebred Golden Retriever, and another parent who is a purebred Poodle. His mother may have been the Poodle, and his father may have been the Golden Retriever — or vice versa. The designer dog was bred intentionally by a designer-dog breeder. A non-designer mixed-breed dog is a dog who was bred either intentionally or by accident. One or both of his parents were *not* purebred dogs.

Even though you have no idea what your mixed-breed puppy will grow up to look like, there *are* ways to be sure he'll still be a good pet. Your good care, training, and love will make him the ideal companion. It doesn't matter what others might think when they see your short-legged, long-backed, droopy-eared, multicolored dog with the overshot jaw and wrinkled forehead. All that matters is your love and devotion to him, which he'll return tenfold.

A Tale of Two Dogs: How Mixed-Breed Dogs Come to Be

The story of mixed-breed dogs is often a sad one. Many people see them as a lower caste of animal — with no heritage and an unknown future. They overpopulate animal shelters and humane societies. They roam the streets in cities, suburbs, and rural areas, menacing wildlife and small pets. In their search for food, they raid garbage cans and alleyways. If captured by animal control, few are claimed, and most are put to sleep.

How to tell where your dog came from

The best way to figure out the breeds that make up your mixed-breed dog is to look through an encyclopedia of purebred dogs. Most mixed breeds have *some* appearance or personality that resembles one of the parent breeds. Often, you just have to look at color, coat type, or size to have a vague idea of which section to look in. For example, if the dog is large, has a beauty mark on the cheek, and has upright ears, there's a good chance he's part Shepherd. If the dog is small, with long silky fur and a short nose, there's a good chance she's part of some Toy dog breed, likely some Pekingese.

Make a list of your dog's attributes. Compare them to those you see in the encyclopedia of purebred dogs or head to Chapter 3, where you can find an overview of the different breed groups. When you have a fairly good idea of your mixed-breed dog's genetics, read more about those breeds to learn about their behavior, temperament, and health-related issues. Doing so will help you know your dog even better than you already do!

Just as people throw out old computers, or clothing that's no longer in style, mixed-breed dogs often suffer the same consequences when their owners no longer want to be bothered to care for them. The most common scenarios:

- Someone falls in love with a mixed-breed pup, but quickly tires of the pup as he grows and develops behavioral problems (because the person treated him more like a toy, than a dog). Broken toys are thrown away; mixed-breed dogs are abandoned in the streets or at local animal shelters.

- Someone wants to let her children experience the wonders of birth. How great is it to watch puppies being born and nursing! How cute the puppies are as they crawl around! Seeing the pups' eyes open for the first time, watching them eat solid food for the first time, and watching them play with each other — what could be better? But when the pups' mother no longer cares for them, the task of feeding and cleaning up after the puppies falls on the adult in the house. And if homes can't be found for the pups, they're abandoned.

- A dog just gets loose. The dog's owner tried to keep him contained, but where there's a will, there's a way, especially if the air is carrying the odor of a female dog in season, which many male dogs can detect from more than a mile away. It's not unheard of for a male dog to climb a high fence to escape or boldly run through an invisible fence's electronic field.

An unhappy dog without companionship will do what he can to get loose and find company. Dogs who are tethered outdoors break their ropes; those in pens dig under the fence; many in yards jump over a fence or take advantage of open gates because they want to find other dogs. And when they find other dogs, they often procreate — and then more unwanted mixed breeds enter the world.

Rarely does breeding of mixed-breed dogs happen intentionally. Though unplanned, many mixed-breed dogs can still bring joy and love to your life. Don't judge the dog on how he came to be, or where he was found — instead, consider how happy and fulfilling a future shared with that mixed-breed dog can be!

Even Toy Dogs Aren't Toys

"Mommy, Daddy, can I have a dog?"

Many families give in to their little one's wishes without thinking long and hard about it first. And many other people give a friend or loved one a dog for a holiday or birthday gift — not knowing whether the person really wants the dog or is prepared to care for him. Unfortunately a good percentage of these "gifts" end up at the local animal shelters just a few months down the road — much like a toy that no longer works or isn't played with anymore.

Dogs take work. Yes, they're adorable — as puppies and adults — but putting time and energy into the care of your dog is essential if you want a happy, healthy companion. Think seriously about how much time you have to give before you commit to getting a puppy or adult dog. If you can't give a dog proper care, you'll do yourself and the dog a favor by not bringing him home.

Proper care goes hand in hand with overall health and well-being. In Part II, I let you know how to give your mixed-breed dog a good home, feed him correctly, groom him, and exercise him. A healthy dog is less likely to develop health and behavioral issues. Bottom line: If you take good care of your dog physically, he's less likely to develop the kinds of behavioral problems that result in many dogs ending up in shelters, without homes.

Training is essential for every dog — big or small. A trained dog is happier, easier to live with, and more accepting of new situations. If all dogs were trained as puppies, the animal shelters wouldn't be nearly as full. In Part IV, I guide you through the training process, as well as help you understand the special problems that can occur in mixed-breed dogs. As your dog ages, he'll have special needs. In Part IV, I also discuss how to recognize signs of age-related behavioral changes, possible physical changes, and when the right time may be to let him go.

Any kind of dog can be a valued family member. What you get from your dog is entirely dependent on what you put *into* the relationship.

They Don't Call 'Em Man's Best Friend for Nothin'

Wondering what you can do with a mixed-breed dog? Anything! You may not be able to compete in purebred dog club shows, but similar certificate-awarding shows are available for mixed-breed dogs. You and your dog are teammates in all performance activities. Your mixed breed can

- **Participate in obedience trials.** These are tests of your dogs' response to obedience commands. See Chapter 16 for more information.

- **Participate in agility.** Not only does this challenge your dog physically, but also tests how well you communicate with him while in action. See Chapter 16 for more information.

- ✔ **Compete in flyball.** This is a relay team event with four dogs/handlers per team. The dogs run down a lane to fetch a ball and return. The fastest team wins.

- ✔ **Take the Canine Good Citizen test.** This test is a way of testing your dog's obedience and temperament in public. (It's not a competition.)

- ✔ **Work as a therapy dog.** Your mixed breed can bring joy to others by going to nursing homes, hospitals, and care centers.

- ✔ **Work as a service dog.** Service dogs perform important tasks for those who are unable to. They are guiding eyes for the blind, ears for the deaf, and hands for those without.

- ✔ **Assist with search-and-rescue operations.** Search-and-rescue dogs find lost people and save their lives.

In Chapter 17, I explain how to travel with your dog. I fill you in on preparing for your trip and help you make sure your dog is safe, secure, and relaxed during the trip, whether you're traveling by plane, train, or automobile. Because many dogs get stressed — or homesick — while traveling, I let you know what to do to help your dog become a traveling gent.

Mixed breeds can perform jobs to help people, save people, and inspire people. They're stars on the screen, stage, and television. They're heroes in the line of duty or while sifting through debris. They keep our borders safe, sniffing out dangerous chemicals and drugs.

Many mixed breeds have a bad start, but you can change that by adopting one that steals your heart. Just one stroll through an animal shelter or humane society, and you're bound to find one, or two, who'll give you the love and devotion you're looking for.

They don't call dogs man's best friend for nothing. Nobody can love you like a dog.

Chapter 2

Designer Dogs: Not Your Mother's Mutt

In This Chapter

▶ Hearing the hype about hybrids

▶ Identifying the pros and cons of hybrid dogs

▶ Looking at the most popular designer dogs

*W*hat do James Gandolfini, Julianne Moore, Uma Thurman, and Jake Gyllenhaal have in common? No, they haven't all won Oscars. They all have Puggles — the designer-dog hybrid of a Pug and a Beagle? Designer dogs are growing in popularity, and they're often more expensive than purebred pups. Why? Because they're unique.

So why would someone pay upwards of $1,500 for a mixed-breed dog when he can go to the local animal shelter and adopt one for $30? Aren't all mixed-breed dogs unique in their own ways? Yes — but not all mixed-breed dogs purposely designed. Not all mixed-breed dogs have pedigreed parents. Not all mixed-breed dogs have a well-documented lineage. Designer dogs are carefully chosen to create a specific appearance and temperament in the offspring. The puppies are calculated, created, and planned. Most mixed-breed dogs are accidents — but there's nothing accidental about a designer dog, and many people are willing to pay more to get one.

Designer dogs are not without controversy, though. Purebred dog *fanciers* (a fancy name for people who are enthusiastic about dogs) are vehemently opposed to mixing their purebred dogs with any other breed. In this chapter, I fill you in on the pros and cons of designer dogs, so you can decide for yourself whether they're right for you. I also let you know which designer dogs are the most popular, and tell you a bit about those hybrids and what you can expect if you get one.

The Pros and Cons of Designer Dogs

Although breeders of designer dogs feel they're meeting the needs of a particular niche of people, purebred breeders and purebred dog clubs, such as the American Kennel Club, think the entire trend is dangerous to all dogs. In the following sections, I offer up both sides of the debate and let you make up your own mind.

The pros

One of the advantages of designer dogs is the sheer number of varieties available. Over 200 different hybrid combinations exist, which means there is a designer dog for every taste. Most of these hybrids are small and designed to have good personality combined with adorability.

Designer dogs are created to fit every need — from pocket-size dogs for easy travel to low-shed dogs for those with allergies. Many of these designer-dog creations are free of some of the traits that can make life difficult for the purebred dog. For example, some purebreds, like the Pug, have a very short snout, making breathing difficult. But the popular Puggle — the hybrid of a Pug and a Beagle — has a longer nose while still maintaining the Pug's wrinkled forehead and loopy gait.

Many hybrid breeders claim their dogs have *hybrid vigor,* a strength that comes from having parents of two different breeds. The offspring of two different breeds rarely inherit genetic defects, because the bloodlines aren't as close as those of purebreds. Purebred dogs often have inherited traits that can cause genetic defects. For example, many retriever breeds tend to have cataracts or epilepsy, many large-breed dogs have hip dysplasia, and many small-breed dogs are prone to dental problems. Mixed-breed dogs rarely inherit these genetic defects, because their genetics are more varied. (Incidentally, this is true of all mixed-breed dogs, not just designer dogs or hybrids.)

The cons

The major con of designer dogs is the price. Most designer dogs cost upwards of $700, whereas many purebred dogs begin at $250.

Although each designer dog was bred for specific appearance and traits, there's a good chance that some or all of them will not develop in the offspring. Mixing breeds is chancy, because the outcome is not absolute. Although purebred dog offspring will always mature to appear like the parent dogs, the hybrid offspring may appear more like one parent than the other, or have a personality more like one parent than the other. So, although you might be searching for a small Yorkipoo, the pup might grow up to be the size of a large Yorkshire Terrier instead of a Teacup Poodle.

As much as the breeders of designer dogs claim that mixing two breeds improves the offspring's overall health, that fact is debatable. Although many of the puppies don't show symptoms of the recessive genetic dysfunctions commonly seen in purebred dogs, many other puppies do. In fact, a hybrid puppy can have the poor luck to inherit the worst physical and temperament traits of both parents.

There are no guarantees when you get a dog — purebred, hybrid, or mutt.

The Major "Labels" in the Designer-Dog World

In the following sections, I introduce you to some of the most popular designer dogs.

I can't cover all 200+ varieties of designer dogs in this chapter. But if you're curious about the wide variety of designer dogs available, a great resource is the American Canine Hybrid Club (www.achclub.com).

Oodles of Poodles

Few hybrids are more popular than those with a Poodle parent. In fact, it was the Poodle mixture that started the entire fad of designer dogs, beginning with the Labradoodle and Cockapoo.

Poodles bring many great attributes into the hybrid crossing, plus they come in four sizes: Standard, Miniature, Toy, and Teacup (a size not currently recognized by the AKC). Plus, they're low- to no-shed dogs with dirt-resistant coats. When combined with a Retriever, or other straight soft-coated breed, they can produce a beautiful wavy or large-curl coat that's very attractive.

The smaller Poodle breeds also tend to live a long time. So instead of having a dog for only 10 to 12 years, you'll have one who will live upwards of 15 years. That, alone, makes a Poodle mix very attractive.

When compared to other purebred dogs, Poodles are rated high on the intelligence scale. They learn quickly and can work their way through problems faster than most other breeds. What's not to like about fast housetraining? Poodles are sensitive, highly aware, and learn by watching others.

Unless very poorly bred, Poodles have few genetic defects, though they aren't totally without health concerns. Their hips are far better than most retriever and shepherd breeds. They aren't prone to heart problems seen in many types of dogs. And they rarely have epilepsy, retinal atrophy, or allergies. Overall, mixing any purebred dog with a Poodle will create great offspring.

Labradoodles (Labrador Retriever/Poodle)

Created as the ultimate service dog, Labradoodles (see Figure 2-1) quickly became popular around the world. Just as the Labrador Retriever is the most popular purebred dog in the United States, the Labradoodle is also the most popular, large designer dog.

Initially, Labradoodles were bred to aid people who needed service dogs, but were allergic to dog dander and fur. Labradoodles are large, solid, strong, and intelligent. They're eager to learn and love to please their human companions. As with the purebred Labrador service dogs, Labradoodles can work all day without tiring. And they're *very* loving. Labradoodles are ideal with children.

Labradoodles don't interact well with assertive people or dominant dogs. Any heavy-handed training technique, such as being yelled at or jerked around on a leash, will cause a Labradoodle to shut down and want to crawl into a corner.

Figure 2-1: Labradoodles have three coat types, two of which do shed.

Goldendoodles (Golden Retriever/Poodle)

Goldendoodles (see Figure 2-2) turn an already perfect family pet into a perfect family pet that sheds less. The mixing of the Golden Retriever and Poodle changes little about the offspring other than coat appearance. The majority of Goldendoodles have coats with golden hue, the structure generally similar to that of the retriever. But the coat changes from a long and smooth, sometimes wavy texture, to a scruffier, curlier, harsher texture.

Golden Retrievers are the ideal dog — they love to please their human companions, play ball, cuddle, play ball, go for long walks, play ball, fetch a stick in the water, or if you're feeling like you want to play fetch for hours, fetch the ball in the water. They're easy to train and easy to care for.

They're energetic and playful outdoors and happy to rest at your feet or join in a quiet game indoors. Many will bark to let you know of visitors, though they don't believe in strangers — after all, *anyone* can throw a ball.

Cockapoos (Cocker Spaniel/Poodle)

In Cockapoos (see Figure 2-3), generally the Poodle is the *sire* (father), and the Cocker Spaniel is the *dam* (mother). Adult Cockapoos mature from 10 to 30 pounds depending on the size of the parents (mainly the size of the sire) and the gender of the puppy. Their coat grows very long and sheds very little, if at all. Cockapoos require grooming every two to four months depending on the desired length of hair. This hybrid is excellent for families with allergies or asthma. They come in a variety of colors: buff, red, chocolate, black, white, and a variety of parti-colors.

Figure 2-2: Goldendoodles are a great combination of two great family dogs.

Figure 2-3: Cockapoos are great medium-sized dogs that shed very little, love to cuddle, and learn quickly.

Cockapoos are very patient and tolerant with children, and because they like to play and are durable, children like them. They may bark to alert you of intruders, but they rarely go beyond making noise — especially once the person is allowed inside.

Some Cockapoos can be very sensitive because both parent breeds have a tendency toward having their feelings hurt very easily. This is a great hybrid for the elderly, because Cockapoos are gentle, cuddly, and easy to care for.

Schnoodles (Miniature Schnauzer/Poodle)

Schnoodles (see Figure 2-4) are very loyal to their families. This hybrid is affectionate, extremely intelligent, easily trained, clever, friendly, fun loving, and loaded with personality! However, because they are half Schnauzer, they can also be willful, stubborn, and prone to excessive barking. Most Schnoodles are good with children and get along fine with other animals. They're great watchdogs because they let you know when someone is near, but they aren't aggressive.

This great companion dog excels in obedience, agility, and flyball. They make excellent therapy dogs. Schnoodles are loyal and loving companions. They're comfortable in any environment — from an apartment to a farm — as long as they're with their families.

Schnoodles are high-energy dogs outdoors, but they're happy to warm your feet indoors. Because neither of the parent breeds — Poodle and Miniature Schnauzer — shed, the Schnoodle does not shed. This hybrid is easily maintained through weekly brushing and bimonthly clipping.

Figure 2-4: Schnoodles are medium-sized dogs with loads of personality.

Teripoos (Terrier/Poodle)

A Terripoo (see Figure 2-5) is any Terrier breed mixed with a Poodle. Because there are so many Terrier breeds, there are numerous types of Teripoos.

Figure 2-5: The Teripoo can learn to work as a therapy dog.

Although most Terripoos benefit from having Poodle blood, they're still part Terrier, which means they have a stubborn streak, tend to be willful, and are prone to excessive barking and overall controlling personalities. However, you can't ignore their adorable appearance and intelligence.

Peke-a-poos (Pekingese/Poodle)

Peke-a-poos (see Figure 2-6) are small dogs, often Toy-size, weighing from 9 to 20 pounds. Their coats are usually white or gray, but some are brown. The texture of the coat is very soft.

Peke-a-poos are fairly low maintenance with few of the common health problems associated with the Pekingese. However, because they are half Pekingese, they can have breathing difficulties common with the shortened nose. The other problem associated with a Peke-a-poo is tearing of the eyes, which can become a serious problem if the eyes become swollen or the tear stains are dark.

Peke-a-poos tend to inherit their parent Pekingese's long, soft fur. Unless you want to brush your dog daily, keep your Peke-a-poo's fur short, because a Peke-a-poo's fur mats into dreadlocks very easily.

Peke-a-poos love to cuddle and have a medium energy level, making them ideal dogs for small homes and apartment living. They love to play outside for a short period of time, then sleep on your lap for a long period of time. Though very affectionate, they can be quite willful and stubborn, making housetraining difficult.

Figure 2-6: Peke-a-poos are lap potatoes, much like one of their parent breeds, the Pekingese.

A basket of Toys

There are more combinations of Toy hybrids than there are recognized purebred Toy breeds. Though small, they're still dogs and should be treated as such — not as mere arm ornaments. Toy hybrids tend to have good longevity, great personalities, and require the special care accorded to Toy dogs.

So-called *pocket dogs* are usually a combination of two Toy breeds; the parents chosen more for their small size than anything else. The mixing of two Terrier-type Toys can mean a challenging personality. Also, the combining of two breeds that already have the tendency toward similar health issues, such as breathing difficulties or skin allergies, will likely result in puppies who have to contend with these same issues throughout their lives.

Bichon Frise hybrids

The Bichon Frise is a small, white, curly-coated dog with an anti-allergenic coat. They require a lot of exercise and consistent training. Bichons are cute and cuddly, but also like to be in charge. Any Bichon Frise hybrid may tend to inherit these qualities, especially if one of the parents is a Terrier-type breed.

The American Canine Hybrid Club recognizes more than 25 Bichon Frise hybrids, ranging from the Griffichon (Bichon Frise/Brussels Griffon) to the Cock-a-Chon (Bichon Frise/Cocker Spaniel). To get the full list, go to www.achclub.com.

Pug hybrids

Pugs are a popular breed for Toy hybrid dogs because they're fairly hardy, sweet, intelligent, and have a short, easy-care coat. For large-dog enthusiasts, the Pug offers the appearance of a Mastiff (their ancestors) without the enormous size.

Pugs do have a few physical issues, however, because they've been bred to have extremely short noses, which cause many respiratory problems, and their legs are known to have problems with knee dislocation. Plus, this breed can be willful and stubborn.

One of the biggest dangers of using Pugs in designer hybrid Toys is their eye configuration (they have protruding eyes) and short noses. Breeding them with other Toys with similar physical attributes can cause dangerous health issues.

Though Pugs are Toy dogs, they have a very ingrained alarm system. For hundreds of years they have alerted their human companions of coming danger, often saving the lives of those in their communities. If your hybrid Toy has Pug blood, you can be sure he'll bark when he hears intruders!

The American Canine Hybrid Club recognizes more than 20 Pug hybrids, ranging from the Pugland (Pug/Westie) to the Puggle (Beagle/Pug), currently the most popular designer dog. To get the full list, go to www.achclub.com.

Maltese hybrids

Though very small, Maltese have large personalities. They're bold, are quick to sound the alarm when they hear something, and can be difficult to housetrain. Some can be snappy with children or with human companions who are inconsistent with their leadership role.

These small white dogs have long, silky fur and can grow to be 8 to 10 inches tall at the shoulder, weighing about 9 pounds. They have large, round eyes with dark rims, black noses, and a fine bone structure. Their bodies are slightly longer than they are tall, as is common with many Toy breeds.

The Maltese may be small, but should not be overly pampered. Pampering makes them jealous of others, causing aggressive reactions. These traits are very possible in the hybrid offspring.

Maltese are prone to sunburn on their skin, respiratory problems due to their very short noses, eye irritation due to their somewhat bulging eyes, and tooth problems, a common Toy dog malady.

The American Canine Hybrid Club recognizes nearly a dozen Maltese hybrids, ranging from the Mauzer (Maltese/Miniature Schnauzer) to the Silkese (Maltese/Silky Terrier). To get the full list, go to www.achclub.com.

Pekingese hybrids

Pekingese have long, straight coats with profuse feathering. They come in all colors and grow to about 9 inches tall at the shoulder, weighing 8 to 10 pounds. One of the reasons for their popularity among hybrid dog breeders is that many Pekingese can be found at under 6 inches in height and weighing under 6 pounds, creating a great parent base for a pocket-size dog.

This Toy dog tends to have a broad head with wide-set dark eyes, a wrinkled short muzzle, and drooping heart-shaped ears with long feathering. Their necks are short and thick. Like the Pug, they have a rolling gait.

Pekingese are very brave, independent, and affectionate with their own people but wary of strangers. They can be obstinate, willful, and finicky. Due to their sensitivity to sound and movement, they tend to be excessive barkers.

This Toy breed tends to catch colds easily and is prone to herniated disks, dislocated kneecaps, *trichaiasis* (eyelashes growing inward, toward the eyeballs), and breathing problems due to their short-ened snouts. Heart problems are also a common health issue in Pekingese. As with many other Toy breeds, they have a tendency to easily become overweight so should never be fed a high-calorie diet.

The American Canine Hybrid Club recognizes numerous Pekingese hybrids, ranging from the Foxingese (Pekingese/Toy Fox Terrier) to the Yorkinese (Pekingese/Yorkshire Terrier). To get the full list, go to www.achclub.com.

Shih Tzu hybrids

Though Shih Tzus look like Lhasa Apsos, their personalities are totally the opposite. Where Lhasas are dominant and willful, Shih Tzus are gentle, easy-going, and very willing to learn. They're happy, hardy, and have loads of character. It's no wonder that this is a popular addition to many hybrid dog combinations.

They grow up to 11 inches tall at the shoulder and weigh about 9 pounds, though they do have a tendency to become overweight because they're very food oriented. They have round heads, short noses, and lots of fur around their faces. Shih Tzus have long, soft overcoats with a woolly undercoat, making them fairly hardy in extreme temperatures for short periods of time. Their tails curl over their backs, and they come in a huge variety of colors.

Because of their short noses, they wheeze and snore, along with having respiratory problems from time to time. They can have spinal disc disease due to their long back and short legs. However, compared to many Toy breeds, their genetic defects are few.

Though it has been done, Shi Tzus should not be bred with other dogs who have similarly short noses and large bulging eyes. This can create some horrendous health issues with the hybrid pups.

The American Canine Hybrid Club recognizes more than 25 Shih Tzu hybrids, ranging from the Fo-Tzu (Shih Tzu/Toy Fox Terrier) to the Bea-Tzu (Beagle/Shih Tzu). To get the full list, go to www.achclub.com.

Pomeranian hybrids

Pomeranians resemble foxes, only with thicker, fluffier fur. Their wedge-shaped heads; straight, triangular ears; and pointed noses are fox-like, as are their babydoll faces. Poms have dark, almond-shaped eyes and a double coat, which can be any solid color, though there are some that are parti-colored, such as black and white.

Descended from Nordic breeds bred to withstand extremely cold temperatures and work all day pulling sleds, Pomeranians are some of the hardiest of the Toy breeds. Poms aren't big enough to pull a sled (though if you put about ten of them together, they'd give it a good try), but they still believe they're big, tough dogs. This makes them willful, bold, and often temperamental — though not stupid. If you use a positive training technique with lots of incentive, your Pom will do whatever you want.

Pomeranians are a popular parent breed for hybrid dogs because they offer the beautiful fluffy coat, distinct facial features, and small size. The average Pom doesn't grow much larger than 12 inches tall at the shoulder and weighs a mere 7 pounds.

Though Pomeranians are tough little dogs, they do have a genetic tendency toward specific health issues, including *luxating patella* (the kneecap slips out of its proper groove and moves against the thighbone), heart and skin problems, as well as eye infections. Also, as with most Toy breeds, they are prone to dental problems and weight gain.

Because Pomeranians have large, bulging eyes and the tendency toward specific health problems, they should not be bred with breeds that have similar attributes.

The American Canine Hybrid Club recognizes more than 25 Pomeranian hybrids, ranging from the Pom-Coton (Pomeranian/ Coton de Teluar) to the Poshies (Pomeranian/Shetland Sheepdog). To get the full list, go to www.achclub.com.

Yorkshire Terrier hybrids

Yorkies are very small toys with a long silky coat that falls straight down on either side. Although the puppies are usually black and tan, they mature to steel gray and gold. This breed has a flat head, medium-length muzzle, black nose, and upright V-shaped ears. This is another Toy dog who doesn't have a small personality — they are Terriers, after all. As tenacious as they come, Yorkshire Terriers have a high energy level, are aggressive with strangers and other dogs, are demanding of attention, and are territorial. Yorkies are often spoiled and catered to due to their small size (a mere 7 inches tall at the shoulder, and hardly ever more than 7 pounds). This coddling creates a mini-monster. Yorkshire Terriers, as with dogs of any size, need structure and leadership.

Yorkies do have some genetic health problems. These include abnormal skull formations, paralysis of the hindquarters caused by herniated discs, and other spinal problems. They are also prone to dental abnormalities and excessive tooth decay. They have a poor tolerance to anesthetics and a tendency toward congenital liver disease.

The American Canine Hybrid Club recognizes more than 15 Yorkshire Terrier hybrids, ranging from the Fourche Terrier (West Highland White Terrier/Yorkshire Terrier) to the Snorkie (Miniature Schnauzer/Yorkshire Terrier). To get the full list, go to www.achclub.com.

Intelligent perceptions: Border Collie hybrids

People who want to create a hybrid based on intelligence and not coat type will often use the Border Collie breed as one of the parents. One of the positive outcomes of using Border Collies in a hybrid crossing is that they have few genetic health problems.

Borador (Border Collie/Labrador Retriever)

The Borador (see Figure 2-7) is often medium to large with large feet, a long muzzle, and light brown eyes; some have upright ears. The coat can be either medium length or short with any combination of colors ranging from all yellow to all black or with typical Border Collie white around the neck, on the paws, and on the nose.

Figure 2-7: Here's a typical Borador. You can see both breeds very clearly in this dog.

These two breeds complement each other well. Where the Border Collie might be overly sensitive, the Labrador Retriever is bold. Where a Lab may not be able to figure something out, the Border Collie puts in reason. Where a Border Collie might constantly want to chase farm animals and round them up, the Lab feels more relaxed about work, more likely to wait for the cues from his human companions instead of striking out to work on his own.

In all, Boradors are easy to care for, easy to train, friendly, and often very healthy. They're wonderful companions.

Bordernese (Bernese Mountain Dog/Border Collie)

A Bordernese (see Figure 2-8) appears much like a Border Collie only larger. The coloring of the coat is similar with black and white, sometimes tan eyebrows. The coat texture is also similar; long, smooth, and thick. Both breeds have long muzzles, dark eyes, and long tails with a slight upward curve.

Figure 2-8: The Bordernese looks very much like a larger Border Collie with the added tan highlights over the eyes.

Both breeds were developed as herding dogs. Therefore, both are very intelligent and easy to train. The difference in temperament lies in the Border Collie being a higher-energy worker than the Bernese Mountain Dog and also far more sensitive. Border Collies generally don't interact well with children, whereas the Bernese Mountain Dog adores children.

Mixing these two breeds together creates a larger herding dog with a medium energy level and fairly outgoing personality. However, Bernese Mountain Dogs don't have the same longevity of a Border Collie, so the hybrid offspring may not either. Another issue with mixing these two breeds together is that both are prone to the same genetic defects such as hip and elbow dysplasia, eye problems, and heart problems. Border Collies also might have horrendous allergic reactions to flea bites, as well as epilepsy. The hybrid offspring are highly likely to not have good hybrid vigor.

Chapter 3

A Little of This, a Little of That: Deciding Which Mixed Breed Is Right for You

*B*ringing a dog into your home is a big deal. Sure, they're all adorable and hard to resist. But before you fall for those puppy-dog eyes, you need to ask yourself some serious questions: Am I ready for a dog? Which dog is the right one for me? Do I want a puppy or an adult dog? Male or female? Big or small? In this chapter, you discover the answers to all these questions and more.

Asking Yourself the Right Questions

Before you can start thinking about which dog you want, you need to ask yourself whether you're ready to even have a dog in the first place. A dog is a commitment.

There are several very important questions you need to ask yourself. If you can honestly answer *yes* to all of them, then a mixed-breed dog *is* right for you and your family.

Do you have enough time for a dog?

Notice I asked this question first? Being a dog guardian isn't just about playing with your dog when you want to — it's about caring for him 24/7, walking him, feeding him, grooming him, training him, making sure he gets the right veterinary care. A dog is not a piece of furniture to be cast aside when you get too involved in your busy life. He's a living, needy, interactive, sentient being who craves your companionship. Unless you're able to give a dog all the time he needs, you shouldn't get one.

Do you have enough money for a dog?

Adoption fees generally range from $40 to $100. A designer dog can cost anywhere from $1,000 to $6,000! But the actual amount it takes to walk out the door with a dog in your arms is *not* the bulk of what your dog will cost. You also need to consider daily, monthly, and yearly expenses of dog ownership. You'll need to buy food, bedding, and toys. A small dog may be easy to handle at only $5 per week in kibble, but what if he requires a special diet? Many dogs have food allergies or physical ailments, requiring prescription diets; these can run upwards of $20 per week, depending on the size of your mixed breed. Obviously, the larger and/or more active the dog, the more food he'll need to eat.

You'll need to pay to have your dog groomed; the more you can do yourself, the less it'll cost, but if you send your dog to a professional groomer, you'll be paying anywhere from $25 to $300 (per visit) for the service.

You may decide to enroll your dog in obedience classes or other training; basic training lessons can cost anywhere from $60 for a set of group classes to more than $3,000 for boarding and training.

And you'll need to see a vet at least once a year — more if your dog gets sick or is injured. A quick trip to the vet is rarely less than $50; it normally costs well over $100 just for the checkup and yearly vaccinations. Plus, there are the monthly expenses of parasite control, at about $25 per month. As your dog gets older or is injured, there are the costs of medications to consider. Some medical treatments can range into thousands of dollars.

Are you ready to give your heart to a dog?

Let's say that you do have the time and money for a mixed-breed dog. Are you ready to love one? There's far more to having a dog than merely taking care of his needs. The emotional attachments will affect you for a lifetime. Along with all the fun you have, there will also be stress and sadness. Are you ready to fill your heart with love, only to suffer the eventual heartbreak of loss 10 or 12 years down the road when your dog dies?

Even though the pain of losing a dog is awful, all the years of fun and joy you have with your dog are worth it — as long as you know what you're getting into. If the idea of losing a pet you love is too much for you to bear, you're better off not getting one.

Looking at the Different Breeds

Each dog breed was developed for specific tasks — guarding, herding, hunting, hand-warming — and these breeds are grouped together by their original purpose. A mixed breed is a combination of two or more breeds. Understanding the appearance and person-ality of the various breed groups will help you understand your own dog, and will also be useful if you're thinking about which type of mixed breed to get.

On the hunt: The Sporting Group

Sporting dogs were bred to aid hunters in locating, retrieving, and flushing game. They can track, chase, freeze, and return with the prize. Two of the most popular dogs in the United States — the Labrador Retriever and the Golden Retriever (see Figure 3-1) — belong to this group. Sporting dogs make great hunting compan-ions and fantastic pets; and they're great with active families. They need a lot of exercise and stimulation (see Chapter 9 for more on how much exercise the Sporting Group needs).

Figure 3-1: The ever-popular Golden Retriever is just one example of dogs in the Sporting Group.

The AKC recognizes 26 breeds in the Sporting Group. The most popular breeds in this group — and the ones most often seen in mixed-breed dogs — include: Brittany, Chesapeake Bay Retriever, Cocker Spaniel, English Setter, English Springer Spaniel, German Shorthaired Pointer, Golden Retriever, Irish Setter, Labrador Retriever, Pointer, Vizsla, and Weimaraner.

Sporting dogs vary from medium to large — 25 to 90 pounds, depending on the breed. All of them have ears that fold over. The retrievers have webbed feet to aid in swimming and also have quick-dry coats. The Setters have medium-length coats with feathering on their legs and tails. Spaniels have fuller coats, also with feathering on their legs and tails. Though many of the Spaniel and Pointer breeds have cropped tails, they're born with long ones.

Sporting dogs are athletic, high energy, intelligent, and hard working. They need a job; if they don't have a job, they'll drive you crazy trying to find one for themselves. They love to sniff out game trails, single mindedly tracking until they find the source. If there's something to get wet in, even a mud puddle, you can be sure they'll find it — and you won't be able to keep them out of it.

All the breeds in the Sporting Group are easily trained and thrive on structure.

Ain't nothin' but a hound dog: The Hound Group

Though the Hound Group, which according to the AKC is made up of 23 different breeds, includes some of the first breeds ever developed to aid hunters, they aren't the type to point, flush, or retrieve (see the Sporting Group). Instead, Hound dogs track scents. They're single-minded when it comes to locating their targeted prey.

Hounds are divided into two categories: those who hunt by scent and those who hunt by sight (called sighthounds).

The most common hounds, and those often found within mixed-breed dogs, are the American Foxhound, Bassett Hound, Beagle (see Figure 3-2), Dachshund, English Foxhound, Greyhound, Norwegian Elkhound, Rhodesian Ridgeback, and several types of Coonhounds. Except for the Greyhound, these are all scent hounds; tracking through odor left on the ground.

Many Hounds have long, silky ears; long muzzles; and large rib cages. Some have predominantly short coats, while a few, such as the Afghan Hound, have long coats that require a lot of maintenance.

Figure 3-2: The Beagle is one of the more popular Hound breeds found in mixed-breed dogs. Don't let his cute looks fool you — he's stubborn and can be hard to train.

Most of the breeds within the Hound Group tend to be stubborn, single-minded, and difficult to train unless properly motivated. Sighthounds (like the Greyhound) are generally energetic; the slightest movement catches their attention.

While occasionally aggressive on the hunt, Hounds are rarely aggressive to people, but they will try your patience.

Workin' like a dog: The Working Group

The AKC recognizes 25 breeds in the Working Group. Most of the dogs in this group are large, bold, and hardy (see Figure 3-3). They were bred to work long hours though not all of them have high energy levels. Working dogs guard, pull heavy loads, herd and, in recent years, search and rescue.

Because most of them are very popular as pets, they're often seen within mixed-breed dogs. The most popular breeds in this group are the Alaskan Malamute, Boxer, Doberman Pinscher, Great Dane, Rottweiler, and Siberian Husky. Though less popular, the Akita, Mastiff, and Saint Bernard are also found within many mixed breeds.

Working dogs are large boned, strong bodied, and strong willed. Many were bred to withstand extreme weather conditions, such as Arctic temperatures or the cold of Northern Europe.

Figure 3-3: The Bernese Mountain Dog is not commonly seen in mixed breeds, but he is a great representation of the Working Group.

Working dogs have extreme intelligence and steadfast working ethics. They are hardy, often energetic, and make great pets as long as they're given appropriate guidance. Some of these breeds were bred to fight other dogs or protect people, so they have the instinct to dominate in many situations and can be very territorial.

Working breeds do not do well if left alone for long periods of time or tied up. This might lead to aggressive and destructive behavior.

A mix containing any of these breeds must have regular obedience training and maintain strict scheduling. Otherwise, the dog believes he's the boss of your household — and you really don't want to deal with a large, powerful dog who thinks he's in charge.

On the other hand, given a job to perform, Working breeds put their entire hearts into their work. They want approval from their human guardians, but the activity alone is positive reinforcement.

Tenacious terriers: The Terrier Group

The AKC recognizes 27 breeds in the Terrier Group. Terriers are small-game hunters. Due to their genetic disposition to go after difficult game, they're tenacious and single-minded while working; though their work is usually protecting their household and all those in it, while telling everyone what to do and how to do it.

The most common Terrier breeds seen within mixed-breed dogs are the Airedale Terrier, Cairn Terrier, Jack Russell Terrier (now called the Parson Russell Terrier), Miniature Schnauzer,

Staffordshire Bull Terrier, the Pit-Bull Terrier (not a recognized AKC breed, but still a popular pet and recognized by the United Kennel Club), Scottish Terrier, and West Highland White Terrier.

Most of the terriers are medium to small in stature (see Figure 3-4). Their coats are generally short and smooth or wiry and rough, with the exception of the Soft Coated Wheaten Terrier, Sealyham Terrier, and Skye Terrier, all of whom have longer, silkier coats than the other Terrier breeds.

Figure 3-4: The Border Terrier is not commonly found in mixed-breed dogs, but they're similar in size and coat to dogs such as the Cairn Terrier and Norwich Terrier.

There's really no structural norm among the Terrier breeds. Their common threads lie more in personality. However, the taller of the Terriers — Airedale Terrier and Kerry Blue Terrier — do have some structural similarities in their long muzzles, foldover ears, long necks, and long legs. The American Staffordshire Terrier and Bull Terrier have large egg-shaped heads and very muscular bodies with short smooth coats. The Scottish, Cairn, West Highland White, Norfolk, Norwich, Australian, and Border Terriers have short legs, long bodies, medium to long muzzles, and sharp high-set eyes, with short to medium-length tails. All these breeds also have a wiry, medium-length coat.

Terriers are high energy, rebellious to authority, and more aggressive than any other breed group. When riled up, they don't readily back down. However, they *do* learn quickly as long as they're properly motivated. Terriers require consistent training and guidance every day of the week, every week of the year. Terriers are easily excited, turning from upset-to-see-you-go to attacking the nearest creature they see *because* they were upset-to-see-you-go.

The last thing you ever show a Terrier is that you are apprehensive or hesitant. This is all they need to fully dominate you in every way — from how they prefer to be touched to possessive aggression and worse.

Although these dominant tendencies don't occur in all Terriers, or in all mixed-breed dogs with Terrier heritage, carefully observe your own dog for these behaviors and deal with them accordingly; with obedience training.

Big personalities in small packages: The Toy Group

The AKC includes 21 breeds in the Toy Group. Toy breeds were initially developed from the major breed groups. Their parentage was chosen from the smallest of the lines, eventually forming the Toy breeds of today. Though they are their own individual breeds, they retain much of their genetic heritage from the breeds from which they were derived.

Toy dogs quickly adapt to any living environment. This makes them especially great traveling companions and pets for those who live in condominiums, apartments, or other community housing. Yet, they also do well living in a suburban neighborhood or in a rural setting, as long as they're kept primarily indoors when you're not with them.

The Toy Group consists of the following popular breeds that are very likely to be part of a mixed-breed dog's heritage: Chihuahua, Maltese, Miniature and Toy Poodle, Pekingese, Pomeranian, Pug (see Figure 3-5), Shih Tzu, and Yorkshire Terrier.

Rarely is a Toy breed larger than 14 inches tall at the shoulder. They also usually weigh less than 20 pounds. Being small is what constitutes the Toy dog label. Other than these attributes, however, they come in all shapes, fur lengths, and personalities. Some are very sensitive to weather conditions, and others are fairly hardy. Some can be easy to maintain, and others are time-consuming.

Big things come in small packages. Though small in stature, Toy breeds have big personalities. If you train and guide your Toy mixed breed, he'll be a tiny gem — fun, loving, and loyal.

Despite their small size, they need to be treated just like bigger dogs — not like windup toys. They're still dogs, and they have the same need for structure and understanding of their environment.

Figure 3-5: The Pug is a key component in the super-popular mixed-breed Puggle, a mix of the Pug and Poodle. Any breed that's part Poodle should inherit the Poodle's good nature, intelligence, and longevity.

All shapes and sizes: The Non-Sporting Group

The Non-Sporting Group includes 17 different breeds, in every shape and size imaginable, from the Standard Poodle to the Bulldog to the Dalmatian to the Chow Chow. Non-Sporting dogs are big, small, wide, and narrow. All are somehow related to other known breeds, though genetically specialized for specific jobs.

The most popular breed in this group, and the most likely to appear in a designer dog, is the Standard Poodle. The reasons for this dog's popularity in the designer-dog set are numerous: They're intelligent, loving, and energetic. They have great longevity. They can be almost any color, though black, white, and chocolate are the most common — and they don't shed.

Other popular breeds found in mixed-breed dogs include the American Eskimo Dog, Bichon Frise (see Figure 3-6), Boston Terrier, Bulldog, Chinese Shar-Pei, Chow Chow, Dalmatian, and Lhasa Apso.

Brachiocephalic facial structure is a dog's muzzle that has been specially bred to be very short to nearly nonexistent. Though this was initially done to improve the working ability of these dogs, it rarely has any purpose other than for appearance. Dogs who have this facial structure include Pugs, Shi Tzu, Pekingese, Boston Terriers, and Bulldogs.

Figure 3-6: The Bichon Frise is a popular Non-Sporting Dog, with a happy and playful personality.

Other than the Standard Poodle, Non-Sporting dogs are bold, challenging, and independent. They require lots of exercise and structured guidance through training and consistency.

The Standard Poodle has lots of energy but is easy to guide in the right direction. They have a high desire to work and love training challenges. Essentially, Poodles can learn anything and do anything, making them ideal dogs for designer-dog combinations. They overcome many of the behavioral and structural shortcomings of those breeds mixed with them.

Round 'em up: The Herding Group

There are 18 dogs in the Herding Group. And these dogs not only round 'em up, but also push 'em along. They were bred to help shepherds and farmers, working long hard days in all types of weather. Because they were bred to work independently as well as in close sync with their handlers, many Herding breeds are extremely intelligent.

The most common breeds within the Herding Group, and those most likely to be found within a mixed-breed dog, are the Australian Cattle Dog, Australian Shepherd (see Figure 3-7), Border Collie, Cardigan Welsh Corgi, Collie, German Shepherd Dog, Old English Sheepdog, Pembroke Welsh Corgi, and Shetland Sheepdog.

Figure 3-7: The Australian Shepherd is a classic Herding dog, and is commonly found in mixed breeds.

The breeds within the Herding Group range from those with short legs (like the Corgis) to those with long, lithe legs (like the Collie). Though none of these breeds has a short coat, several have thick medium coats, and most tend toward long fur, making them appear more like the animals they were bred to control.

Herding dogs have high energy. They can run an entire day and make you tired just watching. Herding dogs are on their best behavior if they're allowed to exercise a lot. They're even better if they receive consistent training on a daily basis — in fact, they thrive on it. Because these dogs were bred to work hard and long hours, they need the outlet that training activities provide.

Herding breeds tend to learn complicated tasks faster than any other breed, making them ideal for agility, obedience, herding, and many other occupations. They aren't great breeds to have around small children, because they will chase moving objects and purposefully bump into them as a means of gathering the flock together. However, they're wonderful pets for people with active lifestyles.

Considering Age: Puppy or Adult?

When you've decided that you want a dog, you'll have to figure out whether you'd prefer a puppy or an adult dog. This question is especially important if you want a mixed breed, because so many of the great mixed-breed dogs who are out there in shelters, looking for a good home, are beyond puppyhood.

When you first started thinking about getting a dog, you may have been leaning toward a puppy. After all, how can anyone resist that fabulous puppy breath, those cute rolly-polly bodies, big inquisitive eyes, playful personalities, and openness to learning. Those attributes are their main attraction. In fact, if puppies weren't so cute, they might not be worth the trouble!

Puppies need to eat more often than adult dogs, need to potty more often, and tend to be destructive because they don't yet know the rules (or forget them quickly) and because they're going through teething between 3 and 9 months of age. They take more of your time, cost more in veterinary bills (for all their initial vaccinations and neutering/spaying), and hurt when they bite and scratch.

Adult dogs may not have that puppy cute factor, but they don't require as much from you either. If you get an adult dog, she may already be housetrained; if not, you can housetrain her easily, because she can hold it longer. They eat fewer times throughout the day. They're over the teething stages so they're less likely to be destructive. Adult dogs aren't as active as youngsters; an adult dog will become a foot warmer far faster than a pup who would rather chew on your feet.

If you're afraid that an adult dog will have trouble bonding to you, remember that regardless of the age of your mixed-breed dog, he *will* bond with you. It's just a matter of time.

Not every adult dog will be a great new pet, however. Many have been abused or neglected, and that can have a huge bearing on their current attitudes and behaviors. Although some dogs end up in shelters and rescue groups because of unforeseen circumstances (like an owner dying), most are given up due to behavioral issues. If you adopt an adult mixed-breed dog, you'll need to commit to hours of training and observation to cure bad habits (like destructive chewing, house soiling, excessive barking, and aggression) and create positive new ones.

All behavior problems are curable. Some may take longer than others, but there are always ways to solve them (see Chapter 12).

Puppies usually arrive open minded and fresh to new experiences. This doesn't mean they may not already have bad habits. If you're adopting from a shelter, your pup is bound to have had something happen that has already formed his personality. However, if you're buying a designer dog, this is less likely, because a careful breeder will give the puppies a good start on life — offering positive treatment and socialization in a safe environment.

There are pros and cons to a dog at any age. Every mixed breed is his own combination of genetics and experiences, so you don't have any guarantees in appearance or personality. Ultimately, you need to choose based on how much time you have and what age you're most interested in.

 Before you go to a breeder's house to look at all the cute puppies, spend an hour or two hanging out at your local humane society or animal shelter, playing with all the adult dogs that are looking for a home. That way, you'll see how great dogs can be at *any* age, and you'll make the decision that's right for you.

Gender Bender: Male or Female?

Gender can play a big part in a dog's personality and size.

Male dogs tend to be larger with bigger heads, bodies, and feet than their female counterparts. Male dogs are usually more territorial, which means they need to potty more often and cover the scent of visiting dogs as well. This tendency also makes them more difficult to housetrain.

Female dogs learn faster and are generally more loyal. Although many female dogs are territorial, they usually mark the spot in one pass. Female dogs are more likely to want to stay home, preferring to stay in their safe territories instead of always looking to expand it.

Male dogs tend to be more dominant than female dogs. Male dogs also tend to carry a stronger body odor than female dogs. But the gender most likely to be a good foot warmer is the male dog, because he's better at relaxing when the time comes. Female dogs are always on the alert for any possibilities. Because female dogs have the mothering instinct, most of their behavioral tendencies are to feed, protect, and nurture their young. Thus, they're always aware of everything going on around them.

Adding It Up: The Right Dog for You

Big, small. Short hair, long hair. Male, female. There are so many choices — how can you possibly know the right dog for you? If you're stymied by it all, here are a few suggestions based on where you live and what your lifestyle is like:

- ✔ **If you live in an apartment or condominium:** Try a small female dog, maybe with Toy or Terrier breeding.

- ✔ **If yours is a single-family home with very young children:** Try a small to medium male or female dog. Sporting dogs do well with youngsters, as do some of the Hound dogs such as Beagles.

- ✔ **If yours is a single-family home with older children, or no children:** Try a medium to large male or female Sporting, Hound, Herding, Non-Sporting, or Toy mix. Sighthounds (such as Greyhounds) aren't recommended because older children have a tendency to leave doors and gates open, and sighthounds can't be trusted not to run.

- ✔ **If you live in a country or rural setting:** Try any size female dog of any heritage. Herding and Sporting breeds will definitely thrive in this setting. Remember: If unneutered, male dogs may have a tendency to wander, which can be deadly, especially in a country or rural setting. (For more on why you should spay or neuter your dog, see Chapter 18.)

These aren't rules — they're just suggestions. Each dog is an individual with genetics that are distinctly his own. Much of a dog's personality rests with the training and quality of the care you give. Your best bet is to take the time to temperament-test (see Chapter 4) any dog you're considering, and take an educated plunge into mixed-breed dog ownership.

Chapter 4

Choosing Your New Best Friend

*W*ith the exception of designer dogs, mixed-breed dogs are far easier to find than purebred dogs, because there are more of them available. In this chapter, I fill you in on where to look.

When you decide on where you'll get your mixed breed, you need to know which questions to ask and how to determine if a specific dog is right for you. I arm you with a list of questions and a series of simple tests you can do with any dog to see if she'll be a good fit in your home.

Finding Your Very Own Mixed-Breed Dog

So many places, so little time. Mixed-breed dogs are everywhere! You'll find them in your local newspaper's classified section, on ads posted at pet shops and grocery stores, at animal shelters and humane societies. If you like surfing the Web, you'll find them there as well. In the following sections, I give you all the details you need.

Breeders

If you're searching for a designer puppy, finding a breeder is the best first choice. The best way to locate a breeder is either through your local newspaper's classifieds section or on the Internet. Based on my observation, accidental breeders (people who didn't intend to breed their dog) are most likely to advertise in the newspaper, whereas designer-dog breeders are most likely to have Web sites. This is just a general rule, though — as with any rule, there are exceptions, which is why you need to know what to look for in *any* breeder, no matter where you found him.

Whether you're talking to a designer-dog breeder, or an accidental breeder of a non-designer mix, here's a list of questions to ask:

- ✔ **Was this litter planned?** If so, it's more likely that your pup will be healthy because the breeder wants to produce good-quality pups.

- ✔ **How long have you been breeding dogs?** If the breeder says that the breeding wasn't intended, it's likely that his dog got loose and was bred by the neighborhood Casanova. If the breeder tells you that he's been doing it for several years, there's a good chance he is knowledgeable about the process.

- ✔ **If the litter was planned, how did you choose the parentage for this litter?** The breeder should relate the good genetic background of the parentage (for example, good health and temperament).

- ✔ **If the litter was planned, what types of health screens were done on the parent dogs?** A responsible breeder will have the parents' hips, eyes, and heart checked for abnormalities.

- ✔ **Can you give me the names and phone numbers of people who have bought puppies from you in the past?** A good breeder will be proud of his puppy placements. References shouldn't be a problem.

- ✔ **What do you look for in a potential puppy purchaser?** A concerned breeder wants the best homes for his pups.

- ✔ **Can you give me a copy of the pup's health records?** All pups should get their first worming at 5 weeks, another at 7 weeks, and their first vaccines at 7 weeks.

- ✔ **What are the puppies being fed?** If they're receiving a good-quality food (see Chapter 7), the breeder cares about giving the pups a good start.

If and when you actually visit the home of the breeder, ask yourself the following questions:

- ✔ **Is the odor overwhelmingly bad, tolerable, or nonexistent?** You want your puppy to come from a place that's clean, so the less offensive the odor, the better.

✔ **Where are the puppies being contained?** If they're inside the breeder's home, they're likely to get lots of early socialization, which is very important to their future behavioral development. If they're outside in a kennel, or merely with the mother, who is tied up outside, the pups probably never received proper handling or care.

✔ **How big is the operation?** Is this the breeder's profession? If so, the kennel may be large, but should not contain more than two different types of hybrid mixes.

✔ **Do you see external parasites (such as fleas, flea eggs, ticks, and mange) on the puppies?** If the pups are kept outdoors in unsanitary conditions, they'll probably have one or more external parasites along with some internal ones.

With all the money to be made on designer dogs, lots of breeders are popping up claiming to have designer puppies, without giving any thought to the backgrounds of the parents. Many of these breeders have become puppy mills, merely churning out pups without regard to the welfare of the animals.

Shelters

Animal shelters (including humane societies) are great places to find a mixed-breed dog. If you get a dog from a shelter, you're helping in many ways. You'll be saving a life. Plus, your adoption fees go toward helping other homeless pets.

Getting a dog from a shelter does carry some risk — you may be bringing home a dog who's sick. But the rewards outweigh the risk. (To minimize your risk, be sure to ask questions — see "Knowing Which Questions to Ask," later in this chapter.)

Rescue groups

Most rescue groups are dedicated to specific breeds, but they often take in dogs who are mixes of the breed they work with. Other rescue groups take in dogs of any breed.

The best place to locate a rescue group is through the Internet. Most rescue groups and humane societies tend to advertise their adoptable dogs on Petfinder.com. The AKC also has a page on its Web site that lists breed-specific rescue organizations (www.akc.org/breeds/rescue.cfm).

Knowing Which Questions to Ask

When you've found a dog you're interested in, your work has only just begun. You need to ask questions (either of the breeder, the shelter workers, or the rescue-group guardians) so that your decision is a rational one, not one based on how adorable the dog is. Here's a list of questions to start with:

- **What breeds are part of the dog's makeup?** The breeds that are part of the dog's family tree will give you a better idea of what to expect in terms of personality, size, and other attributes. (See Chapter 3 for more on all this.) The dog's current guardian may not be able to recognize every breed, but she should be able to give you an educated guess.

- **Which vaccinations has the dog received? Has the dog been neutered or spayed? Is the dog receiving heartworm and flea preventative?** Some shelters, such as those in rural areas, don't have the funds to handle these health issues, whereas most rescue groups make certain that these things are immediately handled upon the dog's acceptance into their group.

- **What is the dog's personality like? How about her social skills?** If the dog you're considering has been in a foster home for a while, the current guardian should be aware of the dog's overall behavior patterns.

- **How much exercise does she currently get? Is it enough to keep her satisfied?**

- **What is her behavior like when she's in the house? Does she live harmoniously with other dogs or cats?**

- **How does she do when walking on a leash?**

- **Has she learned any obedience commands?** If so, what are they? Be sure to ask how to perform those commands with her if you decide to adopt the dog.

- **What is the dog eating? Does it agree with her?** The best way of checking this is to ask whether her feces are solid (they should be) and medium to dark brown in color; that her weight is normal; and that she has bright eyes and a healthy coat.

- **What are the dog's feeding and relief schedules?**

- **Where is the dog comfortable sleeping?** In a crate? In a pen? In the bedroom? Somewhere else?

You need to find out as much as possible about this dog, so don't be afraid to ask. In fact, the dog's current guardians will be more likely to accept you as the dog's *new* guardian if you ask the right questions with a genuine interest in the answers.

Matchmaker, Matchmaker, Make Me a Match: Temperament Testing

When you've found a dog you think is right for you, you'll want to do what's known as temperament testing. Temperament testing is just what it sounds like — a way to test the dog's temperament and be sure she's right for you and your home. It informs you of the dog's overall personality — how she prefers to be touched, what frightens her, how she feels about being a family member, and whether or not she'll want to share her toys. It will also give you some insight into what her strengths may be (such as enjoying a game of retrieving or having strong herding ability).

There are five general tests you can perform with your potential new dog prior to bringing her into your life. I cover all of them in the following sections.

Be gentle: Testing for touch sensitivity

This test lets you know whether a dog has any special sensitivities in specific areas, as well as how she feels about being touched in a dominant manner. It's also a great way to break the ice, because most dogs *adore* being touched and will quickly become great friends with those who offer it.

Here's how to test a dog for touch sensitivity:

1. **Begin by petting the dog: Rub the top of her head, her back, and then her chest and tummy.**

   Most dogs, even overly excited ones, will calm slightly when getting a belly rub.

   Progress slowly while petting a fearful dog. Be patient if she moves away and allow her to approach you. Some dogs aren't familiar with being touched in certain areas such as their ears, tail, legs, or feet.

2. **When the dog has accepted touch on her upper body, move your hands down her legs: Lift her feet (see Figure 4-1), touching her paws and toenails.**

   Here are some possible reactions you may see:

   - **The dog growls.** If the dog growls, stop all temperament testing and move on to another dog. She may be injured or ill; ask her current guardian if the dog has shown any symptoms.

- **The dog moves away, growling.** A dog who moves away while growling may be aggressive and unsocialized. Don't force yourself on this dog — she might display fear aggression. Give her the opportunity to return to you without force. She may be injured or ill; again, ask the dog's current guardian if she's shown any symptoms.

- **The dog cringes but allows you to touch her.** A dog who allows you to touch her but cringes may be friendly but also may have been abused at some point in her life. She would do well in a quiet home with adult guardians who have lots of patience and time for her.

- **The dog allows touch, but doesn't react.** A dog who allows you to touch her but doesn't react may be ill or traumatized. It's highly unlikely that she won't respond to *some* form of touch — dogs love being massaged and touched, especially on their backs, chest, and tummies. Look closely for a sly grin — you may have missed it.

- **The dog allows touch and responds by moving closer.** A dog who moves closer as you touch will be a great candidate for most environments except for being left alone for long periods of time. This is also a dog who might display separation anxiety because she has a great need for pack unity. She'll likely work out well in a busy family home where there are family members who would like to include him in their activities.

Figure 4-1: Lift the dog's feet and touch her paws and toenails to see how sensitive she is.

What's that? Testing for movement and object sensitivity

Some dogs enjoy new sights and sounds; others get nervous in the same situation. Dogs raised in loving homes or with a conscientious breeder will likely be more inquisitive than frightened at seeing something new rolling around, while a dog who hasn't had exposure to new things, or had some bad experiences, might become frightened and move away.

This test helps you understand a dog's reaction to new things and moving objects. Here's how to do it:

1. **Collect several objects, such as a ball, squeaky toy, and bone. Have a baking pan, car keys, and a heavy book on hand.**

2. **Lay all the objects on the floor and allow the dog to investigate (see Figure 4-2).**

Figure 4-2: Be sure to include a variety of objects to see how the dog responds.

Here are some possible reactions you may see:

- **The dog moves away:** A dog who moves away is very fearful of new things. Unless you're very patient and live in a quiet household, you shouldn't adopt this dog.

- **The dog has no reaction:** If the dog doesn't react, she's indifferent to new things — or at least to *these* new things. If you have very young children or elderly parents living with you, this dog may be ideal.

- **The dog starts to investigate but stops and moves away:** A dog who starts to investigate but moves away will take time to acclimate to new situations.

- **The dog investigates the objects:** The dog who investigates the objects is inquisitive but not bold. She'll do well in most any home.

- **The dog investigates and interacts with the objects:** The dog who investigates and interacts is confident. She'll do well in a home with children and an active lifestyle.

3. **One at a time, pick up all the objects and roll them across the floor, observing the dog's reactions as you do.**

Begin with the object least likely to cause a reaction, such as a ball. Then try a bone, a squeaky toy, and car keys. Finish by dropping a pan or book.

Some possible reactions that you may see include the following:

- **The dog moves away:** A dog who moves away is fearful and should not be in an active home. This dog may react fearfully when overwhelmed by new events, sights, or sounds.

- **The dog has no reaction:** A dog who has no reaction is a very accepting dog who should do well in most environments.

Most healthy dogs have *some* reaction, though, so be sure that she at least watched the movement or responded somehow to the sound. Otherwise, you may want to check the dog's health.

- **The dog starts to chase but loses interest:** This dog may work out well in a quiet environment, but is unlikely to want to play much with toys. She may like chewing a bone, though.

- **The dog chases, grabs, and carries the object away from you:** This dog is bold, possessive, yet playful. She needs to be in a home with structure and consistency.

- **The dog chases, grabs, and brings the object to you:** This dog will be ideal if you have an active family. She loves to play, retrieve, and interact with the world.

Who's the boss? Testing for dominance and submission

This test will help you gauge a dog's dominant or submissive tendencies — very important to understand, because a dominant dog may be more difficult to control.

You may not see the full extent of a dog's dominant tendencies in her foster home, because she's one of many brought into a temporary environment. When she develops a sense of "home," she may begin to become territorial. Dogs test their boundaries as they're settling in.

There are several ways to test for dominance. Following is a list of all three tests.

Always begin with the least-invasive test (Step 1) and work your way to the more difficult (Step 2 and then Step 3). If you're at all unsure and the dog is reacting negatively, you may want to find another dog to bring home.

1. **Pick up the dog's front end, holding just behind the front legs (see Figure 4-3).**

Figure 4-3: Lifting the dog's front legs is a way to test her dominance.

Possible reactions you may see in the dog include the following:

- **The dog struggles, growls, and tries to bite or mouth you:** This reaction shows a very dominant dog. If you adopt her, you must remain assertive at all times and make sure you and she go through a lot of obedience work.

- **The dog struggles, but eventually gives in:** This reaction shows a bold dog, but not an overly dominant one. She still needs an assertive household and might do okay with older children who won't be afraid of her if she jumps on or chases them.

- **The dog shows extreme fear and yips:** This reaction shows a very fearful dog. This dog should live in a quiet home where her guardians will be patient and understanding.

I've seen dogs who have this reaction turn from being fearfully submissive to being in charge of their household. This can happen when overly permissive guardians give the dog a lot of leeway because she seems afraid. Dogs are smart — she may be displaying the fearful reaction *because* she wants to be allowed a dominant role. The bottom line: Let her make the first approach, but don't let her run the household.

- **The dog gives in readily, but moves away when released:** This reaction shows an insecure dog. This dog just may not feel at home in her current environment.

- **The dog submits and relaxes, remaining with you when released:** This reaction shows a secure dog. This dog would likely do well in any environment, with conscientious children of all ages. She'll learn quickly and enjoy every minute with you.

If you were able to perform Step 1 without the dog showing any aggression, and you feel comfortable with the dog, move on to Step 2.

2. **Sit and stare into the dog's eyes. Don't look away first.**

    Possible reactions you may see in the dog include the following:

    - **The dog stares back at you and growls:** This reaction is one of a very dominant dog. This is *not* a dog you'll want to live with — she'll challenge you every chance she gets.

If she's showing dominance at this point, you most definitely don't want to move on to Step 3. She may just be stressed in her current location, but you have no way of knowing that she won't be similarly stressed at some point after you bring her home.

- **The dog stares back at you and doesn't look away:**
  This reaction is still a dominant dog, but one who can
  be. Doing so will take consistency and diligence, as well
  as an assertive guardian who will make the dog work for
  everything. This dog will be happiest in a very structured environment.

- **The dog stares at you a moment and then looks away:**
  The dog who stares and looks away is unsure of her
  position. She may be testy in specific situations, such as
  when she really wants something, but she'll easily back
  down if her guardian remains assertive and insistent.

- **The dog never looks you in the eye:** The dog who never
  looks in your eyes is very submissive and accepting.
  This dog will do well in most environments.

If you were able to perform Step 2 without the dog showing
any aggression, you can give Step 3 a try. If the dog has
shown any dominance in the other tests, do *not* move on to
Step 3. Step 3 puts the dog in a totally submissive position
where she feels vulnerable.

3. **Roll the dog over onto her back.**

   Possible reactions you may see include the following:

   - **The dog struggles, growls, and tries to bite you:** This
     is the reaction of a very dominant dog. She's not a good
     candidate for anyone with children or an active home.
     She will do best with a single, assertive owner who will
     work with her and maintain a structured environment.

   - **The dog struggles but eventually gives in:** This is the
     reaction of a dog who has some dominant tendencies
     but who understands when she's not in charge. She'll
     do well in a home with assertive owners, but not with
     young children.

   - **The dog has no reaction and remains on her back with-
     out any struggle:** This dog will do well in any home. The
     dog feels comfortable and secure in her environment.

   - **The dog gives in quickly, cries, and moves away when
     released:** The dog who gives in but cries and moves
     away is very submissive and possibly fearful. She should
     live in a quiet home.

   - **The dog gives in quickly and remains with you when
     released:** This dog should work well in any home, though
     she should always be approached in a positive manner
     and be given lots of praise for everything she does.

I'll get that! Testing for possessiveness and retrieval ability

You want your dog to play fetch with you, so the mere fact that she runs after the toy is a great sign. Though, you'd really appreciate her bringing the toy back to you so you can throw it again. It's the give and take that makes the game.

Some dogs have the genetic tendency to play fetch following the rules; other dogs have different ideas. Some dogs would rather just chase the ball and take it elsewhere so that nobody else can play with it. Other dogs think you're nuts if you think she's going to chase that thing when she'd rather be sleeping or chewing on a bone.

This test will let you know which tendency is most likely in a dog. There are two parts to this test, and I cover both in the following sections.

Give and take

The reaction a dog has to this test will depend on the value of the object you give and take away. For example, for some dogs, a squeaky toy might be fun to play with, but a food-filled bone is of higher value, and the dog may not give it up easily.

Begin this test with a toy of lesser value, such as a stick or rubber toy, and gradually work your way toward something of higher value, like a tasty bone.

To do this test, just give the dog the item. Then gently take the item away, either offering another one in its place or caressing the dog as you take the object so as not to present a threatening situation.

Possible reactions you may see in the dog include the following:

- ✔ **The dog growls:** This dog is possessive. This dog is certainly not right for a family with anyone who isn't assertive.

- ✔ **The dog holds the object, but eventually gives it up:** This reaction shows a dog who is possessive but not aggressive about it. This dog will do well in a home with assertive owners, but not with young children.

- ✔ **The dog readily gives up the object or the dog drops the object and runs away:** Dogs who have these reactions will work well in any environment, but if the dog does run away, her guardians need to be patient with her, because assertiveness may overwhelm her.

Chase and retrieve

To do this test, take one of the dog's favorite toys, and throw it a short distance.

Possible reactions you may see in the dog include the following:

- ✔ **The dog goes after the toy, picks it up, and runs off:** A dog who runs off with the toy is possessive. She likes to chase her toys, but she doesn't want anyone else to share them with her.

- ✔ **The dog goes after the toy, picks it up, and lays down with it:** This dog may not be in a playful mood, but definitely wants to possess her toy.

- ✔ **The dog goes after the toy, sniffs it, and turns away:** This dog doesn't have much interest in the toy. Are you sure you chose a favored toy? If not, try again. If you did choose her favorite toy, this dog is one who just doesn't like to play fetch, or who is so stressed that playing isn't in her current itinerary.

- ✔ **The dog doesn't go after the toy:** This dog just doesn't like toys or doesn't care about that particular toy. Try additional toys until you get some response. If the dog doesn't have any response, the dog likely either hasn't gotten the point of toys or hasn't found anything that floats her boat.

- ✔ **The dog goes after the toy, picks it up, and returns it to you:** This dog is highly interactive and social. She wants to play with you and is a natural retriever. She'll likely do well in an active environment with children of all ages and people who spend lots of time with her.

Follow the leader: Testing for social skills

This test is important if you have other animals at home or live in an animal-filled neighborhood. The last thing you want to deal with is a dog who is aggressive to other dogs or wants to chase cats.

The only way you'll be able to do this test is if the dog is currently being housed in a facility where there are other animals. If she's currently in a foster home, she's probably already acclimated to living harmoniously with other animals so this test may not be necessary. But it can be useful if the dog is in a shelter or humane society without direct contact to other animals on a regular basis.

Here's what to do: Walk her by the kennels of the other dogs. Then walk her in the cat area.

Possible reactions you may see in the dog include the following:

- ✔ **The dog goes after any other dog or cat:** This is a dog who shouldn't go into a home with other dogs or cats or into a neighborhood that has many other dogs or cats in close quarters.

- ✔ **The dog only goes after other aggressive animals (those jumping, barking/meowing, or growling/hissing as she goes by):** This dog will fight if challenged. Again, not a good candidate in a home with other dogs or cats, or in a neighborhood where other dogs or cats are living or walking nearby.

- ✔ **The dog doesn't show aggression, but does show an eagerness to say hello to a quiet dog or cat:** This is a friendly dog who should do well in any environment.

- ✔ **The dog walks by with no reaction:** This dog should do well in any environment.

- ✔ **The dog runs by and tries to get away from the aggressive dogs and cats:** This dog should do well in a home with other dogs or cats, but should be introduced carefully and with as much positive reinforcement as possible. She's probably never had the opportunity to socialize with other animals and just needs some time to acclimate.

Some dogs react negatively toward cats but love other dogs. And believe it or not, some dogs love cats and can't stand other dogs. Pay close attention to how the dog reacts to dogs as well as cats — she may be fine with one species and not the other. Do keep in mind your neighborhood, though. For example, if you live in an apartment complex with other dog owners, and the dog you're considering doesn't like other dogs, you could run into trouble every time you take your dog out for a walk.

Part II
Living with Your Mixed-Breed Dog

"He's part Greyhound, so I always mix a little fast food with his kibble."

In this part . . .

1 tell you what you need to do to dog-proof your home and get it ready for your new best friend — everything from removing chewing hazards to stocking up on supplies to setting aside a comfy place for your dog to sleep.

When you bring your new dog into your home, you don't want to let her loose and see what happens. Instead, take her on a guided tour to investigate her new digs and new family members. In this part, I tell you how.

Your biggest challenge will be scheduling time for your new dog. I give you all kinds of suggestions to make sure you give your dog all the time she needs.

I also give you pointers on what to feed your new dog. I tell you what to look for in commercial dog foods, and provide some recipes you can try if you want to make your own dog food.

I tell you everything you need to know about grooming your dog. From dental hygiene to pedicures to checking for parasites, the information in this part will help you keep your dog clean and healthy.

Finally, I let you know how much exercise your mixed-breed dog needs and fill you in on some fun activities you and your dog can enjoy together.

Chapter 5

Getting Ready for Your Dog's Arrival

Clean, hide, remove, and buy. This chapter covers all the things you need to do to prepare your home for your new mixed breed — from getting rid of safety hazards to setting up his new abode. If you've found your dog and you're just waiting to pick him up from the shelter or breeder, you've come to the right place!

Dog-Proofing Your House

Put everything away. And I mean everything! A dog who hasn't grown up and/or been shown how to live in a home could be into anything that looks edible — from books and magazines, to eyeglasses, TV remotes, telephones, and MP3 players, your dog will see something interesting and set his teeth on it.

Your mixed-breed dog isn't necessarily inherently destructive — not any more than a human toddler who tests everything by putting it in her mouth. He's just investigating his environment to see what might taste good and what's just fun to play with.

In time, you'll be able to get your home life back to normal, but until your new mixed breed learns what he can and can't play with, be safe — and until you can trust him — you need to keep your home dog-proofed. Not only is this better for your relationship with your dog, but it's less of a health hazard for him (some dogs swallow things that can poison them or otherwise wreak serious havoc with their insides).

In the following sections, I fill you in on the major steps you need to take to make sure your home is safe for your new friend.

Removing chewing hazards

If your new dog is older than 2 years old, removing chewing hazards isn't as big of a deal. This issue is more important with young dogs, because they're still exploring their environment and tend to chew anything, especially between 3 and 9 months of age (when they're teething). An adult dog may chew if he has separation anxiety when you're not nearby.

Empty your trash cans daily. They're very enticing to a dog, especially if the trash contains discarded food. Get a covered can for your kitchen, or place the can inside a cabinet so your dog can't get into the garbage. Remember: This isn't just to prevent a mess — the trash can include all kinds of dangerous things, like chicken bones, batteries, plant cuttings. Even the ink on paper can be poisonous or become clogged in your dog's intestines.

Electrical cords are a huge hazard. Not only can a dog pull on them and yank the appliance down on top of himself, but if he chews on the electrical cord, he could die. Either make sure that all electrical cords are up out of his reach, or cover them with steel conduit to prevent him from chewing the actual cord. Keeping electrical items unplugged when you're not available to watch your dog is also a good idea.

Put your poisonous houseplants (see Chapter 7 for a list) in a room where your dog can't get to them, or arrange them on a high enough platform that he can't get to them.

Many household supplies — including bleach, detergents, moth balls, pine and citrus oils, insecticides, rat baits, antifreeze, and batteries — are also very dangerous to your dog. Make sure that they're all out of reach of your dog.

Outside there are other hazards — some poisonous, others merely destructive. Put away the garden hose, any potting supplies, lounge-chair cushions, and children's toys. If you have candles or small lanterns on tables, place them in a safe area as well — especially citronella candles. The only things you can't put away are your land-scaping plants and the large patio set, though if any of the furniture is made of wood, either put it out of reach, or cover it daily with a product like Bitter Apple. Or you can always keep an eye on your mixed breed when he's outdoors and redirect him away from the furniture toward a toy.

If you have a garden within an area available to your dog, put a secure fence around it.

Protecting your furniture

In my house, the dogs aren't allowed on the furniture. I've made this a house rule for several reasons:

- ✔ It prevents my furniture from being destroyed by muddy paws and sharp claws.

- ✔ It maintains my dogs' understanding of their place in my household. Many dogs who are allowed on the furniture feel as though they're superior to others (including the people in the house) and become dominant.

- ✔ It keeps my guests from being walked over by my dogs.

- ✔ What if my dogs are used to lying on the couch and they get sick? I've never wanted to have to clean vomit and diarrhea off the upholstery.

If you'd like to keep your dog off of your furniture, and if your new dog is a pup, have lots of nasty-tasting spray on hand to make sure he doesn't develop a taste for wood. Several products — such as Bitter Apple, Fooey, Bitter Lime, and more — are readily available at pet shops for just this purpose.

If you're bringing an adult dog into your home, and you think he might like jumping up on the furniture, there are things you can do to prevent this. In fact, you may want to implement them prior to bringing your mixed breed home so that he quickly learns that the furniture is off limits:

- ✔ Put things in the way so that he can't become comfortable on the couch.

- ✔ Put a ScatMat (an electrified mat that tingles the paws when pressed) across the furniture so that if he tries to get up, his toes get a tingle. (They're available in most pet stores or through www.contech-inc.com.)

- ✔ Place some pans across the couch so that they make noise when jostled, either chasing him off the furniture or at the very least letting you know that he's trying it again so you can redirect his actions.

- ✔ Close off the room so that he can't access the furniture that you don't want him jumping on.

If you've read all this and you're thinking, "Hey, half the reason I'm getting a dog is so I can curl up on the couch with him and watch movies or read a book," you may want to look into furniture covers so your upholstery won't be ruined by his claws. Or you can use a thick throw blanket to cover the areas where you'll allow him to sit. You can also restrict which pieces of furniture he's allowed up on. Maybe you let him up on the couch in the family room, but not on the furniture anywhere else in the house. Whatever works for you — the important thing is to be consistent with your dog.

Pushing up daisies: Giving your dog a place to dig

Dogs will dig. The trick is to give your mixed breed a place where he can dig without destroying your home or yard. If a dog doesn't have an opportunity to dig (or to get some other equally fun form of exercise), he'll search for other activities — such as chewing your furniture, digging up the carpet, pulling up linoleum, eating drywall, or something else along those lines.

Digging is a form of exercise for your dog. So, instead of merely letting him outside to race around the yard by himself, go with him. Play tag, play hide and seek, throw toys. If at any time he starts to dig, redirect him into another game. As long as he stays busy and happy, he won't dig.

Dogs also dig to create a cool place to lie down. If it's hot outside and your mixed breed can't go into a cool house, he'll dig around bushes and the house foundation. Offering a small wading pool with cool water will help fulfill this need to make a comfortable resting area. Keep the wading pool in the shade so that the water doesn't become too hot to be comfortable. Throw some floating toys in the pool to make it more enticing. Better yet, go in there with him and splash around. It's more fun with two!

If you'd like a place to allow your mixed breed the freedom to run and dig, partition part of your yard for this purpose.

If you have a small dog and want to set up a special play area for him, consider using some baby gates to keep him contained within a specific room. Put lots of toys, blankets, and a few small children's outdoor play toys in the room. This may sound extravagant, but if you meet your dog's need to dig, he'll stay out of trouble elsewhere.

Born to run: Making sure your dog can't escape

A secure yard is very important when you own a dog. If you got your mixed breed at a shelter, it's likely that he became a stray because he was left in an unfenced yard and he ran away. If dogs aren't happy, they'll seek other accommodations. If they're lonely, they'll seek other dogs to socialize with. If they're abused, they'll try to escape. If they're bored, they'll look for ways to occupy their time.

The best fencing is a wood privacy fence. Not only does this offer a solid barrier, but it also keeps other dogs and pranksters from tormenting your dog. With this type of fence, your mixed breed is less likely to run the fence, chasing other dogs. The height of the fence depends on the size of your dog. A dog under 10 inches at the shoulder should be fine with a 3-foot-high fence. A dog up to 18 inches at the shoulder should be safe with a 4-foot fence. Any dog over 18 inches at the shoulder, especially one who can jump high, needs a 6-foot-high fence.

Alternatives to wood privacy fences include

- ✔ **Chain link:** This is a good way of keeping your dog at home — it's just not as pretty as a nice wood fence and it doesn't give you and your dog the same level of privacy. The same guidelines regarding height apply to chain link as apply to wood fencing.

- ✔ **Wire mesh:** This works well as long as it's installed correctly. Wire mesh may be less expensive than wood or chain link, but it's even less attractive than chain link and often not as secure. I don't recommend this type of fencing for anything other than a small dog who isn't prone to digging and jumping.

- ✔ **Invisible fencing:** This is great if you live in a neighborhood with rules against fencing. It's also good for fencing in large areas, giving the dog lots of space to run. However, an invisible fence doesn't keep others out, which leaves your dog open to attack from other dogs or people who are looking to steal him. Dogs learn the boundaries of an invisible fence within a week and adhere to them, though some dogs will test the collar batteries now and then to see if they can make a run for it.

    Invisible fencing consists of a wire that's buried 1 or 2 inches around the boundary of your yard and attached to a transmitter that maintains the boundary distance, most commonly set at 6 to 15 feet. The dog wears a collar that beeps if he gets within 2 feet of the set boundary. If he continues and enters the "no zone," he gets a mild electric stimulation. Be very careful if you intend to use this type of fencing. Remain with your dog until he's aware of his boundaries and feels comfortable enough to use the yard.

If you don't have the luxury of being able to fence a yard, you'll have to take your dog for walks on a leash. Walks aren't a bad thing — they're actually very positive, because you get to spend lots of time with your dog. In fact, even if you have a fenced yard, you should make an effort to walk your dog at least once a day. This becomes a special time that your mixed breed will look forward to.

Many neighborhoods have fenced dog parks. These areas are great for letting your dog freedom to play in relative safety. It also gives him a chance to socialize with other dogs and people — a great combination. However, some dog owners aren't conscientious about cleaning their dog's mess, or teaching their dogs to not play aggressively. Always keep a watchful eye as the dogs play and remove your dog from any sticky situations.

Your Mixed-Breed Dog's Bedroom

Dogs need a place to sleep where they feel safe and secure. You have a few options, so before you bring your dog home, think about what will work best for you and your dog.

Crate or pen? Your dog's first place to sleep

Many dogs who don't yet know the house rules will have accidents indoors or play with something that isn't a dog toy. Until you know for sure that your mixed breed won't have an accident in the house or be destructive, contain him in a crate or pen when you're not around to watch him — including during the night. This will become your dog's private room where he can go when he wants some peace and quiet, as well as a place for him to sleep.

Furnish the crate or pen with a bowl of water, a couple of toys, and a comfortable bed (see the "Bedding" section, later in this chapter). Be sure to acclimate your dog to his bed using positive reinforcement, teaching him that it's a nice place to be. The crate should never be used as a place of punishment, nor should the dog be imprisoned within it for long periods of time every day.

Although a crate offers the safest sleep area, a pen may work for a dog who feels too cramped within a crate. An exercise pen consists of eight 2-foot-wide side panels. The pen can be folded for storage, or opened to the full extent, giving your dog 16 cubic feet of space. If your dog likes to climb or is in any way an escape artist, a pen is not the place to contain him, because he'll easily climb out.

Thinking outside the box: Letting your dog sleep outside a crate or pen

Don't let your dog sleep outside a crate or pen unless you're absolutely sure she won't get into trouble when you aren't watching her.

Start by keeping him in an enclosed room, such as the kitchen (if during the day) or your bedroom with you (if at night). When your mixed breed proves reliable with these areas, you can gradually open up your house a little more.

Even if you're adopting a dog with a proven housetraining background, you may still want to initially restrict him to smaller areas of the house because dogs sometimes soil indoors when moving into a new home.

Bedding

The type of bedding you give your dog depends largely on the situation and size of your dog. For example, a small dog can be spoiled with one of those canopy luxury beds, while a big dog might be most comfortable on a big pillow or hammock type dog bed.

The main consideration when shopping for a bed is ease of cleaning and durability. I've found that the beds with a structure made of PVC pipe are the hardiest and easiest to clean — you just hose them off. This is a great bed for indoors or out, and few dogs will have a tendency to put their teeth to work on them.

A good bed for the crate is a pillow or mat-type bed. Look for something thin enough to go into the washing machine, or a bed that has a removable outer shell.

Some dogs make it a point to destroy their beds or soil on them. If your dog falls into this category, don't give him any bedding at all until these tendencies go away.

If you live in an area where fleas are an issue, a cedar-filled bed will help control the pests and protect your pet. Cedar is a natural flea repellent and great for filling up a pillow bed, giving your dog a comfortable place to sleep. This is great for an outdoor bed or if your dog's bedroom is located in the basement or a storage area.

Don't buy your dog an expensive bed until he's proven that he won't eat it or soil it. At that point you can go and get him that bedroom set you've been eyeing.

Giving Your Dog a Place to Eat

The most convenient area to feed your dog is usually the kitchen, because the flooring is easy to clean and most people prefer to keep food in one area of the house. Plus, your dog will like the consistency of knowing where he eats.

Dogs should always have access to fresh water. However, if you want to prevent water spillage, offer your dog his water in a raised feeder appropriate to his size. Place this in his eating area.

Stocking Up on Supplies

Ah, the fun part! You get to go on a shopping spree for your new dog! Although it's loads of fun to go to a huge pet-supply store, it's also more expensive than shopping via catalog or online. (See the Cheat Sheet in the front of this book for some online resources.)

The basic supplies include a collar (more than one if you want to be stylish), a leash or two, food and water dishes, a bed (see "Bedding," earlier in this chapter), and toys. You may also want to get a travel carrier (see Chapter 17), a home crate/pen, and grooming supplies (see Chapter 8). Prior to bringing your new mixed breed home, you also need to stock up on his food (see Chapter 7).

Collars and leashes

Many different types of collars and leashes are available. The type you choose depends on your dog's temperament and how you intend to use the collar. If you're using the collar to make a fashion statement, get a separate collar for training purposes. And if you have a training collar on your dog, be sure to remove it the moment you're done with the training session.

The typical buckle or snap-on collar is great for making a fashion statement and for displaying your dog's rabies tag, ID tag, and license.

If you're looking to get a training collar, there are many to choose from. I recommend getting a head halter (Comfort Trainer and Halti are two good brands), a Gentle Leader Easy Walk Harness (www.gentleleader.com), or a SENSE-ation Harness (www.softouchconcepts.com).

In terms of leashes, your dog will walk best with a 4- to 6-foot walking leash that isn't overly heavy or difficult for you to hold. I find that a ½-inch leather leash offers optimal comfort for both the dog and the person — and it lasts a long time. Cotton leashes are also generally comfortable, but not practical if your mixed breed pulls hard. Nylon is fine for a dog who doesn't pull at all.

Dishes and bowls

Which dishes and bowls are right for your dog depends on his size and temperament. Here are a few things to consider:

- ✔ **Size:** If the dog is large, don't get a dish that's barely big enough to fit his nose. Make sure he can fit his entire face in it as he eats his food. On the other hand, you may not want to use a large bowl for a small dog. He'll spend more time chasing down the flying kibble than eating it. For dogs with long ears, get a bowl that's narrow at the top and flares out at the bottom — this will keep his ears from getting into the food.

- ✔ **Material:** If your dog is likely to play with his dishes, you don't want anything breakable. Ceramic is out of the question, regardless of how heavy-duty it appears. If he'll chew the dishes, you don't want plastic ones. It doesn't matter if the plastic is very thick — he can get his teeth into it and have a great time demolishing the dish. Also, some dogs develop contact allergies (hypersensitivity to plastic).

  Stainless steel dishes are my dish of choice. They last a very long time, can't be destroyed (even if your mixed breed has all sorts of games planned for his dinner dish), and are easy to clean.

- ✔ **Elevation:** Whether you put your dog's bowls on the ground or in an elevated feeder depends on the size of your dog and how he eats. A small dog is fine with his dish on the floor. A medium to large dog should have a raised feeder if he tends to eat quickly or likes to play in his food or water. The raised feeder will prevent him from putting his paws in his food and tracking it around the house.

Toys

The types of toys you should get are totally dependent on your dog. Obviously, you want to get a toy that's the right size for your dog so he can get the most use out of it — big dog, big toy; small dog, small toy.

Stay away from anything that can cause choking, diarrhea, or allergic reactions. This means no rawhide sticks, chips, or edible toys that contain cornstarch, wheat glutens, or chemical preservatives. I know this rules out a lot of the things that dogs like chewing — some of which even claim to be good for dogs' teeth and gums — but if you don't want to have to take your mixed breed to the vet for expensive allergy tests, steer clear of these items.

There are lots of interactive toys that are safe and fun for your dog. Toys that have hollow areas to put kibble or squeeze treats (like cheese that comes from a squeeze can) are always popular.

Small dogs may do well with plush toys that have squeakers, or even vinyl squeaker toys. However, I don't recommend these toys for dogs over 25 pounds, unless the dog has proven that he won't shred the toy.

All dogs do well with real beef shank bones. The bones have thick walls, and are hollow on the inside, offering a great place to stuff food and treats. These toys last for years — they're indestructible.

Hollow bones are great for dogs who teethe. They can be filled with canned food, and then frozen. Give it to the dog when you can't watch him for an hour or two. He'll stay busy and get some relief for his gums.

There are lots of toys to choose from. Consider the size and temperament of your mixed breed before you splurge on items that'll end up in the garbage or lodged in your dog's intestines. Start out with one toy and see how he likes it. Add additional toys over time. And when you've accumulated a bunch of toys, rotate them out, keeping some set aside in a closet or someplace where the dog can't get them — then rotate the toys every once in a while, and your dog will think it's his birthday all over again!

Chapter 6

Bringing Home Your Mixed Breed

*B*ringing your new dog home involves more than just leading her through the front door. You want your dog to walk into a loving home where every experience she has is a positive one.

In this chapter, I give you tips on introducing your new dog to the people and animals she'll be living with. You'll show your mixed-breed dog where her food, water, and bed are, as well as where she should go to relieve herself.

If your mixed-breed dog recently left her brothers and sisters, or a foster home where she had become attached to someone, she'll be feeling mighty lonely without her special friends. In this chapter, I let you know what to expect and how to help your dog feel safe and comfortable in her new home.

Finally, you need to schedule time for your new mixed breed. You need to figure out how your new family member fits into your own busy schedule, when and where she'll get her exercise, what times are good for meals, and when you'll take her out to relieve herself. In this chapter, I offer some tips on all these topics.

Giving Your Dog the Guided Tour

You want to introduce your new mixed breed to your home — and everything and everyone in it — in a controlled, calm, and loving manner, from the first minute you arrive. Proper introductions will help her settle in faster and feel secure in her new home.

Walking her in and showing her around

If you're driving your mixed-breed dog home, be sure to put her on a leash and walk her from the vehicle to your door. This prevents her from running off, especially important because she has no idea where she is and could easily become lost (not to mention hit by a car).

The other reason a leash is important is because you want to have some control over where she goes after she's inside. You want to take each room slowly, so that your dog won't feel overwhelmed. Here are some basic steps to follow:

1. **Walk her into a room.**

2. **Let her sniff around the room, still on the leash.**

3. **In each room, tell your dog to sit. If she doesn't listen, place her into position and reward her so that she learns the meaning of the word, Sit.**

4. **After she sits, praise her, pet her, and give her treats.**

5. **Move on to the next room.**

   Repeat these steps until you've gone through every room in your house — even rooms you plan on keeping off-limits for your dog. This approach will help her feel more comfortable.

 Dogs react to the emotions of the people around them. If you remain calm, you'll help your new dog feel more relaxed.

Put other family dogs outdoors when bringing in your new mixed breed. This will prevent any territorial disputes and help your new dog settle in faster. When she's comfortable, allow her to meet other four-legged family members one at a time.

Greeting the family

Everyone probably wants to be the first to greet your new dog. But the last thing you should do is let everyone come up at once. Being swarmed by a bunch of strangers is way too overwhelming for your new dog. Instead, make sure that each family member has a treat in hand and then take turns allowing the dog to come and accept the treat. As the dog eats the treat, pet her gently on her chest and talk to her in a happy, calm tone of voice. When your dog is done with the first treat, repeat with the next person until everyone in the family has had a turn. The meeting will be positive, and the dog will learn that everyone in your family is a source of all kinds of love and treats.

Always closely supervise children as they interact with your new dog. They need to be taught responsible handling techniques and that the dog should sit for them prior to giving her a treat or petting.

To a dog, being the source of treats means good things. You definitely get on a dog's good side through her stomach. Gentle massages are great, too — especially the ears, tummy, and back.

Meeting other pets

Introducing your new dog to your other pets is something you need to put a little thought into. An unplanned introduction can go very badly for the new dog, as well as your other pets.

Don't make the introductions at the same time you enter your home with your mixed-breed dog — it could be threatening to the existing family pets, who may become territorial and assertive. Keep your other animals in a safe area away from where your new dog will be entering and exploring your home.

Do the first introductions in neutral territory. A great meeting place is anywhere that your current pet doesn't spend much time, someplace where she won't feel territorial.

Introductions to other dogs

The best way to ensure that your new mixed-breed dog will be welcome into a home that already has a dog or two is for you to take your current dogs to meet the new family member prior to bringing her home. If they do well together, then the canine welcoming committee will be more favorable. If not, then you know to not adopt that particular dog.

The best way for dogs to meet is on their own terms. This means off leash (or if you're unsure, allow the leash to drag) in a safely fenced area where they can greet each other in their own way. You'll see lots of rear-end sniffing, nose-to-nose sniffing, *posturing* (walking around stiff-legged, putting a paw over the other dog's shoulders, or fur raising along the spine, among other things), and maybe some whining, whimpering, or barking.

Regardless of what you see, most dogs work it out well on their own without your help. In fact, getting in the way of this initial canine socializing can cause problems as you aren't allowing the dogs to do what they need to do to figure out where they stand within the pack pecking order. After the dogs figure out where they stand, one dog will bow down and invite the other to play. Then they're off and running, lifetime friends.

Here are some signs that the dogs may have some difficulty getting along:

- ✔ **One of the dogs is snarling.**

- ✔ **The dogs rush at each other growling.**

- ✔ **Both dogs posture and try to get on top of each other.**

- ✔ **One of the dogs shows complete disinterest and tries to walk away, but the other dog persistently tries to gain that dog's attention.** This might happen if one of the dogs is very old and has no interest in playing with another dog, but the other dog wants very much to play. The older dog may snap or injure the persistent younger dog. Or the younger dog may inadvertently injure the older dog.

- ✔ **The dogs stare at each other for a long time, challenging dominance.**

If you notice any of these signs, separate them immediately.

A good means of acclimating dueling dogs is to walk them together. Initially, have one person walk one dog and another person walk the other dog. Walk the dogs side by side, but make sure the dogs are separated by one or both of the people. When both dogs are paying more attention to their people than to each other, you can bring them closer together while walking.

When the dogs can walk in the same direction together, they'll need to learn to pass each other. Start them at a distance where the dogs don't react to each other. Each time the dogs can pass each other without reacting, bring them a little closer together on the next pass by.

When both dogs are working well together, they can have the freedom to play together in a neutral area, such as a park or down the road from your house. However, if you're still uncomfortable with allowing the dogs to interact, or you see something in their actions that is bothersome, contact a professional dog trainer or animal behaviorist right away. It never hurts to get a second or third opinion on the dogs' interactions.

Projecting a positive attitude

When you're helping two dogs acclimate to each other, keep your emotions in check. In order for the dogs to gain comfort, you need to remain passive yet positive about the situation. Your first dog will be directly affected by your emotions, showing edginess if you're pensive, or aggression if you're totally scared of the two dogs getting together. The new dog will quickly pick up on this negative energy flowing from you. Keeping your thoughts — and your energy — positive will help the two dogs acclimate to each other quickly.

Introductions to cats

Introducing your new dog to a cat can be dicey — some cats won't be as open to greeting your new mixed-breed dog as the dog is to saying hello, often with enthusiasm, to a running, screeching cat. If your mixed-breed dog believes cats are there to be chased, their relationship will be off to a rocky start.

All meat-eating animals have a *prey drive,* a desire to hunt that's triggered by something (or many things). For dogs and cats, movement is one of these triggers; scent comes in a close second. Most dogs chase cats merely because they move (usually running away from dogs). The dog isn't chasing the cat because she's hungry — the movement merely triggers the dog's instinctual desire to hunt.

You have to quickly let your dog know that the cat is supposed to be a friend, not prey. In order for the dog to get the message, you have to keep the cat still during the initial introduction. Have someone hold your cat as you introduce your mixed-breed dog to her. Here's how to hold your cat:

1. **Hold her paws in your hands.**

   Front paws in one hand, rear paws in the other.

2. **Place one arm around the cat's haunches to control movement of her back end. Place the other arm around her shoulders for control of the front end.**

3. **Sit and keep your kitty on your lap, holding securely.**

When you're ready to introduce your new dog to your cat, follow these steps:

1. **Put your dog on a leash.**

2. **Allow your dog to push her nose at the cat, with a loose leash.**

   As your kitty remains still, your mixed-breed dog's prey drive will not be initiated.

3. **Offer both the dog and the cat some tasty treats.**

   This will make the experience of meeting each other a more positive one. It will give them both good associations in each other's presence.

   Don't let go of the cat until your mixed-breed dog begins to lose interest and turns away. Instead of just letting go of the cat, place her in another room. This will ensure that she doesn't run and trigger your dog's prey drive.

It may take several such meetings in order to ensure that the two creatures become friends. However long it takes, the time spent is well worth it. Not having to separate your pets and teaching them to be comfortable together not only gives you less to worry and fuss about, but also gives them the chance to be companions instead of enemies.

Feline/canine companionship rarely entails the rough play that you see between dogs. It's more of a comfort level in each other's presence.

Taking her out to do her business

Shortly after introducing your dog to your house, your family, and your other animals, you'll need to show your new dog where she should do her business.

Because your dog is new to your household, you need to go with her to show her where to relieve herself. Just letting her out the door might make her uncomfortable. She's not yet familiar with the yard and she'll want to come back inside with you, where she may potty on the floor — not the behavior you were looking for.

Instead, take her to her potty zone — on a leash if your yard isn't fenced. Have some treats with you. Wait with her as long as it takes for her to relieve herself. Your dog has been busy with all the activities, so you can be sure she has to go. Walk around a bit with her, allowing her to sniff. Make certain the leash is very loose at all times.

When your dog does her business, praise her enthusiastically and give her treats. This positive reinforcement tells the dog that you're happy that she relieved herself outside, in the area you want her to do her business.

Until your mixed breed is familiar with the yard, you'll need to continually accompany her to the relief zone, giving treats the moment
she does her thing.

Many dogs, especially those new to a pack, will follow the behavior
patterns of the established pack. This helps them be accepted by
the other dogs and, even better, learn the house rules faster.

Showing the dog her sleeping area

In order to feel at home, your mixed breed will need to know where
to sleep. After all the commotion of introductions and being walked
around on the leash, she'll be very tired. Before leaving your dog to
her own devices, show her where you'd like her to rest.

Place her bed in a quiet area, offering safe containment. This can
be an alcove with a baby gate separating it from the rest of the
house, an exercise pen, or a crate (see Chapter 10).

Prior to placing your dog in her area, put fresh water within easy
reach and include at least three toys along with a comfortable bed.

Remain with your new dog for a few minutes. *Remember:* You're
her source of comfort. Show her the toys — interact with her and
the toys to increase her interest in them. Stroke her gently and
speak in a soothing tone of voice. All these things will help your
dog relax.

You'll know you can leave her in her room when:

- ✔ She lays on her hip.
- ✔ Her head lowers.
- ✔ Her breathing is calm and slow.

Toyland: Choosing the right toys

So many toys, so little time. You really won't know which toys your dog likes until
you've tried a few of them and gauged her reaction. Some dogs merely mouth their
toys while others demolish them.

The safest bets are heavy-duty toys that you can fill with food treats — such as
sterilized hollow shank bones, Kong toys, Buster Food Cubes, and others along those
lines. A delectable toy will maintain your dog's attention, preventing her from using
her bed or your walls as chewing outlets. Offer a variety at all times.

If she gets up when you leave (which is a possibility, because her source of comfort is no longer nearby), don't give in and return. Unless you plan on always sleeping with your dog, she needs to get used to the idea of being alone in her area. Go about your business and don't look at her. She'll either turn her attention to the toys or return to napping.

Fighting Those First-Night Blues

Being in a new place with a new family is tough, especially when your dog may have been attached to people or other animals in her last home. The first night in your house may be very frightening — she's found all kinds of new smells, new people, and new companions. It's a lot to take in all at once. Where's the dog she used to cuddle with? What are all those new sounds?

It may take a day or two for your new mixed-breed dog to acclimate to her new home. Until then, you need to understand why she's unable to relax and figure out how to help her.

Whether you got your mixed-breed dog from a breeder, picked her up from a rescue group, or adopted her from a humane society, she was probably living with other dogs (or puppies) and had formed a relationship with them. Dogs are pack animals, social creatures. They want the company of other canines and they're very lonely when they're separated from them. Your new mixed breed will likely miss her former friends until she feels at home with you.

This situation can be far different if you already have another dog, as long as the other dog has accepted your new dog and is willing to allow her to remain nearby at night. However, if your new dog isn't readily accepted as part of the pack, she'll likely pace, whine, and scratch to get to you.

The first tendency of new dog owners is to take their anxious dog into bed with them, thinking this is the best way to alleviate the poor dog's insecurity. Unless you're planning on always doing this, don't. Yes, your dog might sleep better, but you'll regret it later if you really want her to sleep somewhere else.

 Allowing your dog to sleep with you is setting a precedent for the future. Your dog learns that whining and scratching will earn her a place in the *preferred* bed. Plus, this will make her feel empowered, in control of the family instead of merely a family member. This situation can be a dangerous one for a mixed-breed dog with dominant tendencies.

The first night may be difficult for both of you, but setting the house rules early in the game will help your new dog learn her place within your family and home. She'll settle in faster, learn her role, and discover the difference between right and wrong.

Here are some things you can do to help your new mixed breed dog settle in:

✔ Sit with her a while at her bed, massaging her chest, back, and ears.

✔ Keep the lights turned low, not off.

✔ Try to avoid sharp noises.

✔ Give her herbal remedies such as valerian root or chamomile tablets an hour before bedtime to help her relax. You can find these at nearly any store that sells vitamins.

✔ Flower remedies such as Equilite brand, Home Sweet Home, or Bach Flower Rescue Remedy (see Chapter 12) are great for helping your dog settle into her new home. You can obtain these online or at many popular pet stores.

Before putting her to bed give her lots of exercise. A tired dog doesn't have the energy to stress.

Scheduling Time for Your New Dog

You got a dog to enrich your life. Your new mixed breed gives you joy and is something you look forward to each day — and you need to be the same for her. You have to make time for her — time for exercise, specific feeding and relief schedules, and an education (see Chapter 11).

When you make a schedule stick to it. Dogs are creatures of habit. Knowledge of what's going to occur, and when, helps your mixed breed dog adjust to her new life quickly.

Exercise and playtime

Exercising your dog is just as important as feeding her. Set aside time each day to play with your dog and work with her.

The amount of exercise she needs depends on her age, her breed mix, and her personality. But you can be certain that without enough exercise, she'll engage in the wrong activities — both to get your attention and to occupy her time.

Walking along on a leash does is great exercise, especially for an older dog, but younger dogs need more than this.

Though training exercises do stimulate your dog's mind, and make her tired, they don't totally exercise her body. Dogs need free play — off leash, preferably with other dogs, provided they haven't ever displayed any aggression to other canines.

A small dog will often get plenty of exercise racing around the house, but that isn't the preferred situation for a medium-sized or large dog. Having an 80-pound dog racing around an apartment or even a good-sized house can be quite disruptive. More so as she jumps over the couch, runs through the kitchen, and barrels over a trash can or two. Having any dog larger than 10 pounds means lots of exercise — outside, in all types of weather.

A fenced yard will help, but your mixed-breed dog will prefer to spend much of her exercise time interacting with you, such as going for long walks, and playing fetch and chase games. Make time for this.

Feeding time

Dogs need to know when they're going to eat. Feed your mixed breed in the same location every time so that she knows where she'll be eating. This will help prevent her feeling that she can eat anywhere in your home, which can set her up for future anxiety (see Chapter 12).

Your mixed-breed dog's feed dish should be somewhere in the kitchen, but not in a direct path with your cooking area. Under a desk, at one end of a kitchen island, or at the edge of the room are generally good places. Place the water dish near the feed dish.

Don't place the dog's dish near a trash can. She might think the can is part of her meals.

Stick to a feeding schedule to help your dog know that she'll be taken care of at a specific time. The feeding times depend greatly on your own work schedule, as well as the age of your mixed-breed dog.

Let's say you work a regular 9-to-5 job. In order to give your mixed-breed dog time to exercise and relieve herself before and after work, try the following scheduling:

6 a.m.	Take her to her relief zone.
6:15 a.m.	Feed her.
6:30 to 7 a.m.	Take her to her relief zone and exercise her a bit before leaving for work.
5:30 to 6 p.m.	Take her to her relief zone.
6:15 p.m.	Feed her.
7 p.m.	Take her to her relief zone and exercise her a lot.

What about if you work irregular hours? Regardless, try to stick to some semblance of a schedule. You may not be able to offer consistent exercise times, but you do need to offer similar feeding times.

Due to their faster metabolism, young dogs need to be fed more often than older dogs. Here's a sample feeding schedule for a dog under 5 months of age for someone who works the regular 9-to-5 job, keeping in mind that there *will* be an opportunity for the youngster to eat and exercise midday — whether you can come home at that time, or have someone do it for you, it's an important consideration when bringing home a young dog.

6 a.m.	Take her to her relief zone.
6:15 a.m.	Feed her.
6:30 a.m.	Take her to her relief zone and exercise her a lot.
12 p.m.	Feed her.
12:15 p.m.	Take her to her relief zone and exercise her a lot.
6 p.m.	Feed her.
6:15 p.m.	Take her to her relief zone and exercise her a lot.

Dogs over 5 months of age can safely be fed twice a day, as long as they don't have a medical condition that requires the dog to be fed smaller meals more often (see Chapter 14).

Potty time

Potty time goes hand in hand with feeding time, because when your dog eats has the most bearing on when your dog needs to go out (see the preceding section). If you want a housetrained dog, you'll have to adhere to a schedule. Make certain you schedule her potty breaks into your day or arrange to have someone available to do it for you.

The younger the dog, the more often she'll need to potty. This is something to keep in mind when you choose a dog. Do you have the time to take her to her relief zone every hour or so? If you want to housetrain a puppy (see Chapter 10), that's what you'll have to do.

The more your pup exercises, the more often she'll need to be taken to her relief zone.

Dogs over the age of 4 months can hold themselves longer, but they still require relief times more often than a dog over 9 months of age. Take your 4- to 9-month-old dog out every three to four hours to be on the safe side. After the age of 9 months, you can wait as long as 6 hours, longer if she has to, but that wouldn't be kind to her on a daily basis.

Male dogs require more time to relieve themselves because they have the tendency to urinate several times instead of letting their bladders empty all at once. They also have to relieve themselves more often throughout the day than most female dogs.

Chapter 7

Chasing the Chuckwagon: The Basics of Feeding

In This Chapter

▶ Understanding the basics of canine nutrition

▶ Identifying the types of food available

▶ Knowing what to feed your mixed-breed dog

▶ Looking at special diets for special dogs

▶ Getting tips on treats

*Y*our mixed-breed dog needs a balanced diet for optimum physical and mental health. If you've been in a pet store recently, or even just the pet-food aisle of your local grocery store, you know how many commercial foods are available — and you may have been overwhelmed by all the options. In this chapter, I tell you what to look for in a dog food, based on your dog's individual attributes.

You don't want to let your dog become overweight, so you need to know how much to feed him as well as how often. If you do some research into this subject (as if you have time!), you'll find varying schools of thought on this topic. I've read the research, but in this chapter, I cut through all that and give you tips based on my own experience with dogs.

As your dog ages, or if he develops allergies, you may need to remove certain foods from your dog's diet or add certain foods to it. In this chapter, I explain how to recognize these special needs, as well as what to do to maintain your dog's health through appropriate nutrition.

All dogs love treats. But you can't give your mixed breed treats all the time — no matter what he tells you. In this chapter, I help you find the right times and places for treats and guide you toward the right treats for your mixed-breed dog.

The Basics of Nutrition

Your dog has a few important needs when it comes to his nutrition. Following is a list of guidelines to keep in mind:

✔ **Give your dog plenty of water.** Your dog needs to have plenty of water available at all times. Refresh your dog's water twice daily — don't just wait for your dog to finish his bowl. Puppies and their moms tend to drink more, as do working dogs. If it's hot out, you can bet your dog will tend to drink more than usual.

✔ **If you need to change your dog's food, do so gradually.** Some dogs have very sensitive stomachs. This is why you don't want to feed your dog table scraps or whatever food happens to be on sale that week. Your dog's digestive system takes time to adapt. Over a period of two weeks, gradually increase the amount of the new food, and decrease the amount of his old food, until you're feeding only the new diet.

✔ **Feed your dog consistently.** Dogs are happiest when they know what is going to happen and when. The number of times a day to feed your dog depends on your dog's age and overall physiology. If your dog is between the ages of 3 and 5 months, feed him three times a day. Most adult dogs do well with two meals each day. But in some situations an adult dog may need to be fed more often; for example, if your dog has a digestive disorder, or a tendency to bloat, you'll want to feed him three or four smaller meals each day. (If you're not sure, as always, check with your vet.)

✔ **Don't free feed your dog (leave food out for him to eat whenever he wants) — control the amount he eats.** If you control how much he eats and when, you'll be able to control his weight better.

Pay attention to your dog's waistline — to be blunt, he should have one. Dogs can develop fat rolls all over their bodies, which not only hinders their ability to exercise but decreases their hearts' efficiency. Reevaluate the amount of food you feed your dog periodically — your dog's needs will vary as he ages, as his activity level changes, and as his lifestyle changes.

✔ **Feed your dog a balanced diet.** I cover the kinds of foods to find your dog in the following section.

✔ **Make sure your dog's food is clean and free of contaminants.** Commercial foods are typically packed to keep contaminants out, but after you open the food (whether a bag or a can), be sure to securely fasten it, refrigerate canned or raw food, and store dry food in a dry location. After your dog has finished a meal, if he's left anything in his dish, throw the food away, and clean his bowl after each meal. (You wouldn't eat off the same dirty plate over and over without washing it, so why should your dog?)

✔ **Consult your vet if your dog experiences any abnormal conditions.** Changes in appetite, thirst, or behavioral changes may be signs of serious health issues.

A shiny dog means a healthy dog. You'll know you're feeding your mixed-breed dog correctly if he has bright eyes, and a shiny coat, and if he maintains a good weight and energy level.

Types of Dog Food

There are more brands and variations of dog food than I can count. You can find many of them at your local grocery store, discount department store, or pet store. Where you buy your mixed breed's food doesn't necessarily mean it's a better (or worse) food than any other. The only way to know for sure is to read labels.

Most store-bought dog food comes in two varieties — dry and canned — so in this section, I go into more detail on what to look for and what to avoid with these two types of foods.

"Wait!" you say. "What about the semi-moist variety?" You may be tempted to go that route, thinking it's the best of both worlds, but here's a serious warning: Stay away. There's a reason that the food is semi-moist — in a word: preservatives. If you feed your dog a food that contains preservatives, you may as well be pumping poison into him. Over time, preservatives affect your mixed-breed dog's liver, heart, and other organs. The result is organ malfunction, organ breakdown, and growth of cancerous tumors.

Commercial dog foods aren't your only options. You can cook your own food for your dog. Or you can prepare a raw diet for your dog, or have one delivered to your door. Homemade and raw diets offer many benefits, but you have to be careful with how they're prepared, stored, and given to your dog. I cover homemade and raw diets in this section as well, to let you know what to watch for.

On the subject of being careful, I include a list of specific foods and plants that can be poisonous to your mixed-breed dog.

Commercial dog food: Canned or dry

The brands of dog food most advertised in the media aren't necessarily the best ones for your mixed-breed dog. You can be sure, however, that the least expensive foods are of the poorest quality, because good quality costs more.

 Pet-food labeling regulations are poor, so you'll rarely get full disclosure of all the included ingredients and nutrients that a commercial food contains. You also won't know all the preservatives either. In fact, although some foods might *claim* to be preservative-free, that only means *they* didn't add anything, not that they didn't obtain ingredients that already had the preservatives in them.

Most of the lower-quality commercial dog foods are high in grains (such as corn, wheat, rice, and barley), which are used as fillers. Although small amounts of rice and barley are healthy, corn and wheat can cause allergic reactions in some dogs. Symptoms of allergic reactions include runny eyes; dry, itchy skin; *lick granulomas* (hot spots); and ear infections.

 When reading dog-food labels look for meat proteins, vegetables, vitamins, and as few grains as possible. The first three ingredients should be healthy proteins — not grain, by-product, or a preservative. You should see lamb, turkey, beef, or chicken. After those first three ingredients, you shouldn't see more than three types of grain within the food. Any more than three and the food is mostly grain filler, not protein-based.

 You'll probably see meat by-products and meals in the ingredient list. *By-products* are often the organs and other tissue of the protein meats used in the foods. Digest is another popular ingredient, especially in chicken-based foods. Chicken digest is the content of the chicken's stomach — often grains. Neither the by-product nor the digest are bad for your dog, as long as the food is meat-protein-based and low in grains and preservatives.

So what should you feed your dog? I recommend a mixture of dry and canned. Here's more on each of these two types of food and why I recommend each of them:

- ✔ **Dry:** It's less expensive, easy to store, and easy to feed. Many people claim that their dogs do better on dry food than they do on canned; the dogs have less loose stool, less gas, and better breath. Dry foods are also good for your dog's gums and teeth. Dry food doesn't spoil or attract ants as badly as canned food. However, dry food also has very little moisture and not a lot of flavor. It's far more processed than canned food, which means it has fewer vitamins and nutrients for your dog. If your dog is at all finicky, he'll likely turn down plain, dry food.

- ✔ **Canned:** Canned food is more expensive than dry food, especially the premium, holistic brands. It can sell for upwards of $2 per can! But canned food is easy to store.

Canned food is not processed as much as dry food, so it contains more of the whole foods that comprise the ingredients and fewer preservatives. This also means more vitamins, nutrients, and flavor.

Canned food contains a lot of moisture. Dogs don't get all their moisture from merely drinking water — they also get it from the foods they eat.

Both dry and canned food offer benefits to your dog. The dry food is good for his teeth and gums, and it gives him more bulk to fill him up. The canned food contains more of the nutrients, moisture, and vitamins he needs to remain healthy, but it is more expensive. To give your dog the best of both worlds, give your dog some of each type of food at every meal.

Homemade food

If you have the time, and a couple good recipes, you can create a healthy, balanced diet for your mixed-breed dog. You'll need to mix together the correct amount of proteins, fat, carbohydrates, vitamins, and minerals. Your dog requires a consistent diet, so if you're going to go the homemade route, be sure you're willing to stick with it.

If you want to give your dog a partial raw diet, add some raw vegetables, fruit, and supplements to your dog's commercial diet.

Here's a basic recipe that you can give your dog without causing him intestinal distress:

1. **Cook some turkey, beef, chicken, or venison until it's no longer pink inside.**
2. **Add some chopped vegetables, such as peas, carrots, and/or green beans.**

   Use raw vegetables for optimum vitamin availability. Cook the veggies slightly if your dog is less than 20 pounds.
3. **For roughage, add cooked brown rice.**
4. **Add some doggie vitamins and a sprinkle of garlic as a parasite repellent.**

If you cook up a bunch of the above, with variations in the meat base, you can freeze it for future use. This will make homemade meals for your dog a little more convenient for you. Frozen into meal-sized packets, you just heat it up a bit in the microwave before giving it to your dog. (Dogs really *do* prefer warm meals.)

For dogs who need to go on a low-calorie diet, restrict the grains to a bare minimum, if you include them at all, and add more green vegetables. Vegetables such as green beans offer a lot of fiber, making your dog feel fuller without all the calories.

For an entire chapter devoted to the pros and cons of homemade diets, along with recipes for adult dogs as well as puppies, check out *Dog Health & Nutrition For Dummies,* by M. Christine Zink, DVM, PhD (Wiley).

Raw diet

You may have heard about the raw diet called the BARF diet. In this case, BARF is short for *biologically appropriate raw foods.* Proponents of this type of diet claim that it is closer to what dogs would eat if they were out in the wild and that it makes them healthier (illustrated by their shiny coats and clean teeth).

The drawback to feeding your mixed-breed dog raw meat is that it often harbors deadly bacteria, such as salmonella or botulism. These bacteria can be fatal to humans, and many veterinarians say it's dangerous to dogs as well. Due to these dangers, I stay away from feeding my own dogs any raw meat, though I often feed them raw vegetables and fruit as between-meal rewards.

Feeding the BARF diet requires more of your time and energy than just a homemade meal. You'll have to store the raw foods safely and also soak the meats in specific bacteria-killing substances such as grapefruit seed extract. As with the homemade diet, you need to add fresh raw vegetables, fruit, and bone meal, as well as fish and/or flaxseed oil to include all the nutrients your dog requires.

Because most vegetables contain cellulose, which dogs cannot digest, raw vegetables will need to be blended so that the dog receives the full vitamins from them.

Cook all grains that you add to your dog's food. Even in the wild, canines rarely eat uncooked grains. They get their grains from the stomach contents of their prey — and that grain has already been chewed and digestively processed.

When feeding a raw diet, your dog will need raw meaty bones every day. You'll also have to alternate the meats so that he gets organ meat as well as muscle meat.

To ensure you always have a consistent raw diet available to your mixed-breed dog, prepare a week's worth of meals ahead of time, place each meal portion in a freezer-safe storage container and then into the freezer. In the morning, take out enough for two meals, heating one in the microwave prior to feeding your dog, and placing the other in the refrigerator for his evening meal.

Raw diets must be frozen for safekeeping. Because raw foods often harbor bacteria, poor food-preserving practices will increase the potency of these bacteria and spread them. Always wash your hands well after handling the raw meats and vegetables and make sure you wash your dog's dishes immediately after he finishes eating.

Don't touch! Foods and plants that are poisonous to dogs

Some plants and foods are dangerous for your mixed-breed dog, and you need to know what they are so you can prevent dangerous accidents. The following is a list of indoor and outdoor plants to avoid. Make sure that you don't leave these items anywhere that your dog can get to them, either indoors or in his outdoor play area.

- Autumn crocus
- Azalea
- Caladium
- Castor bean
- Cyclamen
- Daffodil bulbs
- Elephant ear
- English ivy
- Foxglove
- Holly berries
- Hyacinth bulbs
- Hydrangea
- Iris
- Kalanchoe
- Laurel
- Lilies
- Lily of the valley
- Mistletoe berries
- Oleander
- Philodendron
- Poinsettia
- Rhododendron
- Rhubarb
- Sago palm
- Tulip bulbs
- Wisteria seeds
- Yew

Here are foods to be sure your dog never eats (whether by being given the food by someone in your family, or by digging through the garbage and finding it on his own):

- ✔ **Chocolate:** The most dangerous of foods to dogs is chocolate. Never, *ever* feed your dog candy or other sweets that contain chocolate or cocoa. Too much is often fatal.

- ✔ **Grapes:** Grapes cause abdominal pain, diarrhea, lethargy, and vomiting in dogs.

- ✔ **Coffee:** Coffee causes not only abdominal symptoms but also seizures, labored breathing, heart arrhythmia, coma, and, in some cases, death.

- ✔ **Onions:** Onions cause intestinal distress, liver damage, convulsions, and sometimes death.

- ✔ **Mushrooms:** Mushrooms cause the same symptoms as onions.

- ✔ **Nicotine:** Nicotine is dangerous to dogs so be sure to watch what he picks up on the sidewalk or street, and if he's picked up a cigarette butt, get it out of his mouth before he swallows it.

If your dog does eat any of these poisonous foods, watch him carefully for any severe reactions, such as diarrhea, gagging, or vomiting. If he does have a reaction, take him to the vet immediately.

How Much to Feed

You can't find the right amount to feed your mixed breed on a box, bag, or can of commercial dog food, though feeding guidelines are clearly printed there. In my experience, if you were to follow those directions, your dog would be a rolling tub of lard in short order, and the dog-food company would be a little bit richer.

Each dog is an individual, with his own needs. In the following sections, I give you some guidelines to go by.

If you read the following sections, and you still have absolutely no idea how much to feed your dog, you can ask

- ✔ **Your veterinarian:** Veterinarians can make an educated guess on the amount needed to give your dog appropriate nutrition.

- ✔ **A canine nutritionist:** This person can give you an even better idea of what to feed your dog, because she specializes in proper nutrition for animals.

- ✔ **The dog's breeder or foster guardian:** This person has been feeding your dog for a while and can give you some advice on what worked while the dog lived there.

After you've had your dog for a few weeks, you'll know whether you're giving him the correct amount of food. You can tell by looking at his body. Search for your dog's waistline — it's just above his hipbones and below the rib cage. That waistline should not protrude wider than your dog's hips or ribs. When running your hands along his abdomen, you should be able to easily feel his ribs. On the other hand, you shouldn't see his ribs protruding either. You shouldn't be able to count his ribs or see the ridges of his backbone; if you can, it's a sign that he's underweight.

A dog with a good energy level is usually of normal weight. This dog can play for a half-hour or more without tiring; whereas a dog who is overweight rarely exercises for more than ten minutes before needing to rest. An overweight dog will pant heavily and take a long time to recuperate. Watching your dog during and after exercise is a good way to judge how much you should be feeding him.

Feeding according to your dog's age

Younger dogs have a faster metabolism than older dogs do, so they require more food, more frequently. Younger dogs are also more energetic — they play more than older dogs.

If you have a puppy between the ages of 4 weeks and 5 months, feed him three times each day — morning, noon, and evening. The morning meal should offer the most nutrition and the most food. The noon meal can gradually decrease in size as the dog ages. The evening meal can be a similar amount to the morning meal, though you may want to offer just a little bit less as the dog ages.

When your dog reaches 5 months of age, he might naturally decrease his midday intake, preferring a biscuit to a full meal. Giving him a biscuit is a great way of weaning him away from three meals a day.

From the ages of about 6 months to almost 4 years, two meals a day will be enough, as long as he gets appropriate nutrients and high protein.

After sterilization (neutering or spaying), reduce your dog's food intake by 25 to 30 percent, because his metabolism will automatically slow due to the lack of reproductive hormones. A popular myth is that sterilization causes dogs to become fat and lazy. The reality is that dogs become fat due to too much food for their metabolism, and they become lazy because they're too fat to exercise. If you monitor his food intake and give him enough exercise, he won't become fat *or* lazy.

When dogs reach middle age (as young as 4 or 5 for extra-large dogs, or closer to 10 for the tiniest of breeds), their energy level decreases, and their metabolism slows, so they don't need as many calories. At this point, your mixed-breed dog should be fed half what he got as a teenager (when he was 5 to 10 months of age).

Senior dogs sleep most of the time. You'll need to put more effort into involving him in exercise activities and decrease his food allowance a little bit more, because he won't burn many calories and has a very slowed metabolism. His diet should be rich in fiber and protein, and very low in fats and carbs.

Feeding according to your dog's size

Toy-sized dogs (those weighing less than 15 pounds) rarely eat more than ¼ cup of food per meal. Regardless of how much exercise your Toy-sized dog gets, don't offer much more food than this. Be sure that each meal is high in nutrients, however, so that your little dog gets the most out of the little bit he consumes as possible.

Small dogs (those weighing 15 to 25 pounds) should get approximately ⅓ cup of food per meal.

The food requirements of medium-size dogs (those weighing 25 to 55 pounds) vary more according to their age and breed combinations. Whereas the younger Sporting, Herding, and Terrier breeds have a faster metabolism and higher energy level, the older ones are far more sedate — with the exception of several Herding breeds who are highly energetic most of their lives. I suggest feeding the younger dogs up to 1 cup of food per meal; for dogs older than 5 years of age, reduce the food to ¾ cup per meal.

Large dogs (those weighing 55 to 90 pounds) should receive at least 1 to 2 cups of food mixture per meal. Some very large dogs need 1 ½ to 3 cups per meal until they reach their senior years, which unfortunately come earlier for large dogs; many by the time they reach 5 years of age. As they slow down, reduce the amount you feed.

Special Dietary Needs

Not all foods are right for all dogs. As dogs age, or even due to genetics, some dogs need special diets to stay healthy and happy.

Here are a few signs telling you that what you're currently feeding may not be right for your dog:

- ✔ Your dog is scratching a lot.
- ✔ Your dog tends to get frequent ear infections.
- ✔ Your dog has really bad gas.
- ✔ Your dog has loose, light-colored stool or diarrhea.

✔ Your dog has lick granulomas on his legs.

✔ Your dog's coat is dry, dull, and coarse.

There's really no way to know for sure which specific ingredient is causing your dog distress without narrowing it down by feeding fewer ingredients. Because the most common allergy is to specific meats, that's the first item you should change. The most common switch is from chicken or beef to lamb, duck, venison, or fish. Another common allergy is to grains, such as corn and wheat, common fillers in commercial kibble. Many dogs have allergies to these grains, which manifests itself in an itchy coat, watery eyes, ear infections, and lick granulomas. Rice can be another culprit; you can easily remove rice from your dog's diet to see if this was the cause of his allergic reactions.

Try eliminating some of these common allergens before giving your dog prescription medications, which treat the symptoms but not the source of the allergies.

Dogs suffering from physical ailments such as cancer, diabetes, or organ malfunction need prescription diets from a veterinarian. For example, you may need a low-sodium prescription diet if your dog suffers from heart disease, a prescription diet high in complex carbohydrates for a dog with diabetes, or a low-protein prescription diet for a dog with liver problems. Only a veterinarian can test for these disorders, so you'll serve your dog best by getting the correctly formulated diets that your vet provides.

It's My Treat: Giving Your Dog a Little Something Extra

Everyone likes giving their dogs special treats. My dogs get one whenever they do something especially well, such as sitting on command, coming when called, or after performing a special trick. They *don't* receive a special treat without first earning it. In fact, they must sit prior to receiving their regular meals.

I try to keep all treats wholesome and free of fillers, preservatives, and other contaminants, so I take the same cautions when buying treats as I do when choosing my dogs' regular food: I read labels.

Freeze-dried liver is the treat of choice for most of the dogs I've known. It's what I call "puppy candy." But just like candy, it's also high in calories, so I don't recommend feeding your dog a lot of it, even during training sessions. I alternate freeze-dried liver with lamb, venison, or buffalo jerky that has been dried and preserved with vitamin E. These types of treats tend to be expensive to buy, but you can make them for not much money (if you're willing to spend the time). Another alternative is to take luncheon meats, microwave them for a few seconds until they're crisp, and serve these as training treats.

On rare occasions I also give my dogs hard edible treats such as gourmet health chews (of various flavors, especially the mint for their breath), Booda dental bones, and raw vegetables such as carrots, broccoli, and green beans. When I'm chopping apples for an apple pie, the dogs get the apple cores. After dinner, they each get a small morsel of leftover meat or vegetable. (***Remember:*** I'm stressing *small morsel* because I wouldn't want to give them enough of anything to cause an allergic reaction, especially for my dogs with beef and chicken allergies.)

Though many people like to give their dogs pizza crusts, bread heels, and commercial dog biscuits, I steer away from these things because they contain grains, which may cause an allergic reaction.

As for special-occasion treats, keep it minimal. After holiday meals, you can give your dog a bit of lean meat, but none of the fixings because those contain spices, which might cause stomach distress.

On hot days, or if you have a teething puppy, bouillon popsicles are a real treat. Here's the recipe:

1. **Boil 2 cups of water.**

2. **Dissolve 2 bouillon cubes in the boiling water.**

   You can use any type of bouillon that is low-salt and free of spices. I usually prefer to use the chicken variety, because it's less messy.

3. **Allow the bouillon water to cool for an hour.**

4. **Pour the bouillon water into an ice-cube tray and put it in the freezer.**

5. **Serve your dog a frozen cube.**

   To prevent a mess inside your house, give it to him outside or on an easy-to-clean surface such as linoleum.

Chapter 8

Grooming Your Mixed Breed

. . . .

In This Chapter

▶ Understanding why grooming is about more than just appearance

▶ Brushing your dog

▶ Cleaning your dog's ears and teeth

▶ Caring for your dog's eyes

▶ Keeping on top of your dog's nails

▶ Bathing your dog

▶ Checking your dog for parasites and other problems

. . . .

Would you be willing to walk out of your home without having brushed your teeth, combed your hair, and changed your clothes? How many days could you last like that? Good grooming isn't just about appearance — it's also about good overall health. Because dogs aren't self-grooming, like cats, we need to give them a hand, or two, to stay clean, healthy, and free of parasites.

In this chapter, I tell you everything you need to know about grooming — from bathing your dog to cleaning her teeth and ears. I also tell you how to keep your dog free of parasites like fleas and ticks. If your dog could tell you to read one chapter of this book, this would be pretty near the top of her list!

Why Grooming Matters: Inside and Out

Does your dog fill with excitement when you pick her up at the grooming salon? Isn't she clean enough to cuddle? What dog doesn't like being loved on and cuddled! Would you do that with a mud-encrusted, parasite-infested dog with bad breath? Of course not. The trouble is, that dirty dog doesn't understand that she's not getting attention because she's dirty — all she knows is she's not getting the attention she needs and wants.

Besides having a clean house companion, there are other sanitary and medical reasons for keeping your dog clean:

- ✔ **A clean dog has a coat free of tangles.** What's the big deal about a few snarls? Try letting your hair get all matted and tangled and get back to me on how that feels. Not only does it look bad, but it can actually hurt.

- ✔ **A clean dog is free of debris between her toes, under her tail, in skin wrinkles, and in other areas you don't want me to go into.**

- ✔ **Regular grooming removes dead skin and brings out the natural oils in the coat.** These natural oils not only make your dog's coat shiny but also help it serve as a better insulator against all types of weather.

- ✔ **When you groom your dog regularly, you quickly locate any injuries or parasites, and you can treat them right away.**

Plus, the time you spend grooming your mixed breed is important bonding time — you're showing your dog that you care about her. And a dog who is clean will be welcome near you — you'll want to run your hands through her coat and give her hugs. What better reason to groom your dog could there be?

Brushing Your Dog

The amount of time you need to spend brushing your dog depends largely on your dog's coat type and propensity for getting dirty. If your dog loves to roll in the dirt, you'll be bathing her a lot. I once had a dog who loved going to the farm next door, rolling in the freshest cow pie he could find, and coming home, prancing with pride at how well he had covered his scent. He wasn't as pleased about the frequent baths though.

Even if your mixed breed is primarily an indoor dog, with little exposure to cow pies, mud puddles, and other digging opportunities, you'll still want to brush her a couple times each week to remove loose fur, dander, and detangle long strands.

If you've been to a pet store lately and looked at the options in the brush aisle, you may have been overwhelmed. Here's a quick guide, based on your dog's coat type:

- ✔ **Short coat:** For a dog with very short fur, use a massaging glove. Not only will this make her groan with delight, but it will also loosen the dead fur and dirt, forming a mat on the glove that's easily removed.

✔ **Medium coat:** For a dog with medium length fur, use a bristle brush. This will loosen the dropped fur, remove debris caught in the coat and detangle. Most bristle brushes are easily cleaned by balling up the fur as you pull it from the bristles.

✔ **Long coat:** For a dog with a long coat, I suggest using a wide-tooth comb. Look for one with rolling tines. The rolling tines help detangle the coat without pulling it and causing your dog distress from painful fur tugging. The comb is great for dogs with feathering on their legs, tail, or chest areas; use a bristle brush for the shorter fur on the back and head.

No matter what kind of coat your dog has, always use a very soft brush for the dog's face, because the facial areas are very sensitive.

Some dogs have double coats — wooly undercoats and long stranded top coats. These require a special tool called a *rake*. It looks like a mini-rake with wide spaced tines along a long, flat bar. Comb the dog's undercoat with the rake, removing loose intertwining wooly hairs. Then do the top coat with the comb. The Nordic dog breeds tend to have this wooly undercoat along with many of the northern breeds.

If your dog has very dry skin, she'll need a spritzing with a mixture of water and leave-in conditioner. As you groom your dog, give a spritz to wet down the fur a bit, and then brush it into the coat with a firm bristle brush. The coat will remain soft, as will the dog's skin, allowing the coat to lay flatter against the dog and be more efficient as insulation against extreme weather conditions. If your dog has dry skin, you'll see little white specs of dandruff in her coat. She'll also be scratching a lot.

Cleaning Your Dog's Ears

Everything from mites to dirt to bacteria can cause ear infections in a dog. If you don't give weekly attention to your dog's ears, she may be more prone to getting ear infections. And ear infections aren't just minor annoyances — they can cause hearing loss, damage to the middle ear, and/or fever from a bacterial infection.

Most dogs will show clear signs of ear irritation and infection. They shake their heads, rub their ears against solid objects, or use their paws to scratch at their ears. If the infection gets worse, you'll likely smell a foul odor coming from the ear, see small granular dirt particles, and notice a topical rash from your dog's constant scratching.

The only means of curing infections is the appropriate ear medication. Your veterinarian will need to inspect the ear and possibly take a sample of the infectious material. The prescribed cure is anything from ear ointment to antibiotics, depending on the cause of the infection.

To prevent infection, clean your dog's ears at least once a week, regardless of the type of ears your dog has. However, you may need to clean your dog's ears more often — such as after bathing or swimming. (Water tends to remain in the ears, especially if the ears have a fold-over structure.) Dogs with upright ears allow moisture to dry out quickly, so you'll only need to do a minor ear cleaning.

Dogs who have Retriever or Spaniel heritage may have smaller ear canals than other dogs, making them ripe for contracting infections. This special structure — along with the heavy fold-over ears — retains moisture, dirt, and bacteria. Other types of dogs who tend to get chronic ear infections are Bloodhounds and Bassett Hounds; they have very heavy droopy ears that don't allow air to flow within the canals to dry out retained moisture. Along with the heavy ears, their length scoops up dirt. So besides cleaning the inside, you also need to clean the outside, or they'll get very smelly.

The next time you take your dog in to the veterinarian for an examination, ask him to show you how to clean your dog's ears. But here are basic ear-cleaning procedures to follow after you've seen it done by your vet:

1. **Squirt a couple drops of herbal ear cleaner into the dog's ear.**

2. **Rub her ear for a couple seconds to loosen any dirt and grease.**

3. **With a soft cloth wrapped around your index finger, gently remove the loosened dirt from the outer canal features and inside of the ear flap.**

4. **Repeat with the other ear.**

Never clean deep in the dog's ear canal. You can damage the dog's ear and hearing that way. If you think something might be located deeper inside your dog's ear, have your veterinarian do a thorough cleaning and exam.

Some dogs have lots of hair in their ears. This can clog the air flow that is needed to dry moisture. From time to time, tweeze these hairs — only those that come out easily — so that the outer ear can remain dryer. If you're not sure how to do this, take your dog to the groomer to have it done professionally.

Look, Ma — No Cavities! Brushing Your Canine's Choppers

Brushing a dog's teeth is a part of routine maintenance that many dog owners overlook. But if you think about it, your dog's teeth are as important to her overall health and well-being as your own. Would you skip brushing your teeth for a couple days? A week? A year? Absolutely not! And, it's not just because teeth that haven't been brushed cause bad breath. Without regular brushing, you can develop gum disease that may cause you to lose your teeth and can even harm organs such as your heart. The same goes for dogs!

 If your dog loses her teeth at a young age, it will shorten her lifespan because she can't eat as she should. Plus, if she loses her teeth due to lack of dental care, the gum infections may cause problems with her internal organs as well.

Introduce your mixed-breed dog to dental cleaning in as positive a manner as possible. Use a meat-flavored toothpaste (they come in beef, poultry, and liver flavors) that your dog will love, along with a long-handled toothbrush or a finger brush.

Place a little paste on the brush and begin brushing the front teeth. These are the easiest to start with because they don't require your pushing the brush farther into the dog's mouth. Brush in a circular motion so that you cover each tooth. Remember to brush the back of each tooth (the side closest to the tongue). Be sure to give your dog frequent breaks to lick the paste off her teeth, which will keep the experience positive for her. When she's relaxed, work on the teeth farther back in the mouth. Gently pull the dog's skin away from the teeth (as shown in Figure 8-1), so you can access the teeth easier.

Talk to your vet if you're at all unsure that you're brushing your dog's teeth correctly. He'll be happy to show you the right way to do it.

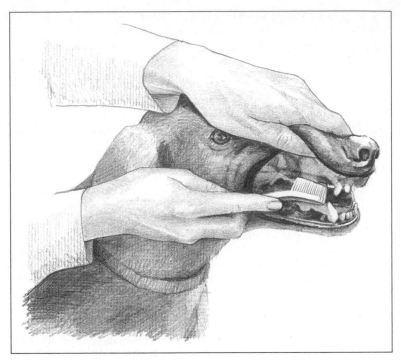

Figure 8-1: Brushing your dog's teeth is a vital part of canine care. Ease your dog into it, and make sure brushing is always a positive experience for her.

The Eyes Have It: Caring for Your Mixed Breed's Eyes

Unless your mixed-breed dog has allergies or protruding eyes, you won't have to do much to take care of them. However, if your dog has allergies, you'll need to apply an optic solution to keep her eyes clear of discharge; your vet can suggest the appropriate solution for your dog.

If your dog has protruding eyes, they're likely to collect dirt particles, causing the dog's eyes to water or become irritated. Dogs with protruding eyes also tend to have constant tearing, which stains their facial fur. Products are available to clean the stains as well as those to clear the eyes of debris.

Cleaning your dog's eyes on a weekly basis (more often if she has protruding eyes) is a good idea. Even if she doesn't have any allergies or problems with her eyes, it will help train her to have her head held gently in case she ever does need medication.

Mani/Pedi Time: Clipping Your Dog's Nails

Dog's nails grow quickly, and you'll probably need to clip your dog's nails every six weeks, regardless of her size, breed mixture, or age. If your dog spends most of her time on soft surfaces (such as dirt, grass, or sand), she may need her nails clipped more often. Even if you walk your dog on sidewalks or along the street, you'll still need to clip her nails on the sides of the feet as well as the dew-claw nails.

If your dog doesn't like having her nails done, you'll need to take her to a professional groomer or to a vet to have them clipped. If you want to do it yourself, however, you'll need to make certain your mixed breed will remain calm while you're clipping — otherwise, you might clip the nail in the wrong place and cause severe bleeding.

Before clipping the nail, look at how it curves. If your dog has at least one white nail, take note at how far around the curve the pink color (known as the *quick*) goes (see Figure 8-2). This will guide you on where to clip — you want to remain at *least* ⅛ inch away from the quick to avoid injuring your dog.

If you plan on clipping your dog's nails yourself, have some styptic powder handy to help stop any accidental bleeding that might occur from cutting too closely.

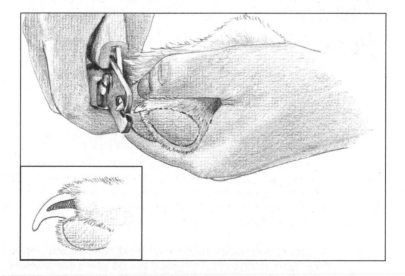

Figure 8-2: Look carefully at where the nail hooks. This is where you'll want to apply the nail clippers in order to avoid clipping too closely.

If you want to teach your dog to accept nail clipping, use lots of treats and take your time. Here are some basic steps to follow:

1. **Show her the nail clippers and speaking in a soothing, pleasant tone while touching her feet with them.**

2. **When she accepts the presence of the clippers, hold her feet and separate her toes while touching them with the clippers.**

3. **Clip one nail, and then allow her to relax as you pet her and speak to her in a soothing tone of voice.**

4. **Clip another nail, and pause again for praising her.**

5. **Repeat this procedure until all her nails are done.**

6. **Release her and play with a toy together.**

Keep all grooming activities positive so that your dog will easily allow you to work with her.

Bathing Your Dog

How often you need to bathe your dog depends on your dog's lifestyle. Obviously, the more she plays outdoors, the more she'll need to be bathed. However, if she has a Poodle or Lab-type coat, she'll likely repel dirt rather nicely, so a quick wipe is sufficient to prevent her from dragging debris into your home. Even so, a dirt-resistant coat doesn't help with odor. Large dogs tend to have strong body odor, especially those who insist on covering their own scent by rolling in dead fish or other carcasses.

Scent covering is a natural instinct in hunting dogs — they want to camouflage themselves from their prey. Rolling in something dead often takes away their predatory smell, allowing them to get closer without alarming the prey animal.

If you have a very small dog, you can bathe her once a week in a sink. If your dog weighs more than 15 pounds, a bathtub would work best.

Most sinks and tubs tend to have a slippery surface. Use a rubber tub or sink mat to prevent your dog from sliding around. A dog who feels secure where she stands will be less likely to get scared during the bath.

Unless you have a smaller mixed-breed dog and have no problem lifting her and placing her into the tub, you'll need to teach her how to enter and exit the tub on her own; as well as how to remain inside the tub while she's being cleaned. Here's a positive proce-dure to help acclimate your mixed breed to the bathing process:

1. **Take your mixed-breed dog to an empty, dry tub and throw some treats inside.**

   Allow your dog to get the treats without forcing her.

2. **Repeat Step 1 until your dog easily jumps into the tub to get her treats.**

3. **Begin asking your dog to remain in the tub by caressing her after she gets her treats. Gently hold her in place while caressing and offering soft praise.**

4. **Each time she enters the tub, gradually increase the amount of time you coax her into staying there.**

5. **When you want to let her exit the tub, coax her to you as you move backward. Give her another reward when she comes to you, and then rub her with a dry towel.**

   This is even more rewarding because your mixed breed will enjoy being groomed and caressed.

6. **Follow the same routine with a little bit of water in the tub.**

   Because your dog has accepted the tub as a positive activity, the addition of the water shouldn't be a deterrent.

7. **When your dog is comfortable getting in with a little water, add enough water for the bath, add soap, and wash her all over.**

   Be sure to give your dog lots of rewards and gentle praise throughout the bathing process so that she continues to enjoy it.

 If you have to wash your dog's face, apply some eye ointment (available from your vet) prior to bathing her. It'll keep your dog's eyes safe from the sting of soap, in case some accidentally gets in her eye. If your dog has protruding eyes, applying the eye ointment should be the first thing you do prior to bathing.

 If your dog has long fur, apply some conditioner to her coat after you rinse off the soap. This will help with detangling her fur, making it easier to comb her out after her bath.

 Don't try to comb your dog's coat while it's wet. Brushing and combing is far more difficult wet than dry, and if you try to do it while your dog is wet, you'll end up pulling harder on her skin, making the process a lot less fun for her (and for you!).

Checking for Parasites

During the warmer months, make a daily parasite check part of the care routine. You can make it a positive experience for your dog by merely caressing her in a methodical manner (see "The Daily Once-Over: Checking Your Dog for Problems," later in this chapter, for some guidelines).

To check for the presence of fleas separate your dog's fur along her back, underside, head, and neck. If you see any little black specs (almost like pepper), that's flea waste. And where there's waste, you can be pretty sure that there are adult fleas present as well. The adult fleas are unmistakable — they're little black bugs crawling along your dog's skin.

If that doesn't creep you out enough, wait till you come across a tick, burrowed into your dog's skin. Like fleas, ticks thrive on your dog's blood. However, unlike fleas, they don't move over the dog's surface — they dig into her skin.

Internal parasites are tougher to detect. You may be able to see tapeworm pieces in your dog's feces, but the other types of worms must be seen through a microscope. Many types of worms — such as heartworm, whipworm, and hookworm — can be fatal. So it's a good idea to take a fecal sample to your veterinarian every six months to stay on top of the internal parasite problem.

There are several ways to prevent all topical and some internal parasite infestations, as well as ways to clear them. I cover all this in the following sections.

Preventing parasites

Apply a topical oil such as Frontline, K9 Advantix, or Revolution to your dog every month. These will kill any topical parasite that lands upon your dog and/or bites your dog's skin. Because the parasite doesn't have a chance to transfer its saliva or lay its eggs, it will also reduce the incidence of internal parasites. Because heartworm and tapeworm are transported by biting fleas, the topical oil will reduce your dog's risk of infestation. A monthly heartworm tablet also reduces the risk of heartworm infestation as well as several other worms such as hookworm, whipworm, and roundworm. Some types of heartworm medications, such as Sentinel, disrupt the reproductive cycle of biting fleas, dramatically reducing their population but don't outright kill them like the topical oils. Frontline, Advantix, and Revolution protect against fleas *and* ticks.

A home remedy that often works to prevent parasites are daily doses of brewer's yeast and garlic tablets. The garlic repels bugs of all sorts while the brewer's yeast is great for your dog's digestive system.

Curing parasites

The cure for internal parasites is prescription medicine available from your veterinarian. If your dog has a heartworm infestation, the treatment is long-term. Most of the other internal parasites can be treated with one or two doses of the appropriate medication.

A dog with a flea and tick infestation can easily be treated with one Capstar tablet. This will safely kill all parasites on the dog's body within four hours. Contain your dog in a small space that's easy to clean during this treatment. While she's being treated, you must treat your home to prevent a reinfestation when she returns. The best type of foggers to use for home treatment are those containing Siphotrol — it's the safest and most effective. Siphotrol kills not only adult fleas, but also the larvae, which many insecticides won't kill.

Here's a great way of ridding yourself of those pesky fleas:

1. **Take the dog to a groomer or vet for a flea bath.**

2. **Before bringing the dog home, fog the entire house and spray the entire yard. Also, spray the interior of the vehicle you used to transport the dog.**

3. **Repeat this program in ten days, because the flea eggs will have hatched and the cycle will begin again.**

If you walk your dog through areas where other dogs visit, there's a high possibility of your dog contracting a parasite. Prevention is the best means of ensuring your dog's health. Use the topical treatments and monthly heartworm pills.

The Daily Once-Over: Checking Your Dog for Problems

Make it a point to go over your dog daily and check for injuries, cuts, bruises, parasites, and suspicious lumps. As your mixed breed ages, this daily check becomes more important. Dogs rarely let you know that they aren't feeling well or in pain — in fact, the dog's nature is to *not* show weakness, so you'll be the last to know when something's wrong.

Sometimes dogs appear lethargic or have a lack of appetite when they're feeling poorly. However, an illness has to progress to an alarming point for this to happen. Daily checks will help you discover something that might be the beginning of a problem — for example, a wound that might become infected, a lump that might be the beginning of cancer, a flea that will bite and cause your dog to have an allergic reaction. All these things, and more, can be detected by a daily once-over.

Here's a great way to do a thorough daily check while also giving your dog a great massage:

1. **Begin at the dog's nose: Using your fingertips, rub her nose in a circular manner.**

   This will allow you to feel any scabby skin or lumps while giving your dog a very relaxing massage.

2. **Move up her head, around her forehead, cheeks, lower jaw, and the base of her ears.**

   Familiarize yourself with her dimples, moles, and whiskers. Often there is lumpy skin around each whisker.

3. **Look inside her ears, and rub the ear from base to tip.**

   This will help locate any extra dirt or grease, as well as ticks. Ticks often latch on to the inside of the ear flap because the skin is moist and warm.

4. **Move down the neck: Still use your fingertips, though you can begin to apply a little more pressure.**

   The skin is a bit tougher than on the face, and you'll have more fur to go through as well.

5. **With the dog's head and neck checked, move your hand along the center of her back.**

   You can move your hands in a straight line down her spine, and then use the circular motions on each side, gently touching the loin area, sides, and tummy.

6. **Check the chest and shoulders: Long chest fur is a prime target for loose debris and tangles.**

   Use your fingers as you would a brush, starting at the top of the neck and combing downward.

7. **Check the legs, again using a circular motion with your fingertips on the skin. At her knees and hocks, enclose her joints in your hand feeling for excessive heat.**

   Heat is the first sign of a joint disorder, swelling may or may not be present depending on the problem.

8. **Check your dog's toes and foot pads.**

   Keep in mind that she walks around barefoot all day and she may cut a pad or get debris entangled between the pads (if your dog has long foot fur).

When you've completed your daily check, your mixed-breed dog is sure to be snoring and drooling!

Chapter 9

Exercising Your Dog

In This Chapter

▶ Figuring out how much exercise your dog needs

▶ Finding fun activities to do with your dog

Dogs are extreme athletes. They require exercise to remain healthy and happy. Few are natural couch potatoes — but they *become* couch potatoes after living with humans for a while. Some breeds don't require much exercise, but the majority of breeds do.

Your mixed-breed dog probably has at least some ancestors who had a drive to work, hunt, or herd. Your dog may not be a purebred hunting, working, or herding dog, but that doesn't mean that his drive to go out and chase rabbits or herd cows has disappeared. Your job is to find exercise activities that can help your dog satisfy his natural instincts.

In this chapter, I fill you in on how much exercise your dog needs and give you some suggestions for activities to try with your dog.

Regardless of how you give your dog his exercise, you can be certain he'll have the most fun if you share the activities with him.

Knowing How Much Exercise Your Dog Needs

A dog's exercise requirements depend on many factors, including his age, breed combination, and size. For example, dogs who have Herding blood need to run and exercise a lot every day, because they were designed to help farmers, while dogs with Sporting blood generally won't need more than a couple of good long games of fetch, because their jobs traditionally were to aid hunters in locating and returning game.

Puppies

Your puppy will go through several stages of development that will affect his level of energy. Some studies suggest that a dog matures the equivalent of 21 human years within his first year of life and 5 years each year thereafter. If you consider the behavioral stages of people (and puppies), this is a good assumption. Imagine taking a child all the way from infancy to the legal drinking age in one year — that's what you have when you bring home a puppy!

Physically, the puppy grows from a little, short legged, roly-poly, round-faced cutie into a dog with a sleek, more angular physique. After the first year, your dog won't change much physically.

Here's an overview of what kind of energy levels (and exercise requirements) you can expect from your pup in the first year of his life:

- **Four weeks to three months:** Between the ages of 4 weeks and 3 months, pups tend to sleep most of the time. They have short little bursts of energy but they quickly tire out. A few minutes outside and they're beat.

- **Three to four months:** When a pup is about 3 to 4 months old, his energy level changes a bit. He'll play more and for longer periods of time. This is when your pup begins testing his position in the pack — he'll display dominance when he plays with you or other dogs. He'll get into tug-of-war games in earnest. Fetch becomes a fantastic idea. Chasing butterflies is also very exciting. On average, a dog of this age requires a half-hour of exercise at least five times a day.

- **Five to seven months:** At the age of 5 to 7 months, your puppy will be at the peak of adolescence. This is the period when he'll need more exercise than he will at any other time in his life. Not only will he be testing his pack position, but he'll be very easily distracted and want to do a zillion things at once (just like the typical teenager). At this age, your puppy needs loads of exercise! An adolescent dog requires *at least* several hours of exercise each day; if your dog is a mixture of the Herding, Sporting, or Terrier breeds, I recommend even more. Your dog will need the freedom to run in a safely fenced area. Play with other dogs is the best means of blowing off steam. Though your pup will quickly tire during training sessions, these aren't enough to rid him of the zoomies.

✔ **Eight to ten months:** Between 8 and 10 months, your young dog is still full of energy, but he's able to channel it a bit better. If you offer him regular activities, he'll be happy to participate. He'll also begin showing signs of maturity, with a better understanding of the house rules. He'll have more moments of lying at your feet than in the previous three months. An older adolescent dog still needs lots of exercise time; I suggest two to three hours each day. His exercise can be a combination of play with other dogs and a regulated activity such as a training session.

✔ **Ten months to one year:** Between 10 and 12 months, your dog has become an adult. Don't worry — he'll still be playful and energetic. In fact, many dogs are energetic well into old age. If you give appropriate exercise outlets, you'll have a happy, healthy, easy-to-manage companion. Your dog will require a regular exercise regimen, but his activity can be more concentrated, such as training time, hiking, biking, or jogging. The zoomies are gone.

Growing dogs need lots of exercise. Confining them daily for extended periods of time is detrimental to their physical and mental development. Young dogs need to stretch their legs and minds as they mature. You'll need to discover the proper balance in order to train your dog the house rules, as well as allow him to "be a dog." Though you should confine him in a safe area when you can't be with him, be sure to observe him closely at play when you're home. Make sure to follow an exercise regimen with your dog. If you exercise *with* him, it can be great for bonding — and for your own health as well as his.

Adult dogs

How much exercise an adult dog needs depends in large part on his breed. Even if you don't know exactly which breeds make up your mixed-breed dog's family tree, you can probably make a good guess about which general breed groups he's a part of. For example, you can generally tell a hound from a terrier. If you're just not sure about your dog, talk to your vet — she'll probably be able to steer you in the right direction.

Table 9-1 shows some general recommendations for the amount of exercise different dogs need based on their breed group. If you know your dog has the genetics of one of these breed groups, you'll have a fairly good idea of how much exercise your dog will need.

Table 9-1	Breed Group Exercise Requirements	
Breed Group	*Energy Level*	*Minimum Hours of Exercise Per Day*
Sporting	High	3
Hound	Medium	2
Working	Medium	2
Terrier	High	2
Toy	Medium to low	1
Non-Sporting	Varies Greatly	1–3
Herding	Very high	4

Table 9-1 lists the *minimum* amount of exercise the dog needs every day. If you have a hound and you want to exercise him more than one hour a day, your dog won't have any problems (as long as you increase the amount of exercise gradually, just as you'd do yourself). But if you have a Herding dog and you only give him an hour of exercise a day, the results could be disastrous. If you're not giving your dog enough exercise, he'll find all kinds of creative ways to burn calories on his own — by chewing and digging holes and doing all sorts of things that'll drive you crazy.

If you have a high-energy dog who needs three to four hours of exercise each day, don't panic. There are ways to work this into your lifestyle. You don't have to take your dog on one long three- or four-hour run. In fact, it's healthier for your dog if the exercise is broken up throughout the day. You can take him out for a long walk first thing in the morning, play tag or fetch with him in the after-noon, and take him for another long walk or training session in the evening. Let him blow off some steam playing with other dogs, too.

If you exercise your dog and give him a structured lifestyle, he'll be a great companion.

Although allowing your dog to run in a large fenced area is nice, it isn't as fulfilling to your dog as taking him for a walk around the neighborhood or hiking in the woods. Your dog wants to exercise with *you*. If you can't do this on a regular basis, you should have more than one dog — dogs will play with each other if you can't be there to participate. However, they *still* would prefer to involve you in the games.

Dogs are athletes. They need to use their energy in a positive manner. Participating in activities with your dog will fill this need, while improving the bond you have with your mixed-breed dog.

Older dogs

As your dog gets older, his energy level won't be what it was when he was a pup. But he still needs exercise — not as much as when he was younger, but definitely a good hour per day.

The trick to exercising your older dog is to break up that hour throughout the day instead of trying to do it all at once. Most older dogs receive plenty of exercise through two to three 20-minute walks each day.

So how do you know if your dog is old? The concept of age is relative to the dog's breed mixture and size. The giant breeds, such as Great Danes and Mastiffs, rarely live more than 9 years, on average. The Retriever and Setter breeds average 10 to 12 years. Large Hounds 10 years, smaller Hounds 12 to 14 years. Spaniel breeds often live 13 to 14 years, but Terrier breeds can live 14 to 16 years. There is a bit of a theme to this that you can apply to your mixed-breed dog: Smaller dogs tend to live longer — they don't age as quickly as larger dogs.

So the age of your dog depends largely on his size, not necessarily the breeds that constitute his genetics, though there are many exceptions to this generalization. For example, English Bulldogs, a mid-sized breed, don't live much beyond 10 years, while other mid-sized breeds, such as Cocker Spaniels, have a lifespan upwards of 14 years.

Whether your mixed-breed dog just entered middle age or has become geriatric, he still needs exercise in order to remain healthy. As dogs age, arthritis and other physical ailments begin to degenerate their skeletal structure. Regular walks help maintain the muscle tone around their joints, improving their overall ability to move.

Finding an Activity Your Dog Enjoys

Actually, maybe I should've called this section "Finding an Activity That *You* Enjoy Doing with Your Dog." Dogs like almost any activity, as long as it's *active*. And they like any activity that you do *with* them. In the following sections, I cover some basic activities that you can do with your dog to exercise him, as well as some activities that are a little more out of the ordinary. Take your pick — the more variety you give your dog, the happier he'll be!

Walking

Most dog owners get their dogs so that they'll have someone to accompany them on long walks. And most dogs are very happy to fill this role.

Regardless of where you live, taking a walk with your dog is fun, healthy, and a great means of developing and maintaining a bond with your canine.

Jogging and running

Jogging or running is probably the best way of ensuring that both you and your dog are getting enough exercise. Most runners are consistent — they go on their daily runs regardless of weather or schedule. This consistency is the best thing for your mixed-breed dog.

Running with your dog has many benefits.

- ✔ It's excellent exercise.
- ✔ Your dog learns to stay at your side regardless of distractions.
- ✔ If you run on a hard surface, your dog's nails won't have to be trimmed often (or at all), because the pavement will naturally file them for you.
- ✔ It's a great way of bonding with your dog.

Though you may run 3 miles or more when you exercise, don't start your mixed-breed dog at this rate. He needs to gradually build up tolerance to this distance. Begin him at 1 mile and over a period of two weeks gradually increase his exercise tolerance to match yours.

Don't feed your dog within an hour before or after strenuous exercise. Some dogs are prone to *bloat* (a twisting of the stomach due to gaseous intake).

Biking

Biking, and having your dog run by your side, is another great way for your dog to burn off his excess energy.

If you decide to give biking a try, take several precautions because you, and your dog, can easily be injured:

✔ **Acclimate your dog to your bicycle.** Some dogs would rather chase bikes than run alongside them. Utilize the heeling exercises in Chapter 11, and apply them to this situation as follows:

1. **Have your dog heel with you as you push your bicycle.**

2. **When he's working well, get on your bike, but keep your feet on the ground to move it.**

3. **When your dog is walking nicely at your side, get on the bike and pedal slowly.**

4. **Gradually increase the speed as your dog performs well moving with you.**

✔ **Make sure your dog stays on the side of you that is away from the road.** This will prevent his being hit by a car if he suddenly lunges outward. You can buy a product that will safely tether your dog to your bike. It's a metal bar that attaches to the bike with a hook on the other end to affix your dog's leash. This will keep your dog with you, while also keeping him a safe enough distance from the wheels.

There *isn't* a product available that will keep your dog watching you instead of wanting to socialize with the neighbors' dog as you go by. Your mixed-breed dog must learn to remain with you regardless of distractions. This takes obedience training (see Chapter 11). You might want to begin with walking and running prior to bike riding, to prepare your dog for remaining with you regardless of your pace.

While you ride your bike or run on a hard surface, your dog is running on that surface — barefoot! Without the benefit of booties your dog might injure his pads. I highly recommend a pad conditioner (just a cream that you can rub on your dog's pads) along with some type of pad protection.

Fetch

Many dogs enjoy this game, and it doesn't take a whole lot of effort on your part. When you develop a routine of playing fetch, you can teach your mixed-breed dog a variety of themes on the game. Here are a few suggestions:

✔ Fetch a specific toy.

✔ Find and fetch a toy.

✔ Go find a person.

✔ Fetch a toy and place it in a box.

✔ Fetch two toys at the same time.

If your dog is not into fetching, you can entice him into it. Any dog can learn to point out something, if it has positive benefits. The following steps teach your dog how to *target* (touch something with his nose):

1. **Take your dog's favorite toy and place a treat on it.**

2. **When he goes to get his treat, make a specific noise, such as clicking a clicker, or saying "Yes!" in an enthusiastic tone of voice.**

3. **Repeat Steps 1 and 2 three times.**

   Now your dog knows something good comes from touching that toy. He'll go touch it without your having to put a treat on it.

4. **When your dog goes to touch the toy, the moment your dog touches the toy make the same noise as before and give him a reward.**

5. **Repeat Step 4 three times.**

6. **Move the toy to a new location and repeat these prior steps.**

You can play this game with any number of objects and can even turn into a retrieving game. It's merely a matter of gradually increasing your criteria prior to giving your dog his reward. For example, you reward him for touching, and he quickly understands that concept. Next you hold out for him to actually put his mouth on the object before making that specific noise and rewarding him. Follow this with not rewarding until he actually picks up the object. In small steps, you can easily teach most dogs to accomplish any behavior you want. And your dog will love the challenge of learning to do what you're asking.

Hiking

Hiking is similar to walking, but unlike a walk, where you're likely in your neighborhood, on a hike, you and your dog head out into the woods or mountains. You may not be able to count on hiking every day, depending on where you live and what your schedule is like, but it can be a great addition to your dog's exercise routine.

 Before you leave for your hike, make sure you're familiar with the canine-related rules for the area. Most state parks require dogs to be leashed. Regardless of where you go, always have a leash with you in case your dog becomes unruly or more interested in chasing squirrels than listening to you.

A couple more items you'll want to pack are a collapsible water bowl and a bottle of fresh water. When dogs exercise — and you can be sure your dog will be getting a lot of that while hiking with you — they need to drink lots of water. Many lakes, streams, and rivers are contaminated with bacteria, so you want to make certain that your mixed breed isn't drinking from them. If you give him a fresh water supply before, during, and after your hike, you shouldn't have to worry about him looking for water elsewhere.

Carry a few treats with you so that every time your dog looks and/or returns to you of his own accord, he gets a reward for doing so. This will tend to keep him closer to you and less likely to run after other hikers.

If you've been hiking for some time and your dog is just starting to go with you, you'll need to gradually increase his tolerance to the exercise. Dogs will keep going until they drop, so be aware of signs showing that he's getting tired. These include

✔ Heavy panting

✔ Lying down whenever you pause

✔ Droopy eyes and ears

✔ A slow pace

Be sure to check his pads when you take a break. He doesn't have the benefit of hiking boots like you do, and you may be crossing rocky terrain that can easily slice his pads. Have a small first-aid pack handy (see Chapter 16), just in case.

Swimming

Most dogs love to swim and can do so naturally. Even those who don't enjoy bathing, may still like wading in a creek or along the shore of a lake or ocean. If your mixed breed reliably listens to you off-leash, he can safely go swimming. You can make it even more enjoyable by throwing some floating toys into the water for fetching games. *Remember:* Your dog will prefer to play games with you rather than just swim around.

Swimming can be a great way for older dogs with arthritis to get exercise. They get a workout without the impact that walking brings with it. Some vets even recommend water therapy for dogs who are arthritic. All the more reason to get your young dog interested in the water — that way, as he ages, you can make swimming an even bigger part of his exercise routine.

Ahoy, matie! Boating with your mixed-breed dog

Few dogs wouldn't like to sit at the bow of a boat with their noses to the wind. Watersports are very popular and lots of fun if your mixed breed can participate. Several kinds of watersports can be dangerous for your dog, so take the appropriate precautions. Some people like to ride with their dogs on Jet Skis. Although it looks like a lot of fun, there's no safety net at all, and you can't concentrate the way you should if you're worried about your dog falling off. Another activity to be wary of is sailboating. Because sailboats usually tilt on their sides when the wind hits the sails, a dog can easily slide off and into the water.

Regardless of the type of boating you do, make sure your dog is wearing a flotation device. Dogs are usually good swimmers, but strong currents, waves, the wake of other watercraft, and undertow can all be dangerous for your dog — a canine life vest is essential in case of emergency. And because you never know when an emergency may strike, put the vest on your dog while you're still on dry land, and keep it on him until he's safely back.

When you can't have your hands on your dog, he should be securely contained either below deck or within a seating area where he can't get his feet up on the side rails or put his nose over the side. He'll appreciate the wind in his nose, but saltwater won't be as pleasant.

Horse and hound

Horse and hound is one of my all-time favorite activities — and it's great exercise for a dog! I love riding horses, and having my dogs with me during our adventures makes them extra special. Horses and hounds have been hunting together for millennia, so there's no reason why your mixed breed can't learn how to respect the horse, watch the horse's leg movements, and listen to your requests at the same time. Dogs are great at multitasking, especially when it means a long run through fields and woods.

Before taking off in a run, you'll need to acclimate your dog to horses. Horses are prey animals, and dogs are predators, so you have to teach your dog to control his natural instincts and to listen to you from a distance as well. The guidelines in Chapter 11 will help you train your dog so that participating in horse and hound is fun and safe for both the hound *and* the horse.

Part III
Training 101

"You got an F in Internal Medicine, an F in Clinical Diagnosis, and you ate the liver out of a cadaver in your Gross Anatomy class?! Shoot, I told everyone you'd never learn to heal."

In this part . . .

Obedience training helps you and your mixed-breed dog communicate. It helps the two of you form a bond — a pack of two. Plus, it increases the likelihood that your dog will remain with you throughout his entire life, because he'll learn how to follow the house rules and listen to you.

In this part, I cover everything from housetraining (the most important training of all) to basic commands like sit, stay, heel, and come. I also fill you in on what to do if you and your dog have encountered some training challenges, and I give you tips on finding a professional trainer to work with.

Chapter 10

Housetraining

*E*veryone who gets a new dog must immediately begin working on the most important task: housetraining. Whether you got your dog at a shelter or from a breeder, whether she's a Heinz 57 or a Labradoodle, the techniques are the same, and I fill you in on the basics in this chapter.

But before you can teach your dog when and where to relieve herself, you need to recognize when she's telling you that she has go. In this chapter, I show you how to read your dog's body language, recognize her warning signs, and reward her at the appropriate moments.

In this chapter, you discover how a crate can help you train your dog, whether she'll have access to a yard or stay indoors. Speaking of indoor dogs, I let you know how you can train your dog to do her business in a designated place inside. I also cover creating a schedule so that your dog will know when she'll have a chance to go. As you schedule your dog's relief times, you'll also teach your dog to potty on command, and in the specific location that you want.

Finally, a large part of housetraining is preventing accidents. I help you do exactly that, so your dog has more successes than failures and gets through housetraining with straight A's.

When You Gotta Go: Looking for Your Dog's Warning Signs

Dogs rarely just squat and potty out of the blue. Your dog will always do something specific prior to letting loose. As you hang out with your dog, look for sniffing, circling, whining, or sitting and staring as she wonders why you can't understand that she really needs to go out *now*. Here's some more of what to expect with each of these common warning signs:

- ✔ **Sniffing:** The sniffing dog is the toughest to detect, because dogs are *always* sniffing in their quest for something edible or fun to play with. Believe it or not, there will be a pattern. Your dog may sniff in a circle. Or she may sniff to detect a specific spot in the house where she had an accident recently. (Cleaning the entire smell off carpet or other flooring is nearly impossible, so it's a good bet that your dog will aim for the same area when she has to go again.)

- ✔ **Circling:** Circling is an easier behavior to notice than sniffing is. Unless they're arranging their sleeping place, dogs rarely move in circles. They prefer to go straight toward a person, other animal, or toy. The classic potty circles are usually small in circumference and are normally accompanied by sniffing. When your dog is getting ready to sleep, she won't sniff while she circles, so if you see the two behaviors together, you know what's coming!

- ✔ **Whining:** The whining dog is, for all intents and purposes, verbalizing her need to potty. A dog who whines when she has to go out is a really smart dog, because she realizes that humans respond faster to sound than to body language (like sniffing and circling). Your dog may sit and stare at you as she whines, or she may go to the door and whine. Either way, she's telling you she needs to go potty. No matter how you look at it, a dog can't make her wishes any clearer than she can by whining.

- ✔ **Sitting and starting:** If your dog silently sits and stares at you, she may eventually give up and go potty directly in front of you. In the beginning stages of housetraining your pup, this behavior isn't necessarily a sign of disrespect. Your dog is merely defining herself. She tried to tell you, and you didn't listen. Next time, if your dog sits and stares at you, get her outside.

If your older dog (older than 6 months of age) has a good idea of where to do her business and she happens to urinate or defecate directly in front of you, this *may* be a sign of disrespect. Essentially, your dog is marking her territory directly in front of you, challenging your authority. If your dog is completely housetrained and she does this, she needs obedience training — pronto! (See Chapter 11 for more on obedience training.)

Some dogs prefer to potty in private. If your dog falls into this category, she'll try to do so by leaving the room or going behind furniture. Later, you'll find out what your dog's been up to, but by then it's too late to do anything besides clean it up. If you've experienced this, keep closer tabs on her. When she leaves the room, follow her. If she heads for the same place as before, take her to her potty area immediately.

Scheduling Potty Breaks

The best way to teach your dog when and where to relieve herself is to be consistent with her relief times. A dog who knows when she'll have access to the relief area will learn to contain herself until those allotted times. In fact, figuring out when your mixed breed has to go, and what she has to do when she goes, will help both of you. You'll know what she needs to do and when. And she'll know that she has the opportunity to do her business in the correct place and that she'll be rewarded for doing so.

The schedule that's right for you and your dog will depend not only on what your dog needs to do, but also on your daily routine. If you're away from home most of the day, you may want to hire a dog walker or place your dog in a securely fenced area with fresh water and shelter — a place where she can have access to a potty zone.

Playtime and potty time: They go hand in hand

If you have kids, doggie accidents are even more likely than they are in a home without kids. Accidents tend to happen more when the kids come home from school or the family is together on the weekend. Why? Because there is more commotion and the adults tend not to pay as much attention to whether the dog needs to go out. Also, the more active your dog, the more often she needs to potty.

Remember: Playtime is a high activity time for your dog, so keep a closer eye on her and watch for those gotta-go signs.

Regardless of your work hours, your mixed-breed dog can adapt to your schedule. You just have to give her some guidance along the way.

If you work away from home all day

Working for a living is a fact of life for most people, and if you're among the many who work outside the home, your dog will have to adjust to your being away. You need to give her a realistic schedule for feeding and potty breaks. The younger the dog, the more often you'll need to schedule her relief times.

Here's a sample schedule. Use this in devising your own schedule to fit your needs:

6 a.m.	Relief time. After holding it all night, your dog will need to relieve herself. She should do her business fairly quickly, allowing you to teach her to potty on command (see the "Training your dog to potty on command" section, later in this chapter).
6:15 a.m.	Feed.
7 a.m.	Take your dog to her relief zone.
7:45 a.m.	Before leaving for work, take your dog to her relief area again.
7:45 a.m.–6 p.m.	If your mixed-breed dog is new to your household, she should be contained in a safe area — such as a crate, pen, or fenced yard — while you're gone.
6 p.m.	As soon as you return home, take your dog to her relief area.
6:15 p.m.	Feed.
7 p.m.	Relief time.
8:30 p.m.	Relief time
10 p.m.	Just before going to bed, take your dog to her relief area.

If your dog is younger than 4 months of age, she should be taken to her relief area:

- ✔ Within 15 minutes after eating

- ✔ Directly after getting up from a nap

✔ During playtime

✔ After each training session

She should also be taken every hour to hour and a half. Waiting longer is setting her up for an accident.

If you work out of your house

You may be home, but you're busy, without the ability to constantly tend to your dog. Although you can take her to her relief area more often, which is great if your mixed-breed dog is very young, you may not have time to do so every hour. Scheduling her relief times is just as important as it would be if you worked away from home.

Here's a sample schedule to help you in setting up your own:

6 a.m.	Take your dog to her relief zone as soon as you get up in the morning.
6:15 a.m.	Feed.
7 a.m.	Take your dog to her relief zone.
Throughout the day	Try to take your dog to her relief area every two to three hours (every one to one and a half hours if she's under 4 months old). **Remember:** If, at any time, you can't keep a close eye on your dog, contain her as described in the preceding section.
5 p.m.	Feed.
5:15 p.m.	Take your dog to her relief zone.
Throughout the evening	The more activity there is in the evening, the more often your dog needs to be taken to her relief area.
10 p.m.	Take her to her relief zone one last time, just before bedtime.

If your schedule changes frequently

Changing the relief schedule for your dog will be as difficult as it is for you — maybe more so. You can go to the bathroom anytime you want, but your dog has to wait for you to take her.

Try to develop a potty schedule for your dog that's as consistent as possible, even if your own schedule changes. You may want to get help from a friend, family member, or neighbor to be sure your dog can stick to her normal schedule.

Dogs are creatures of habit — taking away or constantly changing something in a dog's routine will create anxiety.

If you must be away for an extended period of time, make arrangements with someone to come and take your dog to her relief area every four hours.

Crate-Training to Prevent Accidents

If your dog is new to your household, if she's young, or if she has behavioral issues, you'll need to keep her in a safe area when you can't be with her. Restricting her access to your entire house will not only prevent her from destroying your home but also keep her from getting hurt. Containment also teaches your dog to contain her need to potty, because a dog who remains still is less likely to have to relieve herself than one who is moving around a lot.

This "safe zone" is commonly a crate, but it can also be a fenced yard or a large pen. Regardless of where you contain your dog, make sure she has shelter from the weather and fresh water at all times.

Shelter from the weather doesn't just mean a roof. Some breeds (like Boxers, Greyhounds, and other breeds with short coats) are very sensitive to extreme temperatures; if your dog is a mix of these breeds, be sure to provide her with a temperature-controlled environment where she won't overheat in the summer or get too cold in the winter.

If you have a fenced yard, install a doggie door to the basement or kitchen. Place an exercise pen just inside the door so that your dog can come inside to escape the weather but won't have free access to your home.

How the crate works

Many people mistakenly believe that crates are cruel. But unless they're abused by being forced into the crate or left there for long periods of time, most dogs don't think so. Crates simulate dens, and dogs like dens because they feel safe inside. The feeling of something solid all around gives them a sense of security. If you introduce the crate to your dog positively, she'll be happy to stay inside while sleeping or go inside whenever she wants a little privacy.

Because most dogs remain still or sleep while they're in their crates, they're less likely to have to relieve themselves. Crates also help teach control while indoors. The crate is a place where your dog can safely reside when you can't watch her. Plus, few dogs will potty in their crates, especially if the crate is the right size (big enough for the dog, but not so big that she can potty at one end and sleep far away in the other).

Most wild dogs build dens as a safe place to sleep or whelp puppies. Instinctually, they never mess in their dens — they always leave the enclosure to do their business in the surrounding area, not only as a means of relief but also as a way to mark their territory.

Crating is a great way to help with housetraining. Let's say you take your dog outside to potty, but she's too distracted to relieve herself. After ten minutes, you bring her back inside, place her in her crate for 30 minutes, and try again. She'll probably have to relieve herself after that half-hour is up. Then you can praise and reward her for going in the correct location instead of being punished for relieving herself in the house.

Crating expedites the housetraining process and prevents accidents, preventing constant negativity between you and your dog.

Never leave your dog locked in her crate for more than four to five hours at a time. She needs to stretch her legs, potty, and exercise. If you're going to be gone longer than four or five hours, consider a safely fenced area or ask a friend to let her out several times while you're away.

Introducing your dog to the crate

You want your dog to have positive associations with her crate, so the first rule to keep in mind is: *Never use the crate as a place of punishment.* Your dog should feel safe and happy in her crate; she should never be forced into it.

Begin by placing the crate in an area where you spend much of your time, such as the kitchen, family room, office, or bedroom. Put a comfortable doggie bed inside, along with a couple of toys and fresh water.

Use a small water bucket with a double-sided clip, and attach the bucket to the wall of the crate. This will prevent your dog from tipping over the water when she gets excited.

To introduce your dog to the crate, sit on the floor near the crate. Allow your dog to sniff the crate and go in if she wants. After your dog has become familiar with the crate, you can start training her to go into the crate on command. Here's how:

1. **When you have your dog's attention, throw a treat or fun toy into the crate.**

2. **When your dog follows the reward into the crate, praise her and give her another reward.**

3. **Allow your dog to come out of the crate as she pleases.**

4. **Repeat Steps 1 through 3 several times until your dog is anticipating and going in the crate on her own.**

5. **Close the door of the crate while your dog is inside eating her treats.**

6. **Praise her and stick more treats through the crate so that your dog sees that she gets nice things when she stays inside.**

7. **After 2 minutes, open the door of the crate and let your dog come out if she chooses.**

8. **Repeat Steps 5 through 7, gradually increase the amount of time the crate door is closed while your dog is constantly being rewarded, until she relaxes comfortably for five minutes.**

9. **Repeat Steps 5 and 6, but instead of standing by the crate, give her a treat and briefly leave the room while your dog remains closed in her crate.**

10. **Peek around a corner and continually praise your dog.**

11. **Return to the room, give her a reward, and open the crate door.**

12. **Repeat Steps 9 through 11, gradually increasing the amount of time you're gone, always returning with many rewards for your dog.**

If your dog eats her treats quickly, offer a food-filled toy instead. A hollow rubber ball, bone, or dental scrubber works well. You can put treats inside or along the edges, so it takes longer for your dog to finish — keeping her occupied for a longer period of time.

When you're home, leave the crate door open so that your dog can go in and out as she pleases.

As you're gearing up to leave your dog in her crate for several hours at a time, you'll need to start small in order to assure her she won't be stuck in there forever. Begin with being away from home only ten minutes. Peek in the windows and check on her. If she's happily playing with her toys or sleeping, return and reward her. If she's showing anxiety, back up a bit and return to remaining home and peeking around the corner or to wherever she was comfortably relaxed.

Never be afraid to regress a little — doing so offers your dog a safe zone where she's comfortable, and it prevents creating a dog with anxieties about being in the crate.

Teaching your dog to go in a specific area

Is your yard filled with doggie landmines? Does it have a polka dotted patina? Maybe you'd like to have your dog do her business in some out-of-the-way place so that nobody accidentally steps in it.

You can teach your dog to potty in one specific area. It can be at the edge of a wooded area, a section of your yard, or somewhere along your walks that is more appropriate than in the middle of the sidewalk.

This won't magically happen, however. You have to train your dog to do it through encouragement and rewards. You must also make the area attractive to your dog. The surface material needs to easily maintain a scent, be soft enough to scratch at, and be near enough to quickly reach.

Young puppies can't hold it long enough to make it down the back stretch. You may want to begin their housetraining by allowing them to potty a little closer to home. After they have the idea of relieving themselves outdoors, you can gradually increase the distance from the house.

Dogs prefer to relieve themselves where they can smell the scent of other dogs. Some dogs also like to leave their own scent through scratching at the ground. As they scratch, they release their scent, covering the odor of the dog who previously visited. Taking your mixed breed to a location where she can catch a whiff of another dog will improve the chances that she'll get her business done quickly.

You can make sure that your dog understands where she must go to relieve herself in a few ways. Be sure to accompany her there. Walk her on the leash to the location, then let her sniff and move around. Eventually, she'll get the idea that this is where you want her to go. *Remember:* Reward her the moment she goes — praise and offer treats.

Eventually, you won't need to take your dog to the location on-leash. You can run there, coaxing her to follow. As she relieves herself, praise and treat or throw a toy.

It may take some time to establish the relief spot. You'll need to be patient and persistent. Also, watch your dog at all times. If she starts to show the signs of needing to potty in the wrong place, quickly guide her to the correct place. One accident in the wrong location will leave a scent, making it more difficult to guide her away from that area in the future.

Teaching your dog to get it done faster

Are you tired of waiting and waiting for your dog to do her business? Your dog may not care that the weather is uncomfortable — she's more interested in the ground odors or the other dogs playing nearby. Why waste a perfectly good opportunity to say hello to someone?

This is where teaching your dog to relieve herself faster will be very beneficial. Moreover, it totally coincides with all the other things you're doing to housetrain your mixed breed. After all, wouldn't you rather she potty within a couple minutes instead of an hour?

You can speed things along in several ways:

- ✔ **Make sure your dog really has to go when you take her out.** If you stick to a specific schedule, you'll know for sure what she has to do and when.

- ✔ **Every time you take your dog to her relief zone and she potties, give her a reward the moment she finishes.** Most dogs want their rewards so much that they'll quickly do their business just so they can get that reward faster.

- ✔ **If your dog won't potty within five minutes, return her to her crate for a half-hour, and then try again.** Repeat this until she *does* go. As soon as she relieves herself, give her a reward.

In less than a week, your dog will not only be letting you know when she has to relieve herself, she'll also do so on command within a short period of time (see the following section).

Other Training Methods

If you live in a high-rise apartment building, you may decide to paper-train your dog so you're not always having to wait for the elevator and hit the pavement before your dog does her business. If paper-training doesn't appeal to you, you can also train your dog to use a litter pan, as cats do.

The procedures are basically the same as when teaching a dog to relieve herself outside:

- ✔ When not in a safely contained area, observe your dog at all times.
- ✔ Watch for those behavioral signs that it's time to potty.
- ✔ Immediately take your dog to that spot (the paper or litter pan).
- ✔ Reward her when she does her business.

In the following sections, I go into some more detail on both of these methods.

Paper training

Paper is the usual surface cover of choice for indoor potty spots. A variety of products are available to create a specific potty zone for your little mixed-breed dog. Potty pads with plastic on one side and an absorbent surface on the other are readily available and very convenient, because they're easy to dispose. Some potty pads are treated with a scent to entice your dog to use them.

Some potty pads also come with a plastic holder that you can use to hold the potty pads in place. Not only does this keep the pads spread out for easy use, but it also offers a surface different from the regular floor, so your dog sees a difference between the potty zone and the remainder of your house.

Home alone

If you have an indoor dog, you can't offer her a fenced yard to play in while you're gone. But she still needs to be confined to a space smaller than your entire home. To set your little mixed-breed dog up for success, in both the housetraining and overall manners categories, confine her in an exercise pen that contains her bed, toys, water, and potty pad or litter box. This area will give her enough space to move around during the day, a place to rest, and her potty zone.

Where you put the potty zone depends largely on the design of your home. If you have many different rooms, you may want to consider several potty zones. I recommend putting each zone on a hard floor, not carpeting. If your dog misses and some of her urine splashes onto the carpet, she may miss more often — on purpose, because the scent is there.

Using a litter pan

Dogs really love to dig, so you may want to use a litter pan instead of paper. The pan may be more enticing to your dog because she can potty in a more natural way.

Litter allows your dog to step onto a totally different surface from normal household flooring, making the potty zone very distinct from the rest of the house. Because pans tend to have high sides, your dog will be able to discern her relief area faster than a surface that might be close to the floor.

Another advantage to this method is that the litter will soak up "the urine, clumping it together for easy disposal (if you get the clumping kind of litter). It can also coat the feces for similar ease of disposal. Plus, the scent remains in the pan and doesn't permeate other parts of your home. Your dog can scratch at the litter, leaving her scent as she chooses, making it even more attractive for use the next time.

Watching for Success

An ounce of prevention is worth a pound of cure. This adage is very meaningful in housetraining dogs. If you can prevent your dog from having accidents in the wrong place and guide her to the areas she *can* relieve herself, you'll improve your relationship with your dog while forming lifelong good habits.

Nothing sours a relationship faster than constant frustration and punishment. More dogs end up at shelters and rescue organizations due to misbehavior than accidental breeding. The owners of these dogs never took the time to guide them toward correct behavior.

Your dog can't read your mind.

Preventing housetraining accidents is one of the most important parts of the entire process. In the following sections, I help you keep accidents to a minimum.

Mixed-breed dogs are every bit as adorable as their purebred counterparts. This dog doesn't know he doesn't have a pedigree! (For more on what makes a mixed breed a mixed breed, check out Chapter 1.)

The Cockapoo was one of the first designer dogs — intentional crossings of two purebreds — in the United States. (For more on designer dogs, including the Cockapoo, turn to Chapter 2.)

Mixed-breed dogs come in all shapes and sizes (see Chapter 3).

Many mixed-breed dogs are abandoned by the side of the road, neglected, or otherwise mistreated. If they're lucky, they end up in animal shelters or rescue groups — and if *you're* lucky, you'll be able to take one home with you. Despite their rocky start, these dogs can make wonderful companions. (For tips on finding your new best friend, check out Chapter 4.)

When you bring home a mixed-breed puppy, be sure to get a copy of her vaccination records to give to your vet. (For tips on finding a vet who will be your partner in caring for your dog throughout her life, check out Chapter 13.)

Your mixed breed doesn't have to have Retriever blood to love going into the water after a ball. (See Chapter 9 for more fun ways to make sure your dog is getting enough exercise.)

This mixed breed is totally submissive, letting his little friend rub his tummy for as long as she'll do it. Dogs and children can become fast friends. Just make sure your kids know that the dog isn't a toy — even if he's a Toy mix! (For more on introducing your family, including other pets, to your new mixed breed, see Chapter 6.)

You are the center of your dog's world, and the more time you can spend playing with her, exercising with her, and just hanging out with her, the happier she'll be! (For ten ways to have fun with your dog, see Chapter 19.)

A crate like this one can be your mixed breed's "den," a safe place he can sleep in or go when he needs a little quiet time. It can also be a huge help when you're housetraining your dog and can't supervise him 24/7. (For more on housetraining, see Chapter 10.)

© Jean M. Fogle

Don't let this cute face (and those ears!) fool you: Like any dog, a mixed breed needs to be trained. With the right approach, training can be a rewarding experience for you and your dog. (Check out Chapter 11 for everything you need to know to train your mixed breed.)

© Andrew Woodley / Alamy

Dogs love to dig holes. If you don't want your mixed breed tearing up your yard, give him a box filled with sand to dig in (see Chapter 12).

Agility is a great form of exercise for any dog (see Chapter 16). This Eskipoo is a natural!

Your mixed breed will want to go with you everywhere you go, even on the water. If you take your dog boating, be sure she's wearing a well-fitting canine life vest before she puts her paws on deck, and keep it on her until she's back on dry land. Even if she can swim, if she falls overboard she'll need this added protection (see Chapter 9).

Dogs love to play tug-of-war with each other. If your mixed breed doesn't have a canine companion at home, try taking him to a dog park so he can make some friends and develop his social skills. Playtime is a great way for your dog to get exercise, too! (For more on ways to stimulate your dog's mind, check out Chapter 12.)

Your mixed breed will love hitting the road with you. No matter where you're going, she'll be ready for an adventure! (For tips on what to bring when traveling with your dog, head to Chapter 17.)

Observing your dog

If you observe your dog closely, you'll figure out exactly which visual cues your dog uses before she does her business. When you recognize the signs, you'll know when she needs to go.

When your dog is loose in the house, you need to be watching her. Burying your head in a book or watching television will only serve to create the very situation you're trying to prevent — accidents in the house.

You need to keep your eyes on your dog. Engage her in play or work with her on tricks. Keep her in the same room with you.

Have your dog wear a leash of at least 4 feet in length at all times. If she begins to leave the room, step on the leash and coax her to return. Praise her when she makes the correct decision. This is especially important for dogs who like to do their business in the next room or behind the couch.

Giving freedom only when she earns it

One of the worst things you can do with a new dog is to allow her total freedom of your home. Leaving your new dog alone, with free roam of your house, is a setup for disaster for both of you. Your dog will have an accident, and you'll have to clean it up — plus, you may get frustrated with her, which does nothing for the bond that you're trying to create.

Dogs need guidance. They thrive in a structured environment. Dogs love following the rules. It gives them a sense of pack structure; something very natural to their own instinctual behavior patterns.

Your dog has to earn everything she gets. Don't allow your dog free roam of your home if she hasn't yet proved she can be trusted.

Getting to the point where you can trust your dog all over your house, without being watched, may take anywhere from weeks to months to years. It's a long, ongoing process, but being cautious and taking your time will reduce your own frustration and improve your dog's understanding of what you want.

Never allow your dog any freedom within your home without first making sure she has done her business.

The initial stages of freedom go hand in hand with close observation. Don't allow your dog to go where she wants without your being close behind. This way you can see any warning signs and whisk her to her relief area quickly. You can also prevent other types of problems such as chewing on the couch or eating something dangerous.

Begin allowing your dog to areas of the house other than her normal containment area by walking with her. Have her heeling at your side. Practice stays (see Chapter 11) in every room. Then allow her some free time to explore under your close supervision. This will teach her manners in all parts of the house.

As your dog learns to behave and contain herself in her one area, you can gradually allow her free access to other areas. For example, you begin with containing her in the kitchen. She has no accidents in the kitchen for several weeks. You can then offer her free access to the breakfast area along with the kitchen. As she proves herself worthy of more freedom, allow her more access to your house.

You can use baby gates to help cordon off specific rooms. Baby gates also keep your dog safely within her containment area without shutting her off from the rest of the house in a negative way, making her feel ostracized from her family pack (which, to a dog, is punishment).

Working on Some Advanced Housetraining Techniques

After your dog is housetrained (meaning, she knows where to go and she's not having accidents in the house), you can take it up a notch and get her to go potty on command, as well as ring a bell to let you know when has to go out. Pretty nifty, huh?

Training your dog to potty on command

Wouldn't it be great if you could teach your dog to come and tell you when she needs to relieve herself? And wouldn't it be great if she did her business the minute she got into her potty zone — a location that you'd prefer she use? The good news is, all this can happen. You just have to be persistent and consistent with your dog, and she'll aim to please you.

Begin by deciding on one specific word that you'll use as a cue, such as *hurry, potty, business,* or *empty.* When you take your dog to her potty spot, say the word repeatedly until she actually relieves herself. When she is in the middle of relieving herself, say in a cheerful voice, "Good potty!", or whatever word you've chosen to use. When she's done, praise and give her a reward. Your dog will realize that her actions earn rewards, and dogs tend to repeat the behaviors that are rewarding. Most dogs pick up on the verbal cue very quickly. Usually within three days to a week.

You may want to choose a word that won't embarrass you in public. I've always used the words *hurry* or *go.* They're far less embarrassing than the word *potty* or the words for the bodily functions. Picture yourself standing in a crowded park with your dog. Would you rather say, "Pee-pee! Pee-pee!" or "Hurry! Hurry!"? I'm bettin' on the latter.

When you follow one of the schedules discussed earlier in the chapter, you can easily use a specific word to cue your dog to potty, especially during the first morning relief times and whenever you've just let her out of her crate and taken her to her potty zone.

One of the best results of having a dog who potties on command is during travel. Stopping at a roadside table, rest area, or service station; taking your dog to a small grassy area; and giving the command is far easier and faster than having to walk your dog around for a long time, hoping that she'll find just the right spot.

You rang? Getting your dog to ring a bell when she has to go

Earlier in the chapter, I cover some of the common warning signs that your dog may have to do her business. But you can bridge the language gap and teach your mixed breed a way of telling you that she has to go out, in a way you *both* understand. You can teach her to ring a bell to let you know she needs to relieve herself. (Be sure she knows how to potty on command before you train her to use a bell. She has to be able to go on command for the bell training to work.)

Several types of bells work well. Jingle bells and cow bells work nicely because their sounds are loud and clear.

Here's how to train your dog to ring a bell when she has to go out:

1. **Hang the bell on the knob of the door leading to your dog's relief area.**

2. Place a small piece of cheese, some peanut butter, or some canned dog food on the bell.

3. Coax your dog to the door and move the bell a little to get your dog's attention.

4. Chances are, she already noticed you putting the food on the bell and she's eagerly waiting to lick it off.

5. When your dog goes for the food, she'll likely move the bell, making it ring.

6. As soon as the bell rings, open the door and take your dog to her relief area.

7. Cue her to relieve herself.

8. Praise and reward her the moment she potties.

Your mixed-breed dog should be ringing the bell on her own within a week or less. Just make sure that you can hear the sound when your dog is loose in the house, or she just might think that you *still* don't understand her and she needs to do her business near the door, trying to clarify her needs.

Chapter 11

Hup, Two, Three, Four: Good Manners and Basic Training

....

In This Chapter

▶ Getting ready to train

▶ Steps to success

▶ Teaching the basic commands

▶ Distraction proofing

▶ Finding a professional trainer

....

*P*art of owning a dog — and ensuring that you're both happy — is training him. A good training regimen goes hand in hand with overall character development, good behavior, and communication. Plus, it's fun!

In this chapter, I give you all the tools you'll need to train your mixed breed from start to finish — from the equipment you need to the basic commands to finding a trainer to help you.

Preparing for Training

Lots of people get frustrated with training their dogs because they haven't done some of the prep work. They just say "Sit," shove their dog's butt to the ground, and expect him to know what that means. If you spend just a little time getting ready to train, you'll be setting yourself — and your mixed breed — up for success!

In this section, I cover a few categories of preparation: targeting, using a clicker, and buying the right equipment.

Targeting: The first step in training

Have you ever gone to an aquarium and watched a dolphin or whale show? Did you see the sea mammals jump up and touch a big ball on the end of a long stick? That ball was called a *target,* and you can do the same kind of thing with your dog. Okay, so he won't jump 20 feet out of a pool of water, but he'll do plenty of exciting tricks of his own.

Don't believe me? Consider this: When you give your dog a treat, does he look at your hand? That's a target, too. A dog who watches your hand when you have a treat in it is a dog who will learn to respond to visual cues.

Targeting quickly teaches your dog what you want him to do. When you motion him to sit, he looks at your target (your hand) and sits. When you motion him to lay down (by dropping your hand downward), his nose and body will follow into position.

Here's how to begin targeting:

1. **Place a small bit of food in your hand.**

   When targeting, use a piece of food that has a strong smell, such as freeze-dried liver, cheese, or chicken. The enticing scent will instantly grab your dog's attention.

2. **Put your hand near your mixed-breed dog's nose, and allow him to sniff.**

3. **When he puts his nose on your hand he is targeting —
   give him the food!**

Using a marker: The second step in training

Though targeting will get your dog started on paying attention, you need a means of letting your mixed breed know that he's doing what you want. You need to offer a specific sound or movement to coincide with the exact moment your mixed breed does what you've asked. This is called *marking,* and marking is usually done with the use of a clicker, a squeaker, or a specific word said in an enthusiastic tone of voice. The key is that the sound must be distinct from all other sounds your dog is likely to hear. For this reason, a clicker (available from most pet shops) may be your best bet.

Here's how to teach your dog to understand a marker:

1. **Begin by targeting (see the preceding section) except
   when your dog puts his nose on your hand, instead of
   giving him a treat, use your marker.**

2. **Then give your mixed breed a treat.**

3. **Repeat Steps 1 and 2 three to five times.**

You can bring together the concepts of targeting and marking. Here's how:

1. **Show your mixed breed your hand holding the treat.**

2. **Move your hand to the left.**

3. **When he moves his head to the left, mark and reward.**

4. **Move your hand to the right.**

5. **When your mixed breed moves his head to the right, mark and reward.**

When your mixed breed understands the way to earn easy treats, it's time to start making him work a little harder. Make him do more to earn his rewards — for example, move his head from side to side or up and down before you mark and reward. This is called *chaining,* because it's chaining together several behaviors prior to marking the moment when your mixed breed has done what you asked. Chaining is a very important part of obedience training — you don't want to give your mixed breed a treat for every single correct response to commands. If you do, you'll have a very fat dog in no time!

Buying the right training tools

So many tools, so little time! With all the collars, leashes, harnesses and other paraphernalia, how will you know what's right for your mixed breed?

The collar your dog wears while he's lounging around the house isn't the collar you'll want to use when you're training. Here's a breakdown of which collars I recommend for training:

- **Gentle Leader Easy Walk Harness:** The Easy Walk Harness is a great training device for young dogs, small dogs, and dogs who don't tend to pull hard at any time. You attach the leash to the front ring (at the dog's chest). When the dog moves ahead, you turn and pull the leash to the side opposite where your dog is heading. Dogs acclimate quickly to this device.

- **Head halter (such as Comfort Trainer and Halti):** Head halters are great for dogs who pull, especially when they're distracted. They're also great for dominant dogs who feel it's their duty to lead you. Several brands of head halter are on the market, but the ones I recommend are Comfort Trainer and Halti, because they don't put pressure on the dog's nose unless you apply it to get your dog's attention.

The type of leash you use when you train your dog is very important. You want to use one that's right for your mixed breed.

Never use an extendable/retractable leash — whether you're training or not! These leashes teach your dog to pull, because the leashes are constantly trying to retract as your dog moves away from you. You want to teach your dog to pay attention and remain at your side, so this is the last thing you need.

The leash that's right for your dog has a lot to do with your dog's weight. Here's a breakdown:

- **10 pounds or less:** A light nylon or cotton leash no more than ¼-inch wide, with a very small clip.

- **11–25 pounds:** A leather or cotton leash no more than ½-inch wide with a small clip.

- **26–55 pounds:** A leather or cotton leash no more than ½-inch wide with a medium clip.

- **56 pounds or more:** A leather leash no more than ⅝-inch wide with a medium clip.

It's not the clip that will keep the leash on your dog — it's your training method. When using a head halter, use a lightweight leash so as not to apply any pressure to your dog's nose without your needing to do so.

Making your voice and body work for you

Your dog will be watching everything you do and listening to every sound you make. In order to make sense to your mixed breed, be consistent with all your vocalizations and body language. This will help him understand what you want.

Use three distinct vocal tones, depending on what you want to communicate:

- **Praise:** A high, happy tone
- **Command:** A demanding, even tone
- **Reprimand:** A low tone

Your voice isn't the only way you communicate. Your dog also picks up on your body language. The bigger you make yourself, the more your mixed breed will pay attention and listen to your commands. The smaller you make yourself, the less he'll respond to your commands. The reason: A dominant dog will make himself look bigger, and a submissive dog will make himself look smaller. Most dogs won't listen to someone they feel superior to. But they *will* respond quickly to someone they respect.

When giving a command, stand up straight, as shown in Figure 11-1.
When rewarding or greeting your dog, crouch down, as shown in
Figure 11-2.

Figure 11-1: Stand upright when giving a command.

Figure 11-2: Crouch down when rewarding or greeting your dog.

Heel

Heeling means that your dog is at your side, shoulder even with your leg. He can walk on your left or your right, whichever is most comfortable for you.

Most professional trainers and those who show dogs keep the dog on the left; in this chapter, I address the training techniques assuming that you'll be teaching your mixed-breed dog to work on your left side, too.

The method you use for teaching your mixed-breed dog to heel depends on his age, size, and how easily distracted he might be. A young pup, for example, should be started either off-leash, or with a light leash dragging from a harness or flat neck collar. A dog older than 4 months old will need a training device, such as an Easy Walk Harness, with a light leash attached and held in your right hand. A dog over 4 months with high reactivity needs a head halter.

Getting started: The basics of Heel

Start by holding the leash loop in your right hand along with your clicker (if you're carrying one). Have a pouch filled with treats clipped on to your jeans or tied around your waist. Hold a treat in your left hand — your target hand.

Get your mixed breed's attention by targeting and marking (see earlier in this chapter). When he's paying attention to you, hold your left hand (target hand) on your left thigh. Your mixed breed will move closer to your left thigh, which is heel position. Both of you will be facing the same direction.

Take a step forward as you say your mixed breed's name and the command, "Heel" or "Let's go" in a commanding tone of voice (see Figure 11-3). *Remember:* You don't need to be loud — dogs hear far better than humans do. Demand, don't ask.

Because the target went forward a bit as you took a step, your mixed breed is likely to follow along, his nose on your hand. As he moves with you, mark after his correct response and reward.

The next time, take two steps, then three, then four, and so on until your mixed breed is walking with you across the yard or down the sidewalk, nose on your left hand the whole way.

Figure 11-3: Have your dog target on your hand as you take a step forward.

The best means of ensuring your dog knows you are giving him a command is to precede it with his name. Use a happy tone when saying his name so that he'll have positive associations when hearing it. In the beginning, it'll help to give him rewards every time he looks at you when you say his name.

If your mixed-breed dog begins to move ahead of you, it means one of two things:

✔ **You've walked farther than he's ready for.** To remedy this situation, just decrease the number of steps you take between marking and rewarding.

✔ **He no longer thinks that the treats are as valuable as that squirrel he sees climbing a nearby tree.** If this is the case, the moment you see his ears in front of your left leg, turn right and make a total 180-degree turn, without looking at or waiting for him.

If your mixed breed moves off to your right — say, something grabs his attention on that side, or he smells something in your right hand — turn left. As soon as you make that 180-degree turn to the left, he's back on your left side watching you. Mark his good behavior, stop, and give him a small piece of treat.

When you're having trouble getting your dog's attention

Of all the obedience exercises in which you might be using a head halter, heeling differs the most from using any other training device. You may pull a bit with a body harness or flat collar — you don't do that with a head halter. A head halter is on the dog's head, so if you pull back, you're turning your dog's head and straining his neck.

The best way to regain your dog's attention while walking is to gently pull downward as you turn right (see the figure). This will turn your dog's head toward you while also making his body follow along — without causing neck strain or injury.

Pulling down with a head halter does several things:

- ✔ It grabs your dog's attention quickly in a way he understands.
- ✔ It causes your dog to be submissive to you as you press on his nose.
- ✔ It brings his entire body around to where you are.

Trying the Heel off-leash

When you and your mixed breed are walking along nicely, you can begin doing so off-leash indoors or within a small, securely fenced area where there are no distractions.

Working off-leash is generally the ultimate goal of many dog owners. It takes lots of time and energy, but it is possible. I've broken this difficult process into two phases.

You know you're ready to begin off-leash heeling when you hardly have to use the leash at all. You can accomplish this by varying your pace, performing quick 180-degree turns, and never stopping to see what your mixed breed is up to if he's lagging behind.

The more turns you do, the more attentive your dog.

Phase 1: Dragging the leash

While you're walking, your mixed breed should be watching you attentively and keeping pace with you. If he's doing so nonchalantly, drop your leash. If your dog moves a little ahead, you can quickly step on the leash with a verbal reminder that he's not paying attention. This should be enough to return your mixed breed to your side and resume watching you — if not, return to the previous phase and work a little longer before trying this again.

Phase 2: Using a pull-tab leash

A pull-tab leash (shown in Figure 11-4) is a very short leash attached to the training device (at this point the training device should be a flat collar, because your dog no longer needs to be physically redirected).

Begin walking with a light hold on the end of the pull tab. As your mixed breed remains attentively at your side in heel position, let go. Keep a close eye on your dog. If he begins to stray out of position, use a verbal reminder in a low tone of voice as you make a sharp turn. If your dog goes in any direction other than with you, he wasn't ready for this phase. Return to leash dragging until you no longer have to step on the leash or use any reminders about remaining in heeling position.

Otherwise, congratulations! Your dog now heels off-leash.

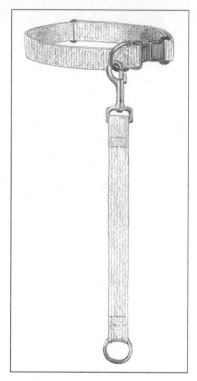

Figure 11-4: A pull tab should be attached to the flat neck collar and hang no longer than your dog's chest.

Sit

Having your dog sit on command is very important in many situations:

✔ He should sit for attention.

✔ He should sit prior to being fed.

✔ He should sit at your side when you stop walking.

Here's how to teach your dog to sit:

1. **Begin with a treat in your hand and target with your mixed-breed dog (see earlier in this chapter).**

2. **When he puts his nose on your hand, mark and reward.**

3. **To lure your mixed-breed dog into a sitting position place your target hand between his eyes, just out of reach of his mouth, but not out of reach of his nose.**

   Be sure to not hold it so high above his head that he feels as though he must jump up to reach it.

4. **As your mixed breed looks upward at his target, his rear end will lower down. Mark and reward.**

5. **Repeat Steps 1 through 4 several times.**

6. **Add the verbal cue — your dog's name and the command Sit— as you place your target hand between his eyes.**

   This will teach him both your word for *Sit* and the visual cue of your hand over his head.

When your mixed breed understands the Sit concept, add it into your heeling routines and use it anytime you want him to stay in one place for a little while. As you teach your mixed breed other commands — such as Come and Stay — you'll want to use this all-important Sit command as part of these requests.

Down

Teaching your mixed breed to lie down on command is very important. Not only can he maintain this position for longer periods of time than a Sit or Stand, but it also places your mixed breed in a less-than-dominant position.

Because of this submissive positioning, many dogs prefer not to listen to the Down command, so you'll need to make sure you approach it in a positive manner and enforce it using rewards. If your mixed breed sees the Down as a way to get treats and belly rubs, he'll respond to your Down command with enthusiasm.

Before you begin, find out what your mixed breed loves above all other things. Is it a specific toy, a piece of steak, or a belly rub? Use this special reward to both lure him into the Down position and keep him there for a few seconds.

Here's how to train your dog to follow the Down command:

1. **Begin with targeting your dog into the Sit (see the preceding section). Mark and reward the moment he's in position.**

2. **Place the special treat directly under your mixed breed's nose.**

3. **As soon as he targets on it, lower the treat to the floor (see Figure 11-5).**

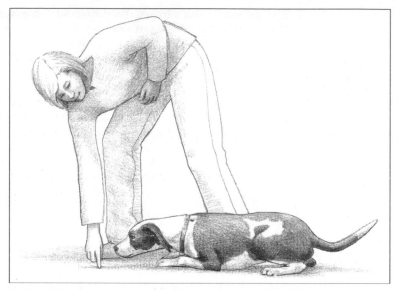

Figure 11-5: Lower the treat to the floor, and as soon as your dog lies down, mark and reward.

4. **As he follows with his head, mark and reward.**

5. **Repeat the exercise again, and don't mark until he has lowered himself a little more.**

   Eventually your mixed breed will lie down completely, enabling you to reward him with a belly rub.

 Your dog doesn't have to go all the way into a down position for you to reward his initial response of lowering his head. Some dogs will go all the way, while more dominant dogs may be reticent to do so. Offer your dog a chance at success in small increments.

Some dogs are so dominant that there is no treat in existence that will get them to demean themselves by lying down at your will. This type of dog needs some gentle assistance into the Down position — but it shouldn't be forceful or harsh. Here's what to do:

1. **Begin with your dog sitting in Heel position at your left side.**

2. **Try targeting him into the Down position with your right hand.**

3. **If he ignores your visual cue, place your left hand on his shoulders as you bring out his front feet with your right hand.**

4. **Apply constant but gentle pressure to his shoulders as you bring the front legs forward.**

5. **The moment your mixed breed's tummy touches the floor, rub his belly and praise.**

If your mixed breed weighs more than 50 pounds, you'll want to *unbalance* him into the Down position. Check to see the side on which he's placing all his weight. (***Hint:*** It's the hip you see the least of.) As you bring the front leg of that same side forward, apply pressure to your dog's shoulders on the opposite side, thereby lowering your mixed breed onto his side as his tummy meets the floor.

When your dog can perform both the Sit and Down on command, you'll be ready to teach him how to remain in these positions through the following Stay exercises.

Stay

Your mixed breed needs to learn to remain in place while sitting, lying down, and even while standing. The stand/stay is great while being examined by a veterinarian or during grooming.

Though your mixed breed can stay for a short period of time in a sit or stand, he can remain in position longer while lying down. For example, a sit/stay is great while looking both ways prior to crossing a street, or while greeting someone, but your mixed breed can't remain in that position more than a couple minutes without needing to move. While in a down/stay, he can learn to remain in his bed while you're eating dinner, visiting with guests, watching television, or allowing a young child to touch him.

There are three components to teaching a solid stay:

- ✔ Time
- ✔ Movement
- ✔ Distance

If you teach your mixed breed with this methodical technique, he'll learn to remain in place regardless of distractions or environmental situations, such as at a dog park, when greeting a guest at the door, or in the presence of other animals.

Time

Wouldn't it be great if your mixed breed remained in the same place for upwards of a minute? In this section, I show you how you can get him to do exactly that.

Begin by doing this in a sit/stay.

1. **Have your dog heel and sit at your side.**

   Always begin a training session with something that your dog knows well and will receive rewards for performing.

2. **As your dog is sitting, target in front of his nose with one hand as you use a specific visual cue with the other hand.**

   I always use an open-fingered hand, with the palm facing the dog (see Figure 11-6).

3. **Hold the target by your mixed breed's nose for only a couple seconds.**

4. **Mark and reward, then continue heeling.**

Figure 11-6: Hold the hand target in the same position as you did with the Sit target while giving the visual cue for stay.

With each successive Stay exercise, hold the target (and thus your dog's attentive sit/stay) a couple seconds longer.

The next step is to add the actual Stay command. Your mixed breed already has an idea of your visual cues for the command, so he'll easily learn the verbal ones associated with your body language. Say your dog's name and the command "Stay" as you give the hand signal in front of his face.

You don't need to actually touch your dog's nose with your visual cue. Seeing it is enough. Also, don't swing your hand toward his face. He might flinch at the motion, making the entire learning process less positive.

If your dog is getting up after a specific amount of time — for example, after he's been staying for 10 seconds — back up a bit (say, to 8 seconds). Work at this level for the remainder of the training session. During the next session, after he's been successfully staying for 8 seconds, try again for 10 seconds. Sometimes you'll have more success with an exercise if you're willing to regress a bit to a comfortable point.

When you've accomplished at least a 30-second sit/stay, do the same exercise with the down/stay.

If your mixed breed has trouble remaining in position, even with his target nearby, apply a light pressure to his shoulder blades any time he starts to push upward. This pressure will maintain his position without your having to replace him with another command or offering another treat.

Movement

Now that your mixed breed can remain in both the sit/stay and down/stay positions, it's time to move around him while he stays.

As with the time factor (see the preceding section), movement should be done in small increments.

When moving around your dog in a sit/stay, begin by moving in front of him. When moving around your dog in a down/stay, begin by moving along his side and then behind him.

Here's how to progress with a sit/stay:

1. **Step directly in front of your mixed-breed dog as you give the stay command (see Figure 11-7).**

2. **After remaining in front of your dog for up to 30 seconds, return to the heeling position, mark his good behavior and reward him.**

3. **Move side to side in front of your mixed breed as he remains in his sit/stay.**

Figure 11-7: The first move during a sit/
stay should be directly in front of your dog,
standing face to face and toe to toe.

4. **When your mixed breed can maintain a sit/stay with you moving in front of him, begin walking along his sides.**

   Be sure to go along both sides equally.

5. **Walk completely around your dog as he stays.**

   As with moving along his sides, do your circles around him in both directions.

Distance

The final step of the Stay exercise is to increase your distance as you move around your dog. This will allow you to tell your mixed breed to stay even if you're not right by his side. You can do this when you're going to answer the door, when you're walking through gates, or when you're going into one room and wanting him to stay in another.

As with the movement part of this exercise (see the preceding section), increase your distance using small increments and always be ready to shorten your distance if your dog can't remain in place.

Begin with gaining 1 foot of distance as you move around your mixed breed. When he proves reliable with this, go to 2 feet, and so on, until you're walking around him at the end of a 6-foot leash. When your mixed breed proves reliable at 6 feet, put on a 15- to 20-foot leash and gradually increase the distance even more.

Increase distance gradually. Sudden distance will cause your dog to move out of position.

Don't move straight backward. Your mixed breed will have a tendency to move toward you if you do this. Increase your distance as you move *around* him.

Come

Of all the obedience exercises, having your dog come when called is probably the most important. Nothing is more frustrating than calling your dog and seeing him run in the opposite direction. Your mixed breed is not doing this because he's vindictive — he just doesn't understand what you want.

If you've already taught your dog the commands earlier in this chapter, you're already well on your way to having your dog listen to your Come command.

The basics

As with all new exercises, start by being very close to your mixed breed so he'll always be successful and see the come command as very positive.

1. **Say your dog's name.**

2. **Mark and reward when he looks at you.**

3. **Repeat several times.**

You'll begin noticing a few things. First, your dog not only turns to you, but he's starting to come to you. Second, he's doing so without any force from you — he *wants* to come.

Now start moving with the request:

1. **Begin with targeting.**

2. **Back up a couple steps and have your mixed-breed dog target.**

3. **Back up a couple more steps and tell your mixed-breed dog his name and the command Come as you back up.**

4. **Repeat until you can back up at least ten steps and your dog is near your toes all the way.**

Taking it up a notch: A game of Round Robin

After your dog has mastered the preceding exercises, it's time to play a game of Round Robin. This game is a great way to teach a young dog to come when called. It's also fun for older dogs and especially great at teaching your mixed breed to listen to the entire family.

Before you begin, make sure that everyone who wants to play the game does the earlier exercise of targeting and saying your dog's name. This teaches your mixed breed that he's rewarded for listening to everyone, not just to you.

Here's how to play:

1. **Have everyone stand in a circle, about 8 feet from each other.**

   Your dog needs some space to move from person to person.

2. **Lean forward, show your mixed breed the target, say his name, and tell him, "Come" in a very pleasant tone of voice.**

3. **As he moves toward you, praise enthusiastically the entire time he's coming.**

4. **As soon as he arrives, mark and reward.**

   If you've been using a clicker, everyone in the game must have a clicker, too. If you're using a verbal sound, make sure everyone can emulate the sound.

5. **Repeat Steps 2 through 4 with everyone in the group.**

Alternate the order in which each person calls your mixed breed, so he never knows what's coming next.

You can vary this game by adding other command elements, such as having your mixed breed sit when he arrives. Or have him lie down. Then add a stay. This way, everyone in the family will be giving him commands, and he'll think it's all a big game and loads of fun to listen. After all, he's earning loads of rewards and attention. What's not to like?

Getting your dog to come from a Stay

Now that your mixed breed is readily coming from one person to another and to you as you move backward, it's time to try the come from both the sit/stay and down/stay.

The most difficult part of this command is gathering the leash as your dog nears you. If you don't gather it, the leash gets entangled under your mixed breed's feet, and disentangling it after his arrival is inconvenient for you (and annoying to your dog).

Try to gather your leash hand over hand as your dog comes to you. Don't pull on the leash — you want your mixed breed to come when called without needing any force.

Here's the step-by-step approach:

1. **Place your dog in a Stay.**

2. **Lean forward, show him your hand target, hold the target near your knees, and call him to you (see Figure 11-8).**

3. **As your dog comes to you, stand upright and gather your leash hand over hand (see Figure 11-9).**

Practice calling your mixed breed from all directions — in front of him, from each side, and from behind him. This will teach him to come from any direction. Also be sure to have your mixed breed perform the come from both his sit/stay and down/stay positions.

The more you vary the exercises, the more attentive your mixed breed will be.

Always begin with the former exercise of calling from the end of a 6-foot leash. But when your mixed breed is reliably responding, you can attach a 15- to 20-foot leash and work from greater distances. Keep in mind that the longer the leash, the more you must gather as your dog comes to you. Also, the farther away your dog when you call him, the faster he'll move toward you — often faster than you can gather the leash! No worries: If your mixed breed arrives before you can totally gather the leash, do the following:

1. **Take hold of the leash near his collar, giving him at least 2 feet of slack between his collar and your hand.**

2. **Move into the heel position, allowing the leash to drag behind your dog as you walk.**

3. **Gather the leash while you're walking with your dog.**

   It will be easier to gather since your dog won't be sitting on part of it.

Figure 11-8: Keep your upper body low and target near your knees as you call your dog to you.

As with gaining distance on the Stay exercises, you want to build on success with the recall as well. Begin with short distances and, as your mixed breed becomes reliable, gradually increase the distance as you vary the location. Practice calling him to you from in front of him, from either side, and from behind.

If you get to a specific distance and your mixed-breed dog is sniffing on his way to you, go back to a shorter distance. Your mixed-breed dog is showing you that he's not ready for that distance yet.

Figure 11-9: As you gather your leash, move your upper body upright.

When your mixed breed is easily coming to you from the distance of the long leash, it's time to move away from the leash a bit. Here's how to do it in *safe* phases:

1. **Drop the leash and move around your dog, but return to the end of the leash prior to calling him.**

   This will allow you to pick up the leash and guide your mixed breed to you if he gets distracted by something along the way.

2. **Call him from near the leash, but not in a direct line with it.**

   Again, this will allow you to reinforce your command fairly quickly if your mixed breed gets distracted by something else.

3. **Move farther and farther from the line of the leash as your mixed breed proves reliable.**

4. **Gain distance from your dog as he proves reliable from any location.**

5. **Hide behind solid objects so your dog learns to stay and come when you're out of sight.**

You may want to have someone help you with this because you won't be able to see when your dog moves before you call him.

Dealing with Distractions

Maybe your beautifully trained mixed breed does super when he's in your house or yard, but not so well walking down the road. But what if you want to be able to go places with your dog and have him still reliably follow your commands?

Your mixed-breed dog must learn how to behave regardless of where he is and what's going on around him. This is a very important part of obedience work. Time for distraction-proofing!

Looking at the different levels of distraction

Every dog is an individual, and that isn't more true than with a mixed-breed dog. Some dogs are distracted by the smallest leaf; others won't react unless they see another dog coming toward them. You've spent some time with your mixed breed, so you probably have a sense — or are starting to get one! — of what grabs his attention.

The things that attract a dog's attention do have some connection to the dog's breed. If you know your dog's mix (or you can make an educated guess), check out the following and see if any of this rings true:

- **Sporting:** Smells of other animals, movement of small animals or toys

- **Hound:** Smells and, for sighthounds, quick movements

- **Working:** Movement of other animals or toys, presence of a dominant dog

- **Terrier:** The presence of squirrels, rabbits, cats, and other dogs

- **Toy:** Other dogs

- **Non-Sporting:** Just about anything — all of these breeds are based on dogs from the other groups, so there's no telling what will distraction them

- **Herding:** Movement of other animal and young children

Although specific breeds (or breed mixes) have a tendency to react more to one type of distraction than to another, a few generalizations can be made about what is least likely to distract any dog and what is most likely to distract. Here's a list of the top-ten distractions, starting with the least likely and ending with the most likely:

- Fallen leaves
- Toys lying around
- Toys being thrown around
- The presence of people
- People moving by quickly
- Children playing nearby
- Children running near and going by quickly
- Dogs barking in a nearby yard
- Dog being walked nearby, especially if coming toward you
- Dog playing with a ball nearby

When working on distraction-proofing your dog, begin with the things like fallen leaves and toys on the floor and gradually work your way up to dogs walking or playing nearby.

Introducing distractions to your dog

Distraction-proofing is far more difficult than teaching the basic commands. It's tough for your dog to pay attention when he'd rather be chasing squirrels, playing with other dogs or racing around the schoolyard with all the children.

You have to offer your mixed breed a positive experience for him to *want* to work for you amid all these distractions. In order to maintain *his* positive attitude, you must always have a positive outlook and offer him high-value rewards so that paying attention to you is more important to him than anything else. You'll also need to reward him very often, so that he has more desire to pay attention.

Be prepared to redirect your dog when there is a distraction too enticing to ignore. Often treats or favorite toys can't compete with the presence of another dog, especially one playing nearby. Your mixed-breed dog won't care if you put a piece of steak under his nose — he feels that the better reward is to go play with that other dog. When this occurs, you need to be able to redirect him. You'll need training tools, namely the head halter.

Here's the process:

1. **Have your dog heeling at your side.**

2. **When you see the distraction, don't react — save your reaction for when your mixed-breed dog *begins* to look.**

   Don't wait for your mixed breed to pull before you react. If he even *looks* at the distraction, he's distracted.

3. **When your dog notices the distraction, pull downward on your leash as you turn.**

4. **Continue walking until your dog is heeling properly.**

5. **Mark and reward.**

6. **Turn and try to get a little closer the next time.**

   Continue with your turning and redirection when your mixed breed begins to look at the other dog. Always mark the moment he returns to his correct behavior and reward him for it.

If you've been trying to get just a couple feet closer than the previous attempt and your mixed breed simply won't allow that, it's time to back off to a safer zone. For example, say you've been working on getting within 20 feet of that yard where the dog is barking and jumping on the fence, but your mixed breed wants to lunge toward the other dog the moment he lays eyes on it. It's time to go back to the area where dog didn't react so adamantly. Work in this area for a while. Then, when your dog is calm and not pulling to go toward the distraction, try to get just a few feet closer.

Helping your dog be reliable off-leash

Don't attempt distraction-proofing off-leash until your dog is totally reliable *on*-leash without your having to redirect, back off, or pull on his collar. When you're off-leash, you can't control your dog's reaction. If he sees something enticing, he may not heed your words of warning.

As you reach a point in your training when your mixed breed is reliable on-leash, without any instances of having to redirect or regress, try working around the distractions off-leash. Begin with the items that are the least likely to cause him to react, such as toys lying around, the presence of another person or child, or someone moving around him. If he handles these well, try working with him near a yard where there's another dog. Finally, with all the other distractions controlled, it's time to attempt the most diffi-cult: dog and toy together.

You may want to have your mixed breed wear a short leash — a pull tab, so that you have something to grab if he decides to look at the distraction instead of you. A light tug of redirection might be enough to remind him that you have far better rewards for him than that distraction does.

Finding a Trainer

Every dog is different, and many mixed breeds bring with them a whole lot of baggage. Negative experiences your dog has had in the past may cause any number of abnormal reactions, so if you're having trouble with training, you'll want to work with a profes-sional trainer.

You need the help of a pro when:

- You've tried to train your dog, but you aren't pleased with the response.
- Your dog continues to disobey no matter how consistent you've been.
- Your dog is very distracted by other dogs or people.
- Your dog has bad habits that are difficult to cure, such as housetraining accidents, excessive chewing, excessive bark-ing, or mouthing.
- Your dog shows signs of aggression, such as dominant postur-ing, staring you in the eye for long periods, being pushy to get what he wants, barking for attention, grabbing hold of you with his mouth, or biting.
- Your dog shows signs of fear, such as backing up while bark-ing and snarling, or biting you from behind.
- You're pulling on the leash so much that you don't want to walk with him anymore.
- You're so frustrated that you're reconsidering dog ownership.

If any of the preceding applies to you and your situation, look into working with a professional trainer.

To find a good trainer, start by asking your dog's vet and groomer. Owners of small pet shops can often recommend trainers as well. (Large, chain pet shops have their own trainers, who may or may

not be what you're looking for.) You can also locate professional
trainers through the following Web sites:

- ✔ **The Association of Pet Dog Trainers (www.apdt.com):** This
  group certifies trainers through testing and education. All
  certified trainers take a specific number of educational credits
  each year so they're current on training methods and scientific behavioral knowledge.

- ✔ **The International Association of Canine Professionals (www.
  dogpro.org):** This group includes only professional trainers
  who have more than five years of experience. When they say
  professional trainer, they mean someone whose main source of
  income is through training dogs. IACP also offers certification
  to members.

- ✔ **National Association of Dog Obedience Instructors (www.
  nadoi.com):** This group has been around longer than the first
  two in this list. It requires certification in Novice, Open, and
  Utility, among other offerings such as Agility and Rally-O in
  order for a trainer to maintain membership. These certifica-
  tions pertain more toward showing dogs than obedience
  training. Someone with the knowledge needed to show a
  dog, however, can often help others with basic training issues.

Chapter 12

Tackling Mixed-Breed Training Challenges

In This Chapter

▶ Helping your dog be okay with being alone

▶ Knowing what to do with your aggressive dog

▶ Making Emily Post proud: Curing bad manners

Many mixed-breed dogs have already learned some less-than-stellar behaviors in their previous environments. These problems are ones you want to identify and correct sooner rather than later. The first step in reversing a particular behavior is understanding why the problem exists in the first place. Is it because of something that happened in the past? Or are you doing something now that's causing the problem? What is it about your mixed-breed dog's personality that makes her act that way? These are the questions that you need to ask — and this chapter is the place where you find the answers.

Regardless of the *reason* for the behavior, you can teach your mixed-breed dog how to get attention (the positive kind) by doing something you *want* instead of something you *don't* want. In this chapter, I show you how.

I start by explaining why many mixed-breed dogs — particularly those from shelters, humane societies, and rescue groups — have special training challenges. Then I cover the most common problem: separation anxiety. Because many dogs also display some form of aggression, or have pushy personalities, I talk about the various types of aggression and how to deal with them. Finally, regardless of where your mixed breed originated, she may have behavioral issues that need to be addressed. I fill you in on some common behavior problems — such as jumping up, excessive chewing, mouthing, and digging — and tell you how to handle these issues in your own dog.

Unpacking the Mental Baggage: Helping a Dog Who's Been Abused or Neglected

Most mixed-breed dogs have had a rough start. Many are a result of the accidental breeding of purebreds who weren't neutered or spayed and, as unwanted puppies, they're treated with little respect and care.

As unwanted pets, mixed breeds are caught by animal-control officers or brought to shelters. Some are found by concerned citizens and given to rescue groups and humane societies. Many accidental pups are dropped by the side of the road and left to fate. Regardless of how the pups or dogs make their way to permanent owners, most have gone through horrible experiences — ranging from a lack of a home with a loving family to outright abuse and neglect.

As the result of having no sense of permanent territory, reliable nutrition, or loving care, most mixed-breed dogs have several serious issues. And as the owner of a mixed-breed dog, it's up to you to manage and help your dog overcome those problems.

Have you ever met a dog who shies away when you raise your arm? Or a dog who's frightened of children or men wearing hats? All these fears are based on past experiences where people of similar demeanor or appearance abused or frightened the dog in some manner.

Past events even affect young pups. Though easily trained at a very young age, they're also influenced by every experience — good and bad. They remember extreme experiences for a long time, until they're totally convinced — by someone like you — that life can be *good,* without fear and deprivation.

Regardless of whether your mixed breed is 2 months old or 2 years old, she's a composite of her past — and you get the wonderful (and sometimes challenging) job of guiding her toward a brighter future.

Alone and Frightened: Separation Anxiety

Between the moment she made her way into this world, all slimy and new, to the moment you brought your dog home, she's likely lived in more than two places. Most purebred dogs get the socialization they need while they're with their litter, mom, and breeder. They're given proper nutrition, handling, and healthcare — and they get nothing but this loving care from birth. Mixed-breed dogs rarely have these benefits.

Unless your mixed breed is a designer dog (see Chapter 2) or was bred by a caring breeder, she has likely had little care, socialization with people or other animals, and possibly long periods of poor nutrition. All these factors form the dog's overall personality.

Usually, after a dog has been in a new home for a period of time, she'll settle into the routine. But if your dog has never had anything like a normal routine, she may suddenly think her world is caving in when you go to work for the day or go to sleep in another room. She's worried that her new family is disappearing. She wonders if she'll ever have another good meal. She's thinking, "Maybe all those poets were right, and love really is a fleeting thing."

If this is what's running through your dog's mind when she's alone, she has separation anxiety. A dog with separation anxiety is very insecure in *every* aspect of her life.

Recognizing the symptoms

The symptoms of separation anxiety can range from barely discernable to extremely destructive. In the following sections, I fill you in.

Excessive drooling

Your dog may drool as she watches you grilling hamburgers and hot dogs, preparing a meal in the kitchen, or eating at the table. This kind of drooling is what dogs are all about. But dogs salivate for several reasons. One of them is because they're dying to grab that piece of meat out of your hands and run away with it. And another reason is because they're anxious.

A dog who salivates due to anxiety doesn't just drip little puddles — she covers herself in moisture as the saliva pours through her lips like a hose that hasn't been turned off all the way. She does this because she doesn't realize that you'll come back at some point, she doesn't understand her environment, she doesn't know how to communicate with you, and she doesn't know what you expect of her.

Dogs with separation anxiety don't just drool when they're left home alone. They may also drool excessively when they're riding in a car (if they're afraid of cars) or when they're frightened of a new place or situation. In other words, fear is what brings about the drool.

The loud protest: Whining and barking

Excessive whining and barking are easy to identify. Your neighbors know it when they hear it: an annoying outburst while you're away from home. If you're living in an apartment, a townhouse, or a densely populated neighborhood with a noisy dog, you'll likely hear from your neighbors that your best friend is upset about being home alone. Your dog may bark and whine when you're home but not right next to her — for example, when you've left your dog outside in the yard or in another room without you.

When you hear your dog whining or barking, your first reaction is probably to run to the poor dog because you can't stand that she's upset. Don't do it! You'll be reinforcing this behavior because you gave her what she had been whining about — your presence. The next time you go somewhere, she'll turn it up another notch or two. Dogs learn very quickly! Later in this chapter, I discuss ways to stop the noise through training, structure, and positive reinforcement.

Self-mutilation: Biting and scratching

Self-mutilation can begin with excessive licking in one spot, making *lick granulomas* (also known as hot spots), which are swelled, raised, and irritated skin. Your dog's behavior can go on from there to pulling out her hair, rubbing her eyes, and doing any uncontrollable motion such as twisting and circling while whining or barking.

Tearing it up: Destructive behavior

Destructive behavior, like chewing your furniture, digging a hole in the carpet, or chewing up your favorite pair of shoes are symptoms of separation anxiety. The more severe the separation anxiety, the worse the destruction.

Dogs who are only slightly upset at their human companions being gone will chew one item, like a book or the TV remote control; dogs who are severely upset will destroy entire rooms of furniture, carpeting, and doors.

From the dog's point of view, she's trying very hard to go find her people. She feels as though she's been left out of the family pack and she's trying to join up with the family again. Being away from the pack is a huge feeling of insecurity. (Given a choice, dogs will typically choose social groupings of more than one individual.)

When you come home to find that your dog has torn up the house, she wasn't doing it out of spite because you left — she was doing it because she was afraid. If you keep that in mind, you won't be as angry and you'll feel more compassionate toward your new best friend.

Aggression

Many dogs don't want to see their people leave the house. They may have tried to get your attention through barking or digging, and you just didn't seem to understand that message. Time for a more direct approach: aggression.

Most likely, the dog isn't showing aggression because she wants to hurt anybody — she's showing aggression as a way of keeping her pack together.

Discerning the difference between aggression associated with separation anxiety and other types of aggression can be difficult. The easiest way to tell the difference is that if the aggression is due to separation anxiety, it only happens as someone walks to the door, and the dog normally attacks from behind. The bite is more a pinch than anything else — the dog isn't doing it to being mean. The bite is fear related — fear of never seeing you again.

Regardless of the reason, when your dog is aggressive, seeking professional help is best. Aggressive behavior of any kind is a serious issue and should be addressed immediately —both for your safety and the dog's future with your family.

Knowing what to do about it

Separation anxiety is something that can be conquered, but you'll need patience, fortitude, and consistency. At times, you may feel that it's just too much work, but keep in mind that a couple months of struggle is nothing in comparison to the many years of joy ahead with your mixed-breed dog.

You can do several things to reduce and/or cure separation anxiety. I cover them in the following sections.

Containing the problem

Most dogs feel overwhelmed when faced with a huge unfamiliar area. Too many scary things might happen: The mail carrier comes up to the house, other dogs walk by the yard, neighbors ring the doorbell when no one's home, cars pass on the street, a squirrel invades the tree in the yard. . . . Your dog is aware of *everything* she can see through the windows or hear outside.

Most dogs seek a small, dark place when they're worried. Such a place makes them feel secure from outside threats. In fact, wild canines always have a den where they can sleep or whelp their pups. A crate can simulate this safe place, because the dog feels something solid on all sides.

Attitude is everything . . . and *yours* is the one that matters

Dogs with separation anxiety tend to be destructive. If your dog has separation anxiety, you may come home to *see* that destruction. Being upset is only natural, but as your dog picks up on your anger, pretty soon she'll feel afraid when you return home instead of being eager to see you.

Teaching your dog to not miss you and returning home with a positive attitude — no matter what you find when you get there — will help alleviate your dog's anxieties.

Placing your mixed breed in a crate will not only give your dog a sense of security, but also keep her from injuring herself through destructive behavior, such as eating carpet strands, chewing on electrical cords, or eating poisonous houseplants. The crate offers safety for your dog and sanity for you — no mess when you get home.

A dog should not be contained in a crate for more than five hours at a time. If you must be away from home for longer periods than this, consider other options, such as hiring a dog walker or fencing off a portion of your yard. Remember to provide a source of shelter and water if you leave your dog in a fenced yard.

Going to obedience training

Obedience training doesn't just teach your dog to come, sit, and heel. It also gives her a chance to learn how to communicate with you and to understand her environment. A trained dog is happier and more relaxed. She has something to look forward to every day. You can use training in many ways to help your relationship with your dog, from alleviating separation anxiety and overcoming many types of aggression to curbing bad manners such as jumping and excessive barking.

In Chapter 11, I cover positive training techniques that help in every aspect of your dog's life.

Sticking to a routine

Structuring your mixed-breed dog's day will give her an idea of what to expect and when. Dogs like knowing when it's time to eat, sleep, play, and greet you at the door. They don't have to look at clocks to know what time it is. Dogs quickly develop a sense of time. Knowing what's going to happen when helps the dog relax — she doesn't have to worry about surprises or unknowns.

Structure can also teach your dog to not miss you, proving to her that nice things happen as you leave.

Here is a regular routine you can practice to help ease the separation anxiety. It works because it redirects your dog's anxiety to something pleasant, something she'll look forward to.

1. **Begin by finding something that has high value to your dog, such as a food-stuffed toy or special squeaky toy.**

2. **If you're keeping your dog contained in a crate, place that special toy or treat in the containment area as you leave the room.**

3. **Peek around the corner and watch the dog's response.**

4. **If she's content playing with her toy, return into the room and praise her.**

5. **Release her from her crate.**

6. **Repeat Steps 1 through 5 a little later, waiting a few more minutes as she plays or chews the toy.**

   Each time you do this, wait longer and longer, until your dog can remain for at least a half-hour in this manner without any anxiety response.

Training your dog not to miss you

Using the reward-when-you-leave system (see the preceding section) is very helpful in teaching your dog that good things happen upon your leaving, but it may not sustain her while you're gone.

You can condition your dog to be more accepting of your absence by starting small. Begin by giving your dog her special treat when you leave the room. Check around the corner where she can't see you. When she finishes with her toy, return and reward her with praise. Gradually increase the time between giving her the as-you-leave-toy and returning with praise. If you see your dog looking around for you before she finishes her treat, you've spent too much time away, too soon. You've conditioned her to look for you instead of enjoying her toy. You may need to offer a higher value toy. Gradually increase your time away, allowing your dog to slowly acclimate to the fact you're gone and that when you return, good things happen.

Socializing with other dogs

Dogs are pack animals. They need the company of others in order to feel secure. If you have long workdays, try to find a way of offering your dog opportunities to socialize with other dogs while you're gone.

Doggie playtime is important to your dog's social development in many ways:

- **Dogs teach each other proper social skills, such as how to get along with others and appropriate behavior in specific situations.**

- **Canine play gives your dog the exercise she needs to remain physically and mentally healthy.** Are you going to get down on the floor and wrestle? Most likely not. You're also unlikely to use your mouth to grab your mixed breed's legs or jump about and race around. In fact, I don't suggest doing that at all, or your dog won't respect you as her leader. There are ways of playing with your dog that offer positive interaction without making her think she's your equal.

You can offer your dog canine social time in several ways:

- **Send your dog to doggie daycare.** Doggie daycare gives your dog exercise and social time while you're at work, alleviating her separation anxiety and reducing her desire to control the activity at home.

- **Find people in your neighborhood who have dogs of similar size and temperament, and arrange a specific time every day or at least several days per week when the dogs can come together and play.** The more often you do this, the healthier for all the dogs involved.

- **Get a second dog.** If you don't have the convenience of neighbors with dogs or a doggie daycare nearby, get a second dog. Your dog will have fewer anxieties if she can cuddle with someone while you're away.

Medications and alternative treatments for anxiety

Homeopathic remedies are available for treating anxiety of many types. Among them are flower, herbal, and aromatherapies. Amazingly, the tiniest essence of specific flowers and herbs help dogs relax and change their mindset. These remedies have been around far longer than modern medicine and have a proven record for working even when prescription medications won't.

I normally try a homeopathic remedy before using a prescription one, because the prescriptions target symptoms instead of the source. Homeopathic remedies target the source of an illness, injury, or behavioral problem. Using homeopathics in conjunction with behavior modification and obedience training will cure a large percentage of dogs with separation anxiety.

Flower and herbal remedies

Ever heard the saying "Stop and smell the roses"? Well, there's a lot to that old adage and not just in the sense of learning to enjoy every day of your life. Flower essences have very powerful healing properties. They can relax, prevent anxiety, and aid in the healing of illness. Ever notice the plethora of aromatherapy products available? Candles, essential oils, soaps, and sachets — they're popular because they work.

Following is a brief list of some of the flower essences that help with separation anxiety. You can apply them via a tincture (directly into your dog's mouth) or you allow the dog to inhale them using aromatherapy:

- ✔ **Chamomile:** This flower essence helps relax a dog's muscles — sort of like a powerful muscle relaxant given to people with pulls and sprains — but it doesn't affect the digestive system as much as a prescription muscle relaxer. People have drunk chamomile tea for centuries as a way to unwind from a stressful day.

- ✔ **Phosphorus, pulsatilla, and arsenicum:** Use these if your dog panics when left alone.

- ✔ **Rescue Remedy Bach Flower Essences:** This blend of flower essences helps dogs with anxieties of many kinds, from separation and fear to grieving. The blend consists of Rock Rose, Star of Bethlehem, Impatiens, Cherry Plum, and Clematis.

Approaching behavioral problems holistically (with herbal remedies) is helpful in many ways. You're addressing the source of the problem — and when the source is removed or modified, the symptoms can be gradually reduced or eradicated. Training and scheduling help remove the source of separation anxiety, and herbal blends help the dog through the transition period, offering a means of remaining calm. Flower essences are often added to the herbal blends.

Here are some herbal remedies I recommend:

- ✔ **Scullcap:** This herbal aids with nervous disorders.

- ✔ **Valerian root:** This helps calm a hyperactive dog.

- ✔ **Belladonna:** This herbal reduces anxiety and calms the dog enough for her to relax when she's left alone.

- ✔ **Vervain:** This is another herb that calms the dog, much like valerian root.

- ✔ **Aspen:** This herbal helps the dog feel secure, less alone.

A professional herbologist has to mix the correct doses of herbs and flower essences, so get prepackaged blends that target specific behaviors. You can usually find these blends at your local health-food or vitamin store. Many Web sites sell good herbal products, too, including the following:

- Equilite (www.equilite.com)
- My Fine Equine (www.myfineequine.com)
- Hilton Herbs (www.hiltonherbs.com)
- NativeRemedies.com (www.nativeremedies.com)
- Alternative Veterinary Hospital (www.alternativeveterinary hospital.com/bach_essences.htm)
- BachFlower.com (www.bachflower.com)

Prescription medicines

The most commonly used prescription medication for separation anxiety is Clomicalm. It specifically targets the symptoms of separation anxiety, not only helping the dog to relax, much like chamomile, but also reducing the dog's reactivity to her environment. Your mixed breed is less likely to get as upset about sudden noises (such as a knock on the door or a delivery truck). The only drawback of Clomicalm is that it can take up to six weeks to see the benefits.

Amitriptyline is another prescription drug used for canine cognitive dysfunction (CCD, which is similar to senility in humans) and separation anxiety. It tends to work faster than Clomicalm but has more side effects, such as retention of urine, loss of appetite, and drowsiness.

These prescription drugs are not to be used for more than a three-month period, under veterinary guidance. They treat the symptoms, not the source, of separation anxiety. Use them in conjunction with behavior-modification techniques aimed at teaching your dog that she won't be left alone forever. Within a few months, you'll have a dog who is well adjusted enough to live without medications.

Severe anxiety: When to seek outside help

Sometimes, nothing seems to work. You've tried everything, and Buster is still displaying the anxiety. At this point you should seek professional help. Your veterinarian, an animal behaviorist, or a professional dog trainer have the experience to overcome these issues using positive reinforcement techniques. It may be time consuming, but the rewards are worth it: a well-adjusted mixed-breed dog who relaxes while you're gone and happily greets you upon your return.

You know you need to get help when:

- ✔ Your dog becomes very upset when left in a crate.
- ✔ Your dog is soaking wet from saliva when you return home.
- ✔ Your dog is eating things that can make her sick.
- ✔ Your dog is biting and chewing on herself.
- ✔ Your dog is biting you or others.
- ✔ Your dog is behaving oddly (circling as she whines, biting at the air, clinging to your heels everywhere you go, sucking on something, shivering and cowering).

There are three specialists who can help:

- ✔ **Your veterinarian:** The first person you should contact for help with severe separation anxiety is your vet. Many sources of behavioral issues are based on physical problems, so it's best to first rule these out. When visiting with your vet, explain what your dog is doing and when it occurs. Your vet will do a full exam. If the vet doesn't mention it, request a full blood chemistry — organ dysfunction (which shows up in the blood chemistry) can be a source of behavioral problems.

    If your vet gives the all-clear and says your dog has no physical problems, call an animal behaviorist.

- ✔ **Animal behaviorist:** An animal behaviorist, who is a veterinary specialist in behavioral medicine, can come to your home and pinpoint the cause of the anxiety, offering ways of solving it. A veterinary behaviorist can prescribe the medications; some will suggest herbal or flower remedies.

    When you meet with the animal behaviorist, explain and try to emulate the situations that produce the separation anxiety as closely as possible so that the behaviorist can observe firsthand. Ask about ways to change the routine, or how to redirect your dog so he can see the situation as something more positive instead of scary.

- ✔ **Dog trainer:** A dog trainer can help you in the long term, because you'll learn how to teach your dog about her environment and how she can communicate with you. Many dog trainers also know the correct herbal remedies and apothecaries to aid in training your dog to overcome her anxieties.

    As you train your dog, you're setting her up for a successful life with you and your family. As with the animal behaviorist, show your trainer what occurs and when so that the specific issues can be addressed. Ask about ways to train your dog to accept the situation or about ways you can change a routine to help her relax or relieve the anxiety.

No More Mr. Nice Guy: The Aggressive Dog

Because of their past bad experiences, some mixed-breed dogs develop some form of aggression, usually for self-defense. Most aggression in mixed-breed dogs has to do with possession — the dog may have had to fend for itself, experiencing a scarcity of food and/or shelter. Your dog isn't intentionally unpleasant to you — she's just developed instinctual reactions to specific situations.

Almost all types of aggression can be controlled or even cured with obedience training, behavioral therapy, and the help of appropriate apothecaries. In this section, I give you the information you need to help your aggressive dog.

Recognizing the types of aggression

Aggression comes in several varieties, and recognizing the type of aggression your dog is exhibiting is the first step toward solving the problem. When you know *why* the dog is behaving the way she is, you can remove the cause and work toward eliminating the behavior.

Always consult with a pet professional prior to tackling any type of aggressive behavior, because an incorrect approach can often cause even worse problems.

It hurts, don't touch: Pain-related aggression

Pain-related aggression is common in dogs who aren't familiar with humane treatment for their pain, or in dogs who hurt so much that they can't control their behavior. This type of aggression can take time to cure. Often, the dog must be tranquilized to be treated for the source of the pain.

This dog won't display any aggressive posturing, such as trying to appear large, snarling, growling or snapping, prior to a bite. If you touch something that hurts, she lashes out.

The need to lead: Dominant aggression

Dominant aggression can be very dangerous. A dog who is dominantly aggressive wants to control you and others. She can display this aggression in a very subtle manner, from demanding attention by pushing against you to outright snapping at you. Although training can help control this dog, there is still a possibility of someone getting hurt.

A dog who is dominantly aggressive will often posture prior to biting. This dog will likely display her teeth, growl, pace, and stare. She makes herself look large by standing stiffly, with her ears forward and tail up, staring at your face with little or no blinking.

Past is present: Fear aggression

There is always a reason for fear aggression. It's the most common type of aggression in dogs who have gone through several homes or were rescued from a bad situation. A dog who displays fear aggression doesn't want to control the family — she's merely insecure and nervous.

Most dogs who end up in shelters suffer from insecurity. They don't understand their surroundings and can't communicate with those around them. Dogs in shelters are like travelers in a foreign country where they don't understand the customs or the language. Think of your dog in this way and you'll better understand why she needs instant guidance and training to alleviate this problem.

You can easily recognize fear aggression through body posturing. The dog will back up, hackles raised, head lowered, and tail down. Don't approach a dog displaying this behavior — she'll feel cornered and lash out. Bites from fearful dogs are usually surface bites, because the dog doesn't want to hurt you (he just wants to warn you), but the bites are painful and frightening nonetheless.

What's mine is mine! Possessive aggression

Possessive aggression is a type of dominant aggression, but it's only seen when the dog has something she wants to keep to herself. Dogs who have had to compete for food or other resources commonly display possessive aggression.

This dog will growl as you near her when she has a toy or food. Her head will be lowered, nose toward the object, her body held very stiff. You might even see the whites of her eyes, because she's afraid that you'll take her possession from her.

Me first, me first! Sibling rivalries

There will always be scuffles of some sort within the family pack as new family members try to determine their place. Most of these scuffles will consist of snarling and posturing. The "arguments" only get worse if people interfere or don't establish their own leadership over the dogs.

It begins with dominant stares and can turn into an all-out war.

Knowing what to do about it

Regardless of the type of dominance your dog has, consult with a professional dog trainer or behaviorist to handle the problem. Controlling and curing these issues require extensive knowledge of canine behavior. Though difficult, most of these behaviors *are* curable.

Here are some guidelines to follow as you help your dog overcome her aggression:

- ✔ **If your dog show signs of pain — such as limping or a sensitivity to light, sound, the presence of others, or touch — go to your vet . . .** *immediately.* Some dogs don't show pain-related behavior. Because part of their instinctive behavior is to not display weakness, your dog may not limp or be lethargic. It's still a good idea to have her checked by your vet, just in case. Internal injuries, bone or muscle inflammation, or organ malfunction can all cause distress, which can in turn cause pain-related aggression.

- ✔ **If your dog is trying to take over the household or wants to always be first, step up your leadership role through obedience training (see Chapter 11) and maintenance of social hierarchy.** Never allow your dog to sleep on your bed, sit on your sofa, or beg at the table. All these indulgences will lead to your dog being the boss.

- ✔ **Build your dog's confidence through regular scheduling of exercise, feeding times, and obedience training.** All these regular activities play a large role in helping your dog feel safe and help her realize that she's in a permanent home.

- ✔ **Because your dog has the energy to display aggression, you need to get that energy under control with lots of exercise.** A tired dog is less likely to be assertive than one with loads of energy. Focus on making sure your mixed breed gets so much exercise that she actually drops with exhaustion upon her return home.

  You can also work her through her predilection for assertiveness. Put her on her leash. Work her at all times, making her heel with you from room to room. Make her sit or go into a down/stay while there. Make her come to you prior to going into another room. Because she has to concentrate on paying attention, and defer the leadership position to you, she'll no longer have the desire to be the boss.

✔ **If your dog is displaying any type of aggression, use apothe-caries such as flower or herbal remedies (see the "Flower and herbal remedies" section, earlier in this chapter).** Using these as you train your dog will help her pay attention and increase her desire to learn — she'll no longer have the "new dog on the block" anxieties to contend with.

✔ **Consider prescription medications.** When you know the reason for the aggression, you and your vet can discuss the type of medication that would be most useful. Amitriptyline is often used to modify the dog's reactivity to her environment. Diazepamis also used to calm the dog. Acepromazine can also be used.

You may need to keep your dog on the medication for several weeks before you can tell whether it's working for her. These drugs aren't to be used instead of training your dog, but rather in conjunction with the training process

Sometimes prescription medication can have adverse effects, causing worse or unpredictable aggression, or side effects involving other organ systems.. Keep a close eye on your dog and maintain close communication with your vet and/or vet-erinary behaviorist.

Jumping for Joy

Jumping on people, furniture or countertops are the most common behavior problems with dogs. It's annoying, frustrating, and disrup-tive. But you can do something about it. In this section, I lay it all out.

Knowing why dogs jump

One of the main reasons dogs begin jumping up is to greet newcom-ers or companions (that's you!) who have returned home. They first touch noses, then go sniff the newcomer's rear end to learn who it is and what her intentions may be. This is the canine way.

Before you correct your dog for jumping, you need to discover why she's doing it. Most likely she's getting some reward for jumping up. Maybe she gets touched or she's spoken to. Some dogs merely like to perch higher than the floor — the old "I'm the king of the castle, and you're the dirty rascal" game. Maybe jumping is such a fun way to get you to play with her that she'll do it every time she wants attention.

The next time your dog jumps on you, note your reaction. Did you push at her? Yell at her? Pet her? Your reaction to her behavior will tell you the reason she does it.

Keeping your dog's feet on the ground

You can do several things to cure the habit of jumping, no matter why your dog is doing it:

- **Greet your dog lower to the ground — and ask your guests to do so as well.** Instead of making your dog reach upward to say, "Hi," crouch down low to allow an appropriate nose touch. This is far better than being jumped on or goosed in your behind. If you don't want your face washed in doggie saliva, keep your head up and offer your hands in greeting, holding them low and allowing your dog to sniff or lick them.

- **Condition your dog to get a tummy rub upon your arrival, by having her sit, then lie down, so you can rub her tummy.** What better way to be greeted than having your dog throw herself at your feet, panting in anticipation as she awaits a belly rub?

- **Try ignoring your dog the next time she jumps on you.** Don't touch her. Don't speak to her. Don't look at her. In fact, step away and hold your arms up so that she can't go to the next level of "I want attention now" and put her mouth on your hand.

- **When you're in a situation where your dog is jumping, tell her to sit.** This will redirect her from doing the bad thing to doing something good — it gives her a way she can earn positive attention. *Remember:* Don't ask your dog to sit too soon after the jumping up or you'll be creating a fun game called Jump and Sit. Dogs learn patterns very easily, and if she thinks she'll be rewarded for jumping and then sitting, she'll be persistent about it.

If you've told your dog to sit and she's too busy jumping to do so, make sure that you place her into position. When she's in position, praise her. Don't get too carried away with the praise, though — you did have to place her into a sit. You can get more excited when your dog sits without your help, especially if she comes to you and sits for attention instead of jumping up for it.

Try not to get frustrated. Your dog didn't learn to jump up overnight, and you won't cure her overnight. Remain calm, focused, and in control. Dogs know when you've reached your breaking point. You have to prove that you have *no* breaking point. Eventually, your dog will understand that you're in charge of doling out rewards and that she has to change her attention-seeking behavior.

Also, be consistent. If you make your dog sit for attention one time, but you're absentmindedly petting her while she has her feet on your lap another time, she won't learn to stop jumping up. If you really want to stop this behavior, you must always follow the law: No jumping up ever. No touching, speaking, or looking at jumping dogs — only sitting dogs get the reward.

Curing the insistent jumper

Some dogs have the jumping habit with little help from their human companions. They simply enjoy the act of jumping up in the air because it gives them thrills and chills. Some of these dogs will hop about without even touching their people. Others will touch occasionally. Some dogs not only spring in the air but also bounce off of their humans as though they were springboards.

Ignoring these dogs won't stop the behavior. Sometimes having them sit for attention will tone it down a little, but only if the dog is jumping up for your attention. Even if you maintain your cool and are consistent with your reactions, you still may not make a dent in this airborne wonder. Stopping the behavior through ignoring won't work either. You'll have to use a correction to change the behavior.

Most dogs respond well to a *sound* correction — something that makes an aversive sound. Dogs have far more sensitive hearing than humans, so certain pitches, volumes, or frequencies can distract them enough to stop a behavior that coincides with the sound.

You can use several objects to create aversive sounds when your dog jumps on you:

✔ **Pennies in a can:** Get a small metal can, such as one used for loose tea, paint, or a small coffee can. Place 15 pennies inside the can and be sure to seal the lid securely. When your dog jumps up, shake the can hard just once or twice. If this aversive sound is going to work, it will work fairly quickly. Your dog will stop jumping and either move away from you or sit. If she sits, praise her. If she moves away, wait until she returns and sits or remains with all four paws on the floor, and then praise her.

✔ **Rocks in a milk carton:** Place small rocks inside a plastic milk jug. Use it in the same manner as the can (see the preceding item). This is not as harsh a sound as the can; if your dog is very reactive to sound, you may want to try this first.

✔ **A bicycle horn:** A honk on a bicycle horn will definitely get your dog's attention. She'll likely step back and have a long look at you as though you've just issued the weirdest noise she's ever heard. She may be looking at you funny, but she stopped jumping, right?

If your dog doesn't like water, you can use a water gun (the Super Soaker brand water guns work best) to squirt water at her when she jumps up. The mere action of something coming at her should be enough to distract your dog and stop the behavior. This won't work with dogs who love water — these dogs will be encouraged to jump *more* in order to play the water game. If your mixed breed has any Retriever or Spaniel in her, I recommend using the aversive sound instead of the water squirt.

Chewing Your Dog Out for Chewing

Dogs love to chew. It's their favorite pastime. You can read books; watch TV; play sports, video games, and board games; or spend time on hobbies. Dogs don't have these things. They chew and dig and chew and run and chew. They chew their toys. They chew on sticks. They chew the sofa. Yikes! That's something you don't want them to chew. Why would your dog chew a sofa when she has her bone nearby? In this section, I tell you why — and help you get your dog to stop chewing things she shouldn't be chewing.

Understanding why dogs chew

Dogs chew for a variety of reasons. The main reason has to do with their age. All puppies chew. They're testing their environment for tasty morsels and for ways to alleviate the pain in their gums. If your dog is younger than 9 months of age, she's teething. Here's how normal teething develops:

- **Between the ages of 3 months and 5 months,** the baby teeth are falling out. You'll see your dog's front teeth being replaced with the larger, adult incisors. Your pup will be pulling at her toys as she explores objects for palatability. Watch out for those electrical cords — they look mighty tasty!

- **Between the ages of 5 and 7 months of age,** your pup's back teeth are falling out and being replaced with new ones. When the new molars grow in, it's very uncomfortable for your dog. She won't be chewing to learn about her environment — she'll be chewing to alleviate the discomfort in her gums. Anything hard is fair game. Wood of all sorts, such as molding, window frames, chairs, table legs, carpeting, shoes, plastic children's toys, books, and more.

- **At 7 to 8 months of age,** the molars are all in, but still a little loose in the gums. Chewing has become more of a pastime than a need, but it's still enjoyable as a way of releasing discomfort, anxiety, or boredom.

That brings me to the other reasons for chewing:

- ✔ **Anxiety:** A dog with anxiety can be extremely destructive. She doesn't just chew — she flings and swings the objects about, tramples and pulls, paws and scratches. Dogs chewing because of anxiety create a huge mess.

- ✔ **Boredom:** A dog who chews because she's bored may not create as large a destructive path as a dog who chews because she's anxious, but the bored dog can still do some heavy-duty damage. Windowsills are typical targets for bored dogs, as are other types of wall molding, shoes left about, or other household items that have fallen to the floor. Toys become old, known things, whereas a dish towel, pillow, or sneaker is like a brand-new toy.

Solving the problem

You can either prevent chewing from becoming a problem or deal with curing a bad habit. Even if your mixed breed arrived with a chewing problem, you can do things to prevent her from continuing her destructive path.

You'll need to be watchful, patient, and consistent. Guide your mixed breed in the right direction much as you would guide a young child — after all, your dog really doesn't know that your couch pillows are off limits, or that the table legs aren't just big chew bones.

Prevention is worth a pound of pillows

The best thing to do when you aren't able to watch your dog is to contain her in an area where she can't get into trouble. Containing your dog when you can't watch her will prevent her from chewing the wrong things — she can't have access to them without your being present. (For more on containment options, see Chapter 10.)

When you *are* able to watch your dog, redirect her from the things she can't chew to the things she can play with. Playing with her will make the items more attractive — dogs prefer interactive games to playing alone.

Because boredom is a main ingredient in developing problem chewing, you can do several things to prevent this from occurring:

- ✔ **Train, train, train.** A trained dog knows the rules and will be less likely to chew the wrong items.

- ✔ **Rotate the toys.** Dogs get bored with the same old toys. Had 'em, mouthed 'em, tired of 'em. If you offer your dog a different variety of toys each day, your dog will think, "Wow! Brand-new toys! This is neat!" It will occupy her time, reducing the chance of boredom.

✔ **Get another dog.** The presence of another dog alleviates boredom.

✔ **Make sure she's getting enough exercise.** A tired dog won't do anything destructive. Take your dog for a run, or long walk each morning before going to work and again when you get home from work. You may want to vary the routine — for example, go for a walk in the morning and play ball in the afternoon. Add some training time to this routine. Teach your dog some new tricks.

✔ **Stimulate your dog's mind.** There are many ways to stimulate your dog's mind:

- **Interactive toys:** You can find all kinds of interactive toys in your local pet store — toys that can be pulled apart and put back together, toys that can be filled with food, toys that involve pet and human or several dogs at the same time. You can never give your pet too many toys. In fact, if you're not tripping over toys, you probably don't have enough. And don't forget to rotate them!

- **Social time:** Doggie daycare is a great alternative for dogs who spend a lot of time home alone. Instead of being left home day after day, bored, you take your dog to a place where she'll have fun socializing with other dogs and people. You come home from work tired, and she will, too. You can both relax.

  If you have a dog park in the area, take your mixed-breed dog there, daily. Make it part of the routine, regardless of the weather. Few dogs care more about a rainy day than playing with other dogs.

Offering your mixed breed these bits of stimulation will prevent her from doing the bad chewing and create a far more positive relationship with you.

Knowing what to do when your dog is in mid-chew

What do you do when your dog has something in her mouth that she shouldn't have? Let's say she just grabbed one of your Italian leather loafers and ran off, initiating a game of chase. The last thing you want is to lose a $200 pair of shoes, so you run after her. Well, she thinks, this is great fun. Now she knows how to get a game started. And guess what? This won't be the last time she does this — unless you offer her a positive alternative.

The Chase Me game is not a new invention created by your dog just because she enjoys the taste of your shoes, laundry, or pillows. It's a common game that dogs play with each other. One dog grabs a toy, tantalizes the other dog with it by pacing in front and dangling it under the other dog's nose, and then when she sees the other dog make a grab for it, she runs, with the other dog racing after her.

You have to offer something better without also rewarding her for the behavior. Dogs often pick up objects they're not supposed to have, such as shoes or other household items as well as trash that may be littering the paths you walk with your dog, you need a way of teaching your mixed breed to drop the item on command, without having to run her down and pry the object from her mouth.

This is called the exchange-and-reward system. You offer your dog a better alternative to the yucky piece of trash or dirty laundry. Here's how it goes:

1. **Put a long leash on your dog and let her drag it around.**

2. **When you see her chewing something she shouldn't be chewing, call your dog to come to you, showing her a food-filled toy or treat.**

3. **When she arrives, and if she's still holding on to her prize, tell her to drop it, using a stern tone of voice to prove you mean it and you're not playing her game.**

4. **Show her the alternative, dangling it in front of her face just as she tantalized you with the shoe.**

   She'll smell the delectable toy. Because dogs tend to have a high food drive, they usually choose the food over a yucky tasting shoe any day.

5. **When the shoe falls from her mouth she'll try to grab the toy.**

   Don't let her grab the treat. Your mixed breed must earn this toy, not be rewarded for initiating a game of tag with your shoe.

6. **Have her perform something such as a Sit.**

7. **When she does so, praise her and give her the food-filled toy.**

What happens if you can't find something that your dog would rather have than that cigarette butt she picked up from the street, or the steak she filched from the counter? You have to teach her the meaning of Drop It. This command will be important when your dog steals your dinner, and it will protect your mixed breed from poisoning herself. You can also use it to teach your dog to retrieve a toy and return it to your hand instead of chasing her down to do another throw.

Here's how you teach Drop It:

1. **Put a leash on your dog so you can back up your commands without having to chase her around.**

   Allow the leash to drag on the ground until needed.

2. **Create the situation by either throwing a favorite toy a short distance or merely dropping it.**

3. **When your mixed breed picks up the toy, bring her to you via the leash.**

   Praise her as she comes closer so that she always believes coming to you is a great idea.

4. **Tell her to sit.**

   If she doesn't do so on her own, place her into position. Again praise, even if you had to place her.

5. **Now, tell her "Drop it," as you hold your hand just beneath her jaw.**

   You can be sure she won't, because she already has a prized possession that is more rewarding than whatever you can offer.

6. **Place your other hand over the top of her muzzle, with fingers on either side of her lips and squeeze her lips into her mouth.**

   Few dogs like to bite their own lips so you will feel her jaw releasing.

7. **As your dog's jaw slackens, praise her.**

8. **When she drops the toy, praise and offer her tasty treats such as freeze-dried liver or cheese.**

   When first starting this, always offer a high-value replacement.

If you're having your dog drop one of her toys, you can offer it to her again so that she learns she isn't prohibited from playing with the toy — she just has to give it to you upon your request.

From Beggar to Chooser: Getting Your Dog to Stop Begging at the Table

How many times have you sat down to eat dinner only to have your dog, or someone else's dog climb onto you or grab something from your plate? Annoying, right?

You can be sure most dogs also prefer to eat in peace, but the mere act of eating overcomes their desire to be peaceful. Many mixed-breed dogs who've experienced starvation or neglect will strive to get food in any way they can. Without learning boundaries, they'll grab at anything that has a tempting odor.

Spoiled dogs have learned that sitting at your chair, salivating, staring, whining, putting a paw on your leg, or outright demanding the food with loud barking will always earn them a reward from your plate. You may have given the dog something to keep her quiet, or you thought she'd like that little piece of leftover steak. Instead of placating your dog, you're creating a begging monster.

Some dogs are very sneaky about getting their stolen goods. They're the counter surfers. Beware of leaving dinner on the counter to cool — it'll be gone before you return. You'll know the counter surfer — she keeps her nose in the air as she walks along the counters in the kitchen. Nothing is safe!

You can prevent your dog from begging for food (or stealing it!) in several ways:

✔ **Never feed from the table or counter.**

✔ **Always make your dog earn her food.** She must at the very least sit before receiving anything, including her dinner.

✔ **Teach your dog how to go to a specific place while you and others eat at the table.** If you place a food-filled toy on a pad or bed nearby, your dog will be lured to the spot and rewarded for remaining there.

✔ **Have a specific area where your mixed breed is fed her meals so that she learns that the only place she eats meals is at her special place.**

Nipping and Mouthing

Mouthing is a lighter form of nipping, common with dogs who are playing with each other. However, as a dog mouthing can become more serious — a means of dominating and controlling. Nipping is started through play. If allowed to continue, however, it can turn into aggressive domination.

Both of these infractions with the mouth must be stopped. At no time should a dog be allowed to put its mouth on you except to lick, which is a submissive sort of *group hug* gesture. Allowing even a light mouthing is setting yourself up for some serious issues down the road.

Understanding why dogs nip and mouth

Dogs use their mouths as you use your hands. They grab, hold, pull, and carry.

Mixed-breed dogs who have spent any time fending for themselves in the wild, or who have learned to fight for food, shelter, or territory, tend to use their mouths to get what they want.

Mouthing and nipping is also a very common puppy game. Dogs use their mouths to explore and to test a playmate for pack position. If they're still with their mom and littermates, they quickly learn that mom won't put up with it. She'll grab their little faces and growl. Littermates will either respond by yipping, or run away from that awful hurtful sibling. Either way, there's a response. How you respond will have a lot to do with whether Princess will continue the behavior.

Preventing the problem

Prevention is the most important means of teaching your mixed breed to not put her mouth on you. Here are a few ways to keep your dog's mouth occupied:

- ✔ Have lots of toys around for her to put her mouth on.
- ✔ Never play with her mouth.
- ✔ If you're playing with her with a toy, the moment she touches you with her mouth the game is over for a little while.
- ✔ Never allow anyone to dangle their hands near her face.
- ✔ Make sure your dog gets plenty of exercise so that she's not nipping at you trying to instigate play.

Curing the problem

Your best bet is to be like mom. I'm not saying to grab your dog's head in your mouth as you growl — you'll be spitting out dog hair for a month. Instead, use your hands, your eyes, and your body.

Never, ever hit your dog!. Mother dog never hits her pups. Even fighting dogs don't hit each other. There are several ways to use your hands to make your point.

Begin by trying to earn your pup's sympathy when you she mouths or nips you. Squeal, "Yipe! Ouch!" Then, whatever you were doing with your dog — a game of fetch, tug, or leg pulling — stop the game.

If your mixed breed has no sympathy for your pain, you'll need to take the mom approach. Put a hand on either side of her head, taking firm hold of her neck scruff. Hold her in place and stare her in the eyes as you growl at her. The moment she blinks or otherwise looks away, let go. Make her do something for you such as a sit. Praise and reward her good behavior.

If the grabbing hold of her neck scruff doesn't work, follow these steps:

1. **Put a hand on each side of your dog's neck and hold firmly.**

2. **Stare into her eyes, growl at her, and roll her over onto her back.**

3. **Continue the stare and growl.**

4. **When your dog shows submission by turning her eyes away from you, blinking, and going limp, slowly release her neck and allow her to get up.**

5. **If she goes back to nipping at you, pin her down again.**

   Repeat this as often and as long as necessary to make your point. It may be a long hold the first couple times, but the length will decrease as your dog realizes that you have no breaking point and she must be the first to give up.

 As with all severe behavior problems, talk to a professional trainer or behaviorist. Nipping and mouthing are not easy to contend with, and implementing the wrong correction can have severe consequences.

Digging to the Center of the Earth

Dogs love digging, but people hate stepping in holes — and having to fill them. Even worse, people hate what a digging dog does to their yard.

Why in the world would your mixed breed choose to dig against the house foundation? Why would she make trenches throughout the yard? Why is she totally thrilled to show up at the door covered in dirt, grass stains, and twigs while wearing a huge smile? In this section, I uncover the mystery of why your dog digs, and tell you what you can do about it.

Knowing why dogs dig

Dogs dig for many reasons, the most common is that it's fun and might yield a snack or two. Who says dead worms and bugs aren't delicacies? Look at it from your dog's point of view:

✔ **Digging is less boring than lying in the shade.** Plus, digging is great exercise.

✔ **There might be something edible to go along with a scent.** Who knows what lies beneath the surface? Gotta dig to find out.

✔ **Dogs feel earth vibrations.** Moles and other underground critters make lots of vibrations. Trenching is a great means of following their paths.

✔ **Holes are often cooler to lie in than surface dirt — never mind that the current hole used to contain an azalea.** The azalea had a prime resting spot.

Digging is a very natural canine behavior — one that cannot and should not be prohibited. Without the chance to dig, you're setting up your dog for failure in other areas of her life, such as proper house manners.

Giving your dog a place to dig

Instead of just screaming at your dog to stop turning your yard into a lunar landscape, give her an alternative. Give her a place where digging is appropriate. If your dog is primarily an indoor dog, a pile of blankets will work fine. A box filled with sand, wood chips, or mulch works well, too. Isn't this better than holes in your carpet?

If your mixed breed is allowed to exercise outdoors in a safely fenced area, think on a broader scale. Here are a couple suggestions:

✔ **Separate your dog's yard from your garden.**

✔ **Give your dog a place to dig such as a sand box or pile of mulch.**

✔ **Fence off your plants so that your dog can't get near enough to dig them up.**

✔ **Fill existing holes and pour vinegar around them so they become less attractive for future digging.** Put your dog's feces in the hole prior to filling.

Redirection of the digging habit will help teach your dog that she has her own place to play. Without this, your dog will continue to dig by your house foundation or under the bushes because it offered some type of reward — a cool place to lie or great exercise.

You can't expect your mixed breed to change her digging location without your help. You'll have to prove to her that the sand pile will offer greater rewards than beneath the English Boxwood. Here's a great means of redirection:

1. **Half-bury a favorite toy or biscuit in the place where you want her to dig.**

2. **Guide your dog to the buried toy and point it out.**

3. **Praise her if she goes for the toy or eats the treat.**

4. **Repeat this many times until your mixed breed runs straight for her digging area each time she goes outside.**

Spend time with your dog in her digging area. Praise your dog when she puts her nose to the sand and even more when she begins pushing her feet into it.

You can try several materials — including sand, mulch, wood chips or topsoil — for your dog's digging area. You want to entice your dog to dig in a special location so use whatever your dog prefers; otherwise, she'll return her attentions to under the hedges.

If your dog is digging holes to escape the heat, provide other outlets for cooling down:

✔ A small child's pool filled with cool water

✔ A dog door so that your mixed breed can come inside and lie on a cool basement or kitchen floor

✔ A doghouse with a fan to cool the interior

✔ A dog bed that can be soaked in water to maintain a lower body temperature

Part IV
Keeping Your Dog Healthy

The 5th Wave   By Rich Tennant

"He's part herder, part worker. So, he'll herd sheep okay, but then he'll go and try and unionize 'em."

In this part . . .

After you have your dog at home, you need to find a veterinarian. In this part, I give you some tips on choosing a vet. I also fill you in on the vaccinations your dog should have, how to control parasites, and how to develop a regular healthcare regimen.

Some dogs are prone to special health problems such as allergies, physical disabilities, or ailments. In this part, I help you recognize and address these issues.

Accidents happen — but I help you prepare for them. I walk you through assembling a first-aid kit and compiling emergency contact information.

Dogs are living longer than ever before. They have better nutrition, healthcare, and home environments. They're members of the family. Senior dogs need special considerations as they age — special diets, exercise, and healthcare. In this part, you discover how to recognize signs of age-related behavioral and health issues, and how to know when the time is right to say goodbye to your old friend and hello to a new canine companion.

Chapter 13

Finding and Working with a Vet

In This Chapter

▶ Finding the right veterinarian for your dog

▶ Spaying or neutering your mixed breed

▶ Making sure your dog can be identified if he's ever lost

▶ Giving your dog regular healthcare

▶ Dealing with chronic health issues

*O*ne of the most important things you can do as the owner of a mixed-breed dog is to obtain the services of a reputable and dog-friendly veterinarian. Just as not every doctor is right for you, not every vet is right for your dog. In this chapter, I walk you through finding a good vet and fill you in on some key issues surrounding your dog's health, including spaying/neutering, getting regular checkups, and alternative treatments that may help your dog.

Choosing a Veterinarian

Your local Yellow Pages lists the names and numbers of numerous veterinarians. The tough part is deciding which one to take your dog to. Convenience may play a big part in your ultimate decision (you'd probably rather go to a vet who's closer to your house than all the way across town), but the most important factors when choosing a vet should be the vet's reputation, the clinic's facilities, and the vet's specialties.

You don't have to get all your veterinary services from one location. For example, I use the services of a local vet for my animals' regular checkups, vaccinations, and stomach upsets. But when it was time for my male dog to be neutered, I took him to another vet because he was the only one within an hour radius who performed laser surgery, and that's what I wanted for my dog. Not every veterinarian can specialize in everything — just as not every doctor can specialize in everything.

The best way to choose a vet is to talk to other pet owners in your area. Check with your family members, neighbors, and friends who have pets — they may be able to give you a referral to one they trust, or let you know of those with whom they had negative experiences.

Here's what to look for in a veterinary clinic:

✔ **A friendly staff:** The receptionist who answers the phone the very first time you call should be friendly, as should every person you come into contact with at the clinic, from the vet tech on up to the veterinarian.

✔ **A clean waiting room and exam room:** If the clinic can't be bothered to keep the areas of the office that you *see* clean, imagine what it's like in the back, where they take your dog for shots or medical treatment.

✔ **Efficient recordkeeping:** You want to be sure that your vet has a complete record of your dog's health and can access it at a moment's notice.

✔ **Knowledgeable and helpful assistants and veterinarians:** You want to be sure that your questions are treated with respect and that you get the answers you need. You don't want to feel rushed through your appointment or as though the vet doesn't have enough time for you.

When you're looking for a vet, you'll need to decide whether to take your dog to a doctor who works alone, or to a larger clinic where multiple vets are on staff. Table 13-1 lists the pros and cons of each.

Table 13-1   Single Vets versus Veterinary Clinics

Clinic Type	Pros	Cons
Single-vet clinic	Your vet will be more familiar with you and your dog and better able to identify problems when they occur. Your vet will be able to spend more time with your dog.	Your vet will likely not be available in an emergency. Your vet won't have other opinions readily available. Your vet likely won't have any specific veterinary specialties to handle difficult cases.

Clinic Type	Pros	Cons
Multiple-vet clinic	One of the vets will likely be available in an emergency. The vets can consult one another on difficult cases and get better insight into medical conditions. Different vets in the clinic may specialize in different areas, such as nutrition or holistic treatments, and you can see whichever vet's knowledge you need at the time, with your records all in one place.	You may see a different vet each time you visit, which means you won't develop as close a relationship to your vet as you would otherwise. Each vet will be very busy and may not spend much time with you.

Here's a list of questions you can ask a vet to help you determine whether that vet is right for you:

✔ **What vaccinations do you recommend and how often should they be given?** Many veterinarians prefer to practice only traditional methods — and traditionally, dogs have been vaccinated once a year, whether they need the vaccine or not. Newer approaches involve blood tests to determine whether the vaccine is needed.

✔ **Where do you send clients who require specialists for their dogs?** You want to make sure that your vet can answer this question and refers her patients to specialists she trusts. You also want to pay attention to how far away that specialist is and, if it seems farther than you'd normally want to have to travel, ask if there's a reason for referring patients so far away. Maybe that vet is the best one in the state, and she only trusts her patients with the best. Or maybe she just doesn't know anyone else. Obviously, the former would be a better answer than the latter.

✔ **Do you offer alternative or homeopathic approaches?** If you don't care about alternative therapies and you're a straight-by-the-book kind of a person, this won't matter to you. But if you'd like to consider alternative approaches, the vet's answer will make a huge difference. Whether your vet offers these alternatives or not, you want a vet who doesn't dismiss them as whacko.

Homeopathy operates on the assumption that like heals like. Similar to traditional vaccines that utilize killed or low doses of live germs to create antibodies, homeopathic remedies take the same path of administering diluted substances to help the dog heal. The dilution is done in several stages to prevent side effects. These remedies come in tablets, powders, liquids, and ointments. Though they're readily available at health-food stores and online, it's best to consult with a veterinarian who is familiar with alternative medicine in order to know the correct substances, dilutions, and doses to give your dog.

✔ **What are your hours?** Make sure that the vet is open hours that are convenient for your life and schedule.

✔ **Are you available in emergencies? If not, what arrangements have you made for your patients?** You probably can't expect your vet to be available at all hours of the day or night, but you can and should expect your vet to have a number you can call in case of after-hours emergencies. It may be a 24-hour veterinary hospital in your area or the number of another vet who's covering her emergencies while she's out of town.

✔ **If my dog is sick, will you tell me all my treatment options and their costs, and let me make the decision that's right for me financially and emotionally?** One of the worst parts about owning a dog is having to make decisions about how far you'll go, and how much you'll spend, to save his life. Some vets believe that anything and everything should be done, and they may make you feel guilty if you question whether a particular treatment is necessary. You want a vet who will respect your decisions and not make you feel like a horrible person for not spending thousands and thousands of dollars to save your dog's life — unless you have the means to. It's bad enough to have to lose your dog without having to deal with a vet's guilt trip in the process.

✔ **When you visit the vet, does she answer all your questions in an easy-to-understand manner and make the effort to fully explain your dogs' health issues?**

Spaying or Neutering Your Pet

Spaying or neutering your dog should be number one on your list of priorities if it hasn't yet been done. Part of being a responsible guardian of a mixed-breed dog is controlling the pet population by spaying or neutering. If you're not convinced of the need to spay or neuter your dog, see Chapter 18.

The procedure really doesn't take much time, but it *is* surgery, so your vet will recommend not feeding or giving your mixed breed any water within 12 hours of the surgery. (If your vet's guidelines differ from these, do what your vet says.)

After surgery, you'll need to keep your dog quiet for a couple days, to give him some time to heal (whether the procedure was done traditionally or via laser surgery). Don't let your dog jump or race around within a week after surgery.

Some dogs will lick or bite at the incision area as it heals, because it can be very itchy. You can prevent this biting and itching in a few ways:

- ✔ **Put a soft Elizabethan or hard plastic Elizabethan (cone-shaped) collar on your dog.** With one of these contraptions on, your dog won't be able to reach beneath him to bite at the incision area. He'll try, of course — and he'll bump that collar on everything he passes. He walks by the end table — bump. He walks by the coffee table — swish go the magazines to the floor. No dog likes wearing one of these collars, but keeping him from biting or licking his incision is critical, so just remember that it's only for a week or so.

- ✔ **Rub a product called Bitter Apple around the area.** I usually apply antibacterial cream directly on the wound and around it, and then I apply the Bitter Apple on top of that. With such a horrible flavor, your dog is sure to not mess with his incision area. You will need to reapply the Bitter Apple several times each day.

No matter what, keep that incision area clean. After your dog goes outside (and remember to keep the play to a minimum), clean the area with a disinfectant solution such as Nolvasan and then reapply the antibacterial cream and Bitter Apple over that.

Microchipping or Tattooing: Keeping Your Dog Safe

I think having some form of identification on your dog is mandatory — I don't care if he spends every minute of every day at your side. In many areas, the law requires every dog to have a rabies tag, license tag, and some form of ID tag that bears the owner's name and phone number. Whether the law in your area requires it or not, it's the only thing to do. If your dog runs away and is taken to a local animal shelter, he could be euthanized if you don't claim him within a few days. Identification helps the authorities find you in case you can't find your dog.

Unfortunately, all this bling can fall off and get lost. I can't count the number of ID tags I've had to replace throughout each of my dogs' lives. That's why every one of my dogs either has a tattoo or has been implanted with a microchip. Here's more on each of these methods:

- ✔ **Tattooing:** A tattoo is usually done on the inside of your dog's hind leg. It takes about five to ten minutes when done by a professional canine tattoo artist or a vet familiar with the techniques. You can choose what to have imprinted on your dog's skin — it can be your driver's license number, your Social Security number, or a number that you register with a national organization such as the National Dog Registry (www. nationaldogregistry.com). Tattoos are easily seen, and if your dog is every lost, you'll be notified. Plus, a tattoo is an outward sign to the people who find your dog that you're serious about holding on to him for life.

- ✔ **Microchipping:** Microchipping is the latest technology for identifying not only pets but also farm animals and people. A microchip is embedded beneath the dog's skin in the shoulder region. It's as easy as an injection, though the needle is a little larger than the kind they use for a vaccination. The microchip contains encoded information, usually a registration number that coincides with your contact information. Most animal shelters, humane societies, and vet clinics own microchip scanners, which can detect the microchip and read the information on it. If your dog decides to take a walk and ends up at one of these places, you'll be contacted.

Keeping Up with Regular Healthcare

Yearly checkups and vaccinations are important for your dog, especially when he's less than a year of age or older than 6 or 7 years of age. You never know what a young pup can get into, and aging dogs tend to develop problems that may not be immediately recognizable.

Not all dogs require yearly vaccinations. After your dog is about 3 years old, your vet can do yearly blood tests to check whether his previous vaccinations are still protecting him. This is called a *titer test.*

Regular checkups and yearly vaccinations

When you bring your mixed breed to your vet for his yearly exam, he'll not only be vaccinated (if necessary), but he'll get a thorough checkup. Your vet will examine his abdomen for lumps and sensitivity, take his temperature, and check his eyes, ears, teeth, and throat. Some vets like to watch the dog in motion; others manipulate their legs and neck, checking for signs of injury or sensitivity.

Only one vaccination is mandatory on a yearly schedule. The rabies vaccine is required by law in every state. The first year it's given it is only considered viable for one year. Every vaccination after the first one is usually viable for three years. Your vet will know the laws in your area.

For your mixed breed's first three years, he should also get the following vaccinations annually:

- ✔ **Coronavirus:** This illness causes diarrhea and dehydration. It's highly contagious, especially among young and very old dogs. It's not often fatal, though it can be debilitating.

- ✔ **Distemper:** This illness is a very common one among *feral* (wild) animals. Symptoms include ocular and nasal discharge. In more severe cases, coughing, vomiting, and fever. Untreated, it's often fatal.

- ✔ **Hepatitis:** Recognizing this illness is difficult — the signs are fever and lethargy, though sometimes there's vomiting and diarrhea, too. It is easily spread through the feces and urine of an infected dog. If it's not caught in time, it's fatal, so vaccinating makes sense.

- ✔ **Leptospirosis:** A dog with this illness will have a fever, will vomit, and won't want to move around much. Leptospirosis is often contracted through the urine of rodents, so if your mixed breed has some varmint-chasing instincts, beware if he displays these symptoms. Renal failure often results from this illness, as does sudden death. If you live in an area where your dog may be exposed to rodents, make sure he's vaccinated.

- ✔ **Parvovirus:** This disease is highly contagious and potentially fatal. It's common in feral animals and easily transmitted from dog to dog. Symptoms include bloody diarrhea, vomiting, fever, and lethargy. Caught in time, dogs often recover with treatment. In young puppies, however, the disease can be fatal. This vaccination is one of the first that puppies must have; they should also should get three sets of booster shots spaced two to four weeks apart to protect them.

There are other vaccinations that aren't as vital, but that are still important for your dog's protection. These include

- ✔ **Bordetella (for kennel cough):** You'll only really need the bordetella vaccine if you're planning on exposing your mixed breed to other dogs (for example, in a boarding kennel or in a dog park — and most kennels require proof of vaccination), but if you're of the better-safe-than-sorry mindset, you might vaccinate him no matter what.

✔ **Lyme disease (to prevent infection of the tick-borne disease):** Within ticks' saliva are several fatal diseases, and Lyme disease is one of them. The symptoms for Lyme disease include lethargy, loss of appetite, and lameness. It's easily treated with antibiotics, if caught in time. If not, the result can be permanent lameness or death. Why chance it?

Baseline tests

A baseline test is just a simple blood test that gives your vet an idea of what constitutes normal function for your dog. If you have one done while your dog is healthy, it'll be a great way of informing your vet of age-related or illness-related changes in your dog down the road.

I always have baseline tests done on my dogs prior to sterilization surgery, to make sure my dogs didn't have any heart or blood problems that might risk their lives while on the operating table.

As a dog ages, baseline testing should be done yearly to diagnose any life-threatening or debilitating diseases at an early stage.

Controlling parasites

Modern veterinary medicine now offers many ways to prevent parasite infestation. On your first visit to your vet, be sure to discuss this. Your vet will prescribe the appropriate preventative for his size and age. If your dog has parasites, he'll be treated for them.

If you got your dog from a shelter, chances are, he's infested with parasites inside and out. If your mixed breed has internal parasites, your vet can treat them through an injection or oral medication. If your dog has external parasites (such as fleas or ticks), he can be given Capstar an oral medication that quickly and safely kills all live adult fleas within 2 hours. After four hours a regular bath will wash out the dead the bugs and clear his skin of the parasites entirely. At that point you can apply a topical flea preventative.

Preventing parasite infestation is your job — believe me, your dog will thank you for it. For heartworm prevention, give your mixed breed the monthly tablet prescribed by his vet. For flea and tick prevention, any number of great topical preventives are available. Talk with your vet to find out exactly which parasites they repel or kill and see which one your vet recommends.

If your dog gets bathed a lot, you'll want to reapply the topical preventative more often than the package suggests.

Addressing Special Health Problems

Not every dog is in perfect health all the time — just as not every human being is in perfect health all the time. Though some dogs display health sensitivities as pups, others may not develop them until they get older. In the following sections, I walk you through some of the most common problems dogs develop and tell you what to expect in terms of treatment and prevention.

Skin allergies

Dogs are commonly allergic to flea and tick bites. One bite is all it takes to drive your mixed breed crazy. Multiple bites will cause his fur to fall out, his skin to thicken and redden, and constant scratching, biting, and discomfort.

Skin allergies also occur when dogs eat something that doesn't agree with them. Some have allergies to lawn treatments or specific types of grasses or plants.

The only way to determine the exact cause of the problem is to take your mixed breed to a veterinary specialist for testing. Knowing what is causing the problem will help you remove it from your dog's environment and speed his healing process. Plus, it'll help you prevent your dog from having the same reaction again.

Food allergies

With all the ingredients that go into commercial dog foods, it's no wonder that some dogs have allergies — with every additional ingredient, there's an additional item that the dog may be allergic to. From dyes and preservatives, to using multiple grains as fillers, any number of these can cause dry skin, itching, runny eyes, and behavioral anomalies.

Your vet will have some suggestions of food brands or homemade meals that will help pinpoint the sources of your dog's allergies and offer your dog a wholesome diet. Consult with a holistic veterinarian or veterinary dermatologist about food allergies, too — she'll have some good insight into the most common foods that cause allergic reactions in dogs, such as wheat, corn, beef, chicken, and rice, among others.

Appetite issues

More dogs have obesity issues than poor-skinny-waif problems. Just as our human society overeats and goes for the extra-large portions of fast food, many dog owners are taking the same approach with their dogs. Overeating is just as dangerous for canines as it is for humans.

Your vet will know whether your dog is a correct weight. Although your vet can let you know your dog is overweight, it's up to you to do something about it. You can

- ✔ **Change his diet to a lower-calorie one.**
- ✔ **Reduce the amount you feed him by half and substitute with raw vegetables.** This will give him the fiber he needs without the calories he doesn't need.
- ✔ **Make sure he's getting enough exercise.**

If your dog is underweight or stops eating, take him to the vet right away. Dogs only refuse to eat when they're very sick. There's a reason for his skipping meals, and it could be very serious. Let your vet examine your dog to discover what's going on.

If there's absolutely nothing wrong with your mixed breed and he still doesn't want to eat, try adding some flavorful gravy to his meals. Adding canned food and mixing it into the kibble can also be helpful in generating interest. Maybe just changing his food altogether to something that's richer, more aromatic, and more flavorful will do the trick.

Skeletal disorders

Skeletal disorders can be caused by accidental injury or genetic inheritance. Either way, your vet will need to do a thorough exam and take X-rays to discover the source of discomfort.

If the problem is degenerative (that is, it happens over time, as the dog ages — such as osteoarthritis), the inflammation can be controlled by several different prescription medications. The one chosen will be based on the dog's age, size, and possible breed combination — not all medications work well with all dog breeds.

You can also use supplements such as glucosamine and chondroitin to help control the fluid levels between the joints and reduce inflammation in the tissue surrounding the joints. If your vet isn't familiar with these supplements, talk to a holistic veterinarian or find another vet who is.

Chapter 14

First Aid: Dealing with Emergencies

....

In This Chapter

▶ Being prepared for any emergency

▶ Knowing who to call for help

▶ Getting your lost dog back

....

*Y*ou could have your dog from puppyhood to old age and never encounter an emergency situation — or you could face numerous emergencies throughout your dog's life. You don't know if or when emergency will strike, but being prepared for any disaster puts you ahead of the game. In this chapter, I help you recognize emergency situations, tell you the basics of canine first aid, and help you find your dog if you ever lose her. Read this chapter while your dog is safe and sound, and tuck the information away for when you need it. It could save your dog's life.

Gathering Emergency Contact Information

There are several numbers you should always have handy in case of emergencies. Make several photocopies of this page and fill in Table 14-1 with all the appropriate numbers. Then keep one copy on your refrigerator, another in each of your cars, another in your canine first-aid kit . . . you get the idea. Just make sure the numbers are easily accessible no matter where you are.

I've left several blank rows at the bottom of the table, where you can add the names and numbers of family members or friends who can help you out in case of emergency. (It's amazing how, in an emergency, you can forget phone numbers that you otherwise have memorized.)

Table 14-1	Emergency Contact Information
Who to Call	*Phone Number*
Veterinarian	
Emergency animal hospital	
ASPCA Animal Poison Control Center	888-426-4435 *
Kennel	
Animal control	
Animal shelter	

* A fee of $55 (as of this printing) will be charged to your credit card to cover the cost of a consultation. The center is available 24 hours a day, 365 days a year.

Preparing for natural disasters

No matter where you live, natural disasters can strike. Being prepared is essential. Here are some tips to keep in mind:

✔ Don't rely on anyone other than yourself to evacuate your pet. City officials and workers will not take on this responsibility.

✔ Don't leave your dog tied up outside. If your dog is tied, she can't escape water, flying debris, wind, and other things that threaten her life.

✔ Don't leave your dog indoors. If there's a tidal surge and your house is under water, your dog can drown.

✔ If you're evacuating in advance of a hurricane and you plan on leaving your dog at a kennel, don't do so anywhere within the hurricane strike zone. As part of your preparation, get contact information for kennels in other states.

✔ Prepare a secure, unbreakable covered pet carrier, marked with your name, address, and phone number. Include two leashes and a harness/collar with your name, address, and phone number on a tag. Bring plastic bowls for food and water; in waterproof plastic containers, put enough food for two weeks. Bring a copy of your pet's health records, her medication, a current photo, plastic bags for waste, and a couple toys to keep her occupied.

Assembling Your Canine First-Aid Kit

Following are all the items you need in a basic, in-home first-aid kit. Though you may not need all the items listed here at any one time in your mixed breed's life, it's a good idea to at least own them and know where you keep them.

- First-aid book
- Adhesive tape or self-sticking Vet Wrap (as of this printing, you can actually buy Vet Wrap online at Amazon.com)
- Cotton balls
- Square gauze pads, 3 x 3 inches
- Instant hot/cold packs
- Cotton-tipped applicators (like Q-tips)
- Antibacterial ointment (like Neosporin or Bacitracin)
- Bitter Apple cream and/or spray
- Hydrogen peroxide
- Clotisol (clotting cream)
- Hydrogen peroxide
- Activated charcoal (in case of poisoning)
- Tweezers and small, sharp scissors
- Thermometer (***Note:*** A dog's normal temperature is 101°F. You can buy ear thermometers for pets at most major pet-supply stores.)
- Aloe-vera gel (to sooth scrapes and cuts)
- Canine antidiarrhea medication (such as Metronidazole, an antibiotic available from your veterinarian) (***Note:*** Human over-the-counter antidiarrhea medications often don't work at all with dogs.)
- Rubber gloves
- Muzzle (***Note:*** Many injured dogs bite first and ask questions later.)
- Something you can use for a stretcher, such as a board, blanket, or floor mat

If you're hiking, camping, boating, or engaging in some other outdoor activities with your dog, place the following items in a zip-top plastic bag and toss it in your backpack:

- ✔ Fresh water, at least 1 pint
- ✔ Antiseptic wipes
- ✔ Sterile gauze pads
- ✔ Antibacterial ointment
- ✔ Vet Wrap
- ✔ Bite/sting stop
- ✔ Tweezers

If you're interested, you can take courses in first aid and canine CPR. One exceptional source for these is Pet Tech (www.pettech.net), which offers information, pet-saver training, DVDs, and pet first aid instructors' courses. Books such as *First Aid for Dogs: What to Do When Emergencies Happen,* by Bruce Fogle, and *The First Aid Companion for Dogs & Cats,* by Amy D. Shojai, are also good sources.

First-Aid Basics

Dogs tend to be inquisitive, which can often get them into trouble. No matter where you live, your dog could have an accident, get sick, or get hurt. Few dogs go through life without *some* physical trauma. In the following sections, I cover the majority of situations, how to recognize them, and what to do if they happen to your dog.

Allergies

Allergies manifest themselves in many ways. The most likely allergic reactions are those to food ingredients, though I've known some dogs who are also allergic to specific types of grass, plants, or indoor fabrics, such as carpeting, upholstery, or window treatments.

When your mixed breed is experiencing an allergic reaction, she may begin sneezing, wheezing, choking, or gagging. She may also develop an itchy rash on her skin. Some dogs will lick and chew themselves. Ear infections can be common symptoms of allergies as well.

If you suspect that your dog has an allergy, you can either take her to a specialist and find out exactly the cause of the allergic reaction, or you can change her diet and see if you notice an improvement before consulting with a vet. If the allergies are due to your mixed breed's environment, you may have to remove some items from her living space.

The only way of knowing for sure what your dog is allergic to is by taking her to an allergy specialist and having her tested.

Bloat

Bloat is a swelling of the stomach from gas, fluid, or both. It tends to occur in dogs with large chest cavities, like Great Danes or Weimaraners, who also like to inhale their food quickly. Dogs prone to this ailment may bloat if they eat immediately after extreme exercise.

The symptoms of bloat include pacing continuously or lying down in odd places, panting, whining, salivating, and agitation. The dog may vomit without anything coming up. She'll drool excessively, make retching noises, and have swelling in the abdominal area.

Bloat is potentially fatal, and there's nothing you can do for your dog to help her other than to recognize the symptoms and get her to the vet *immediately*. Surgery must be performed to save her life. Bloat has a 30-percent fatality rate, mostly due to dog owners who either don't recognize the symptoms or are too slow to react.

Broken bones or dislocations

You can never be sure whether your dog has broken or dislocated a bone without the help of your vet. The only symptoms you'll be able to recognize are your dog being unable to use a limb or the limb appearing to be at an odd angle. If the dog has a rib, shoulder, hip, or back fracture, she may not move at all.

If bleeding is involved, try to control it (see "Puncture wounds," later in this chapter, for tips on controlling bleeding), but *don't try to fix the fracture*. Protect the area with cotton padding. If it's a limb, apply a splint of some sort (two long pieces of wood) and secure them with bandaging such as Vet Wrap. Carefully place your dog on a makeshift stretcher — a rug, blanket, or wide board will work — so that she won't further injure herself by moving. Take her to her vet immediately.

Some injured animals are prone to aggression, due to stress and pain, so I recommend muzzling your dog before applying the splint. Not only will this prevent injury to you but it will prevent further injury to the dog.

Burns

You'll know your dog is burned if you see singed fur, blistering, redness of skin, and/or swelling. Take your dog to the vet immediately. If you have someone who can drive while you flush your dog's injury with cool water that would be ideal. If not, just go to your vet immediately.

Choking

You'll recognize the symptoms of choking by noticing that your dog is having difficulty breathing or swallowing. She might paw at her mouth, and her lips and tongue could turn blue from lack of blood flow.

Look inside your dog's mouth and throat. Clear it by using pliers or tweezers — if you stick your finger down her throat, you can easily lodge the object farther down her throat.

If the object is too deep and you can't get it, perform the Heimlich maneuver by putting your hands on either side of your dog's rib cage and applying firm, quick pressure. Another way you can perform this is to place your dog on her side and press against her rib cage with the palm of your hand. Repeat until the object is dislodged.

 Get someone to take you and your dog to a vet as you are doing the Heimlich. You may not be able to totally dislodge the entire object, and the sooner you can get veterinary attention, the better chance your dog has of surviving.

Cuts

Wash the area with cool water and pat dry. Apply hydrogen peroxide to the area. If it has stopped bleeding (and after the area is dry), apply an antibacterial ointment and then spread a little Bitter Apple ointment around the *edges* (*not* in the cut) to prevent your dog from licking off the ointment.

If the wound is deep or doesn't stop bleeding, apply a pressure bandage and take your dog to the vet immediately.

Diarrhea

If your dog has diarrhea, the best thing to do is to withhold food from your dog for 12 to 24 hours. Give her plenty of ice cubes and water — she'll need to stay hydrated.

Some dogs get diarrhea after eating something that doesn't agree with them, so after that initial 12 to 24 hours, keep your dog on a bland diet of boiled rice and chicken, or beef (as long as she's not allergic to these ingredients) for a couple days and gradually transfer her back to her normal food.

If the diarrhea doesn't cease within a day, take your dog to the vet and bring a stool sample with you for testing. If the consistency of the diarrhea is mucousy, if it's light in color, tar black or if it contains blood, take your dog to the veterinarian immediately.

Heat stroke

If your dog has a short nose, heavy fur, or large structure, don't exercise her at all in hot weather conditions — her body can't handle it. For other dogs, keep all exercise on hot days to a minimum. Stick to allowing your mixed breed to run in early mornings and late evenings during summer months to prevent any temperature-related illness.

The symptoms of heat stroke include difficulty breathing, vomiting, high temperature, and collapse. If the dog isn't treated immediately, heat stroke can be fatal.

The best treatment is to immerse your dog in a tub of cool water. You can also gently soak her with a garden hose or wrap her in a cool, wet towel. You'll need to lower her temperature gradually, so don't put her in a tub of ice — this could go in the other direction and cause hypothermia or shock. If she'll drink, give her some electrolyte-supplemented water, such as Smart Water.

Take her temperature often and stop the cooling process when her temperature reaches 103°F.

Hypothermia

Hypothermia happens when the dog becomes too cold. It's most common in small dogs or those with a short coat and no body fat. If this describes your mixed breed, be sure to never leave her outdoors for a prolonged period of time during winter weather conditions; especially below 35°F.

The symptoms of hypothermia are similar to heat stroke (see the preceding section), only the dog will be shaking to try to stay warm, and she's not likely to vomit. Her limbs will be stiff with cold.

Wrap her in warm blankets and rub her vigorously to maintain a healthy blood flow to all parts of her body. Place her on a heating pad, but be sure to put a towel or blanket between your dog and the pad to prevent burning.

As with all emergency situations, take your dog to the vet as soon as you can.

Insect bites

If your dog ventures outdoors at all, you can't avoid it — she will be bitten by bugs. Numerous blood-sucking parasites may attack your dog — including fleas, ticks, and mosquitoes. Some bugs may sting her, especially if she's chasing them. Other bugs like to fly into eyes, ears, or noses, irritating your mixed breed.

If you see swelling or redness, or if you notice your dog scratching or appearing to be in pain within an hour of the bite, be sure to investigate it further. If there's a stinger, try to remove it using tweezers. Then apply a cold pack for a while to reduce the inflammation. A topical cortisone or anti-inflammatory ointment can be used on the bite area. Some dogs require oral antihistamines due to allergic reactions.

If symptoms persist, call your vet.

Poisoning

Dogs will eat nearly anything, so poisoning is always a possibility. It may be mild (such as eating fallen nuts) or it can be severe (from eating garden poisons or antifreeze).

The symptoms of poisoning include vomiting, convulsions (in severe cases), diarrhea, salivation, weakness, depression, or collapse. Also in severe cases, if it isn't caught in time, poisoning can be fatal.

Give your dog activated charcoal mixed with a small amount of canned food in the case of poisoning.

If you saw what your dog ate, write it down and try to note the amount she ingested. Call the ASPCA Animal Poison Control Center at 888-426-4435 (a fee of $55 may be charged to your credit card) and give the operator the information. Or, if you prefer, call your vet.

Don't induce vomiting unless your veterinarian directs you to do so. If the poisoning is topical (on her skin or coat) from substances such as oil, paint, or chemicals, wash her with a mild soap and rinse well.

Puncture wounds

Punctures commonly occur when animals fight. They also happen when dogs go after wild creatures with sharp teeth. If your dog has gotten into a fight, you may not be able to see all the puncture wounds unless they're actively bleeding.

Apply firm direct pressure over any bleeding areas until the bleeding stops. Hold that pressure for ten minutes and don't bandage it, because the wound needs air circulation for proper healing. Then take your dog to the vet for a thorough investigation and treatment.

Many vets will put drains in place to ensure the wounds don't become infected and can heal properly from the inside out. The drains normally remain in place for three days, at which point they're removed and the wounds kept clean and dry for another week. Your dog will likely be on antibiotics for a period of time.

Run-ins with wild animals

If your dog has a run-in with a wild animal, clean the wound with large amounts of water and dab it with hydrogen peroxide. Any large, open wound should be wrapped to keep it clean. If it's a puncture or bleeding profusely, apply pressure until the bleeding stops.

Take your dog to the vet. Saliva has a high concentration of bacteria, so your dog will need to be given antibiotics to prevent infection.

If your dog has a run-in with a porcupine or foxtails, take her to the vet to have them removed. Don't try to remove them yourself.

Seizures

Some dogs inherit seizures, others develop seizures due to poisoning or illness. The symptoms include salivation, disorientations, violent muscle twitching, an inability to control their excretions, and, sometimes, loss of consciousness.

The first thing you should do if you see these symptoms is to move your pet away from any objects that may be harmful — furniture, floor fixtures, children's toys, and so on.

Don't put yourself at risk during your dogs' seizure. Dogs are apt to lash out without control while having a seizure, so don't try to restrain her. Time the seizure so that you can tell your veterinarian how long it lasted. Most last approximately two to three minutes.

If your dog experiences multiple or prolonged seizures, take her to the vet immediately; she may have been poisoned and will need immediate treatment. On your trip to the vet, try to keep your dog quiet. Speak in a soothing tone and try to prevent her from seeing anything that might excite her (like another dog).

Shallow wounds

Do you go to see a doctor every time you cut your finger? Probably not. Unless your wound is deep, you probably just apply hydrogen peroxide and antibacterial cream, and slap a bandage on it, and go on with your life. If you've got these items for yourself, you have all you need to treat your dog's minor wounds.

Always clean a cut or abrasion thoroughly to remove any dirt and debris. Allow it to dry, then apply hydrogen peroxide (to further clean the wound). When it's dry, apply the antibacterial ointment. Some dogs will lick off the ointment — to prevent this, either apply a bandage or, if the area can't be bandaged, apply Bitter Apple around the wound. She'll be less likely to lick off the antibacterial cream again.

Shock

Shock can occur after a serious injury, fright, or a reaction to extreme temperatures. Shock is a means of the body protecting itself from trauma, but it can also threaten a dog's life. The symptoms are irregular breathing, white gums, and dilated pupils.

You'll need to keep your dog gently restrained, warm, and quiet. Also elevate her lower body.

Take your dog to the veterinarian immediately. Only your veterinarian is equipped to treat your dog for shock.

Snake bites

Snake bites are rare but extremely dangerous for your mixed-breed dog. There are many venomous species that, with one bite or spit of venom, can damage your dog's nerves or body tissue on contact. Many types of snake bites can be fatal to dogs.

Once bitten, the skin will swell quickly. You'll notice a skin puncture. The dog will display pain in the bitten area. All you can do is to clean the area and rush your dog to the veterinarian to be treated.

Vomiting

Dogs vomit a lot — from mother dogs regurgitating meals for puppies to older dogs who enjoy eating grass, vomiting is part of a dog's life.

You don't need to be concerned about vomiting unless your dog is doing it many times throughout the day, or more often than she normally does. Also be aware of the consistency of the vomit: If it's mucousy, there may be a serious problem. If it's merely a meal that was eaten too quickly, it's probably not anything you need to see a vet for. Sometimes, if the dog is ill, she'll vomit up her meals. If she continues vomiting with nothing coming up, you can be certain there's something to be concerned about — she could be choking.

If your dog is vomiting her meal, isolate her from other pets to prevent possible contagion. Stop feeding her for 12 to 24 hours, but make sure she gets plenty of water and ice cubes.

Take your dog to the vet to have her checked for disease or any other possibilities.

If You Lose Your Dog

Although it's easy to go crazy when you lose your dog, you need to remain level-headed and calm to give your dog the best chance of making it back to you safe and sound.

Before your dog is lost: Getting proper identification

Modern microchipping is the best way of ensuring that, if found, your dog will be returned to you. A microchip is a small transmitter bearing your name, address, and phone number that is easily scanned by a handheld device owned by most veterinarians, humane societies, and animal shelters. The microchip is injected under your dog's skin along her shoulders. There is very little discomfort to the dog during the insertion, and it's a permanent form of identification, giving you peace of mind.

Another great way of permanently IDing your dog is a tattoo. A tattoo does cause some discomfort to your dog during the inking process, but it lets people know how to contact you if the dog is found, and it's highly visible — no scanner is required as with microchips. Tattoos are often placed on an inner thigh of the dog's hind leg. The number inked can be your driver's license number or a specific number registered with a national registry. Either way you will be contacted. As with a microchip, the tattoo cannot be removed or fall off. Whether your dog has her collar on or not, the tattoo is with her.

Even though ID tags can either fall off or be removed, I always make sure my animals have theirs on their collars along with their rabies tags and licenses. An ID tag should list your name, the city where you live, and your phone number. You can also get a dog collar with your information stitched into the material.

What to do when your dog is lost

If your dog is lost, start by contacting your neighbors. Chances are, they've seen your dog and either are holding on to her for you or saw the direction she went.

If nobody near you saw your dog escape, contact your friends and family and ask for help searching for your dog. Fill them in on your dog's canine friends she hangs out with, a pond she enjoys swimming in, a park she where loves to run. Search all these places. Most dogs prefer to remain in familiar territory — they just like to go on social walkabouts from time to time.

If a search of your dog's favorite places turns up nothing, notify the local animal-control office and shelters. Often, when people find a stray dog, that's the first place they call. Even if nobody has called yet, leave your name, phone number, and a description of your dog in case someone calls in the next few days.

If your mixed breed hasn't been found within 24 hours, make signs with a recent photo of your dog. Be sure to list your contact information, written large and clearly. If you can, offer a small reward. Don't specify the amount on the sign — just say, "Reward Offered."

Chapter 15

The Special Needs of Senior Dogs

*G*etting old is never easy, but you can make the transition a smoother one for your mixed-breed dog. In this chapter, I help you identify when your dog is really a senior, fill you in on his special health needs, and give him the kind of care he deserves. I also cover the most difficult decision of all: knowing when to let your best friend go.

 Owning a dog is full of fun and excitement, and though the aging process can be sad, if you approach it with the right attitude, it can be a time for you to connect with your dog on an even deeper level than you already have.

How Old Is Old: Knowing When Your Dog Has Earned Senior Status

How will you know when your dog becomes a senior? He's not going to suddenly need a cane to walk with. And you won't need to puree his food one day when he was chewing on bones the day before. In fact, you may not see any outward signs at all. He may appear the same as he always has, at least for a while.

But over time, you'll see a huge difference in your dog's behavior, movement, physical appearance, and overall health. Age deteriorates the bones and muscle tissue; reduces the efficacy of internal organs; and dulls the senses. If your dog had any serious injuries when he was younger, the scar tissue surrounding those injuries will become inflamed. If he has a degenerative disease, such as hip dysplasia or spondylosis, it will take a firmer hold.

Here are some general guidelines on the aging process in dogs based on their size:

- **Small dogs (up to 20 pounds):** Many small dogs live upwards of 15 years, some as long as 18 to 20 years (though these often have some Poodle heritage — Poodles generally have a long lifespan). Small dogs can be considered seniors by the age of 11. In human years that's about 60 years old; for each year beyond this, they age by 4 human years. So by the age of 12 they're 64, by the age of 13 they're 68, and so on.

  Though your small dog may be a senior by 11 years, he may not really show this until a little later. Small dogs aren't as prone to joint problems as bigger dogs are, but they do experience organ malfunction more prominently than their large cousins. Doing baseline testing (see Chapter 13) will be extremely important to ensure you catch any health problems early.

- **Medium dogs (21 to 50 pounds):** Medium dogs tend to live anywhere from 13 to 15 years. They become seniors by the age of 9. In human years, this is equal to approximately 58 years old. If your medium-sized mixed breed lives to the age of 16, he's equal in human years to an 83-year-old person, so you can be sure he'll have slowed down and gotten cranky about his aches and pains.

- **Large dogs (51 to 90 pounds):** Large dogs tend to live about 10 to 12 years. They reach senior status by 8 years of age. At this time, they're equal to a human who is 61 years old. The arthritis sets in, it's tougher to move around, and the eyes and hearing get weak. Between the pain of achy bones and lack of seeing or hearing, they don't respond as quickly as before. Your dog isn't coming when called because of being stubborn — he didn't hear you. By the time a large dog is 11 years old, if he reaches this age, he's having extreme difficulty moving and responding to you. This old dog prefers to sleep and eat, and that's about it.

- **Extra-large dogs (over 90 pounds):** Extra-large dogs generally live about 9 to 10 years. Extra large dogs are considered seniors by the age of 8. Dogs of this size age 7 to 10 years for each of our human years.

The Early-Bird Special: Feeding Your Senior Dog

As your mixed breed ages, his body changes. You shouldn't feed him the same food in the same manner as when he was a pup. His metabolism has slowed down with his reduced exercise, and he won't need as much food, or the same type of food (with both high calorie and fat content) as he used to.

Most dog-food brands offer a senior formula. When you're deciding which one to buy, look for the following ingredients on the label:

- ✔ **Vitamins C and E:** As your senior dog's immune system becomes less efficient with age, he'll need a diet that contains a large amount of antioxidants such as vitamins C and E. This will help his immune system operate more efficiently, thereby reducing his risk of digestive-system problems and the drying of his skin and coat.

- ✔ **Gamma-linolenic acid (GLA):** Older dogs also need a diet that contains gamma-linolenic acid (GLA), which is an omega-6 fatty acid. This acid is normally produced in your mixed breed's liver by the enzyme action on dietary fat. However, in older dogs, these GLA levels are diminished. If your dog's favorite senior food doesn't have GLA in it, you can add borage oil, a natural source of this acid, to your dog's diet. You can find borage oil at most vitamin outlets. One tablet is usually sufficient.

- ✔ **Fructoligosaccharides (FOS):** Older dogs have more frequent intestinal problems than younger dogs do, so your dog will need to have a diet containing fructoligosaccharides (FOS). This is a unique fiber source that aids in maintaining a healthy bacterial population in his intestines. Beet pulp is a good source of FOS and provides energy for the cells that line his intestine, which helps with proper stool formation. It's often already added to most commercial senior dog diets.

Don't feed your senior dog a food with more than three grains — they're tough to digest (see Chapter 7).

You probably won't need to change your mixed breed's feeding schedule or how he eats, though it's always a good idea to elevate his food bowl at least a little to help the food go down smoother. This is especially helpful for senior dogs who have trachea problems, such as a collapsed trachea, making swallowing difficult. (You can find special elevated feeders at any major pet store or online pet store.)

As your dog becomes older, make sure you feed him in a quiet environment where other family pets won't disturb him. Many older dogs eat slowly and will feel challenged by the other animals.

Your dog will let you know if you're feeding him too often: He simply won't eat the meal. Don't fall into the "always hungry" trap though, or your senior dog will quickly become overweight, which in turn will stress his heart and skeletal system, shortening his life.

Use It or Lose It: Exercising Your Senior Dog

Senior dogs need exercise. Keeping him in shape will help him deal with his physical and emotional changes. Exercise maintains muscle tone, in turn supporting his weakening joints. It also helps his digestive system and circulatory system.

Don't keep your dog locked up just because he's limping from arthritic joints. This will quickly increase the deterioration. Exercise promotes healthy bone growth and keeps your mixed breed happy. A dog who isn't exercised quickly declines.

Social time with other dogs

Your old mixed breed may not be able to keep up with the younger pups, but he'll have fun trying. And it's not just a matter of having fun. It's a type of exercise you can't offer — unless you're willing to lie down on the ground, gnaw on his ear, roll, jump, and chase him. (I didn't think so!) But these are all things dogs do when they play.

If your older dog has health issues, such as arthritis or breathing problems, be cautious with his choice of playmates. Let him play with a dog who isn't super-energetic or dominant.

Not only is playing with other dogs good for your old friend, it's also good for the younger dogs, because your old dog teaches *them* important social skills. Your old dog has been around the block a few more times than they have, and he has all kinds of wisdom to pass on to those youngsters.

Walks with you

Your old dog may have a great time playing with other dogs, but he'd really prefer to spend time with you. Both of you will benefit from walks together. It's a healthy, low-impact means of exercise, and you can hardly have more enjoyable company.

If your older dog can't rough-house and race around with other dogs, walking will be his only way of moving around and keeping his muscles toned. You can regulate his exercise regimen — his speed, distance, and terrain.

If your mixed-breed dog is arthritic or suffering from an old injury, walk him on a soft surface (like dirt), not a hard road or sidewalk. This will cushion each foot fall, making each step less jarring.

Identifying Health Problems Common to Seniors

There's no helping it. All our bodies wear down as we age, and your dog is no different. You can slow down the degeneration with proper diet and exercise, but ultimately it's unavoidable. That said, deterioration is different in each dog. Larger dogs tend to develop arthritic joints before losing their eyesight or hearing, whereas smaller dogs are just the opposite.

In the following sections, I walk you through the most common age-related problems that dogs face.

Hearing loss

It doesn't matter which breed mixture your dog is when it comes to hearing loss — deafness is seen in all breeds.

Hearing loss happens either because of damage to the inner-ear components from an ear infection, from trauma to the head and nerves, or through the use of various drugs such as the antibiotics Gentamicin, Neomycin, and Kanamycin. Over time, the ear components can also degenerate, causing a gradual deafness.

Your vet can perform tests to discover the extent of your dog's hearing loss, but there are ways you can detect the loss of hearing in your mixed breed on your own. A couple of the main symptoms are difficulty arousing from sleep and awakening with aggression. His verbalizations will be higher pitched. And he'll also have difficulty figuring out where sound is coming from.

Most dogs adjust to this loss of hearing quite well, and there are ways you can also adjust to it, too. You can begin by using more visual cues or lights to get your dogs' attention — laser lights are great for this.

Blindness

All dogs have decreased vision as they age (and you probably do, too!) — it can't be avoided.

Loss of sight is normally due to changes in pupil size and the loss of focusing correctly. Due to the aging process other disorders and diseases occur because of the downward shift of eyelid tissues and atrophy of the orbital fat.

Your dog's vision may be reduced as he ages, but he'll easily adjust to this, and it most likely won't affect his overall quality of life. You can help by not changing the furniture around, and not leaving objects on the floors that he can't easily detect.

Arthritis

There's no avoiding arthritis. (Are you sensing a pattern here?) If it doesn't occur from an old injury, it most certainly sets in with age.

Arthritis is a disease in which the cartilage in the joints deteriorates. Without the cartilage, the bones of the joints rub together, causing painful movement.

The symptoms of arthritis are obvious: difficulty walking; limping; a stiff, slow, ungainly gait. Sometimes you can hear a dog's joints creaking and crackling. You may even hear your dog's nails scraping against the floor as he walks.

There are many ways you can help your arthritic dog. Exercise helps maintain mobility and flexibility. You don't want to push your dog too much, but one or two very short walks a day (maybe around the block) will keep him moving. (You're better off breaking his walks into multiple sessions instead of taking one long walk.) Another way to ease the pain of arthritis is to make sure you don't let your dog become overweight. The heavier he is, the more stress is put on his joints. Also, numerous supplements are available that contain glucosamine and chondroitin — these nutrients lubricate the joints causing less friction between the bones. You can find them in chewable tables that your dog will eat up like treats.

Digestive disorders

Many old dogs get some sort of inflammatory disease of the gastrointestinal tract — a chronic irritation in his bowels, stomach, and/or intestines. When your dog has this disease, he'll vomit and/or have diarrhea. Left untreated, he'll lose weight and not be able to eat normally.

The symptoms can be caused by food allergies or stress. Sometimes emotional trauma can bring on the symptoms of intestinal disorders.

A diet change is often the first step. Your vet may suggest corticosteroids and other drugs if diet control isn't enough. Talk to your vet to see what she recommends.

Cancer

Cancer is a very common ailment in dogs — and it's often fatal. Because older dogs tend to be weakened with age, knowing whether to put your dog through the difficult and expensive treatments necessary to control the disease is tough.

Cancer of the organs is normally fatal. Skin cancer, however, can often be treated with removal of the tumor and chemotherapy or radiation applied to the affected area to kill any remaining cancerous cells. Dogs tend to become ill when given the first chemotherapy treatment, but they tend to tolerate subsequent treatments fairly well.

You may want to investigate some alternative therapies. Nutritional and herbal components are currently being tested in dogs, and some are looking very promising. Talk with your vet about all your options, and don't hesitate to seek a second opinion if you feel it's necessary.

Dementia

If your dog has Cognitive Dysfunction Syndrome (CDS, or dementia), he might exhibit the following behaviors:

- **Disorientation:** Your dog might be confused, wander aimlessly, go to the wrong side of doors, or get stuck in corners or behind furniture.

- **Change in sleep patterns:** Your dog will sleep more during the day and less at night. He may tend to wander aimlessly throughout the night.

- **Housetraining regression:** Your dog may go outside, forget why, and then comes inside only to relieve himself on your floor.

- **Avoiding family interaction:** He may walk away from you instead of wanting attention. He won't want to play as he used to.

Other symptoms include obsessive/compulsive disorders, separation anxiety, fear biting, environmental phobias (such as fear of thunder or other loud noises), and overall aggression. The aggression can be a variety of types, from fear biting to your dog being more territorial or possessive.

A medication called L-Selegeline can be prescribed by your vet that will help with the early symptoms of CDS. Most dogs show some improvement within the first couple weeks, but there are some, such as those in whom the CDS is quite advanced, who won't show any improvement at all. The medication has few side effects, but some dogs have mild gastrointestinal upset when they're on the drug. Those dogs who improve with Anipryl must remain on it the rest of their lives, or until the CDS progresses to the point where the drug is no longer effective.

If you think your dog may have CDS, talk to your vet. She'll be able to diagnose the condition and tell you about your treatment options.

Depression

Dogs are emotional and form lifelong attachments. So when they lose someone they dearly loved — whether a human companion or another animal — they can develop depression, just as humans can. Depression can also be brought on because of a change of scenery (maybe you moved to a new home) or because of weather changes or health changes.

Regardless of the cause, the symptoms include

- Excessive barking
- Lethargy
- Anxiety or nervousness
- Obsessive behavior such as excessive grooming, self-mutilation, or destructiveness
- Weight loss or gain
- Sulking
- Aggression
- Increased clinginess

When you recognize these behaviors as depression, there are steps you can take to help your dog. Your vet can prescribe antidepressant medication. You can also improve the quality of your dog's life by increasing his activities and social life. Keep him busy!

Left too long, depression can turn into a life-threatening physical condition.

Recognizing Behavior Problems That Sometimes Come with Age

Along with the physical changes that come with age, your mixed breed will also experience behavior and emotional changes. In fact, you're likely to see the behavior changes before the physical ones, because most dogs won't exhibit signs of physical weakness or injury — doing so decreases their standing within a dog pack.

Physical problems can actually cause behavioral problems. The onset of arthritis, for example, creates chronic pain, which in turn makes your dog increasingly grouchy. If cancer is growing, your dog may appear distracted, may not listen well, or may have the tendency to strike out aggressively without reason.

Overall, your older dog will be less likely to respond to obedience commands. If he's in pain, it hurts to move. If he can't hear you call him to come, he won't. If he doesn't see your visual cues to sit, he can't. If he doesn't remember what your cues mean, he doesn't know how to respond to them.

Dogs who once allowed young children to crawl all over them may suddenly lash out or go hide when they get older. Some dogs who once loved playing with other dogs no longer want to do so. Then there's the personal space issue — as dogs age, this becomes more prominent. Their personal-space needs increase, because they don't want to be stepped on or jostled by a person or another dog.

There are reasons behind all this impatience and aggression. The most common is pain from arthritis. Another reason is that your old dog doesn't see or hear well enough to be forewarned of another presence. And, sadly, as dogs age, some develop dementia; the neurons in their brain aren't firing as efficiently as they once did. All these can cause your dog to be impatient.

Pain causes bad moods. If someone were to touch a very painful place on *your* body, you might yell at him. A dog may bark, snap, or even outright attack. All your dog knows is that someone who touched him caused the more intense pain.

If your dog is experiencing dementia, and doesn't understand his world anymore, he'll tend to be more touchy and aggressive. He won't remember his people or other animal pack members — they'll be strangers to him. If they get in his personal space, watch out!

If your dog is in pain or is suffering from Cognitive Dysfunction Syndrome (CDS, or dementia — see the "Dementia" section, earlier in this chapter), keep other animals and small children away from him.

Your vet can tell if your dog is suffering from dementia, and he'll also be able to gauge how much pain your dog is in from arthritis or other health problems.

If your dog can't hear or see something coming, how can he prepared when it comes? Dogs rely heavily on their senses to understand their world. If they can't sense someone coming from behind them, or are awakened suddenly, their first instinct is to lash out. This can be especially dangerous in a home with youngsters, because they don't understand why their dog has suddenly become less loving.

If your dog is losing his eyesight or hearing, you'll need to change how others interact with him. There are ways you and your kids can inform your dog of your approach. For example, if your dog is losing his hearing, clap your hands or stomp loudly on the floor before you get close to him. Your dog still feels vibrations fairly well, and this will alert him. If he can't see well, try flashing the lights on and off to grab his attention.

Saying Goodbye

As dogs age, they become debilitated by illness. You love your dog and you hate to watch him suffer. Though most dogs try to hide pain, you need to know what to look for beyond the obvious. Here are some behaviors that might give you an indication of your dog's level of discomfort:

- ✔ Limping
- ✔ Obsessive scratching
- ✔ Licking an area
- ✔ Unusual mouth movements or excessive panting
- ✔ Frequently turning his head to look at his painful area
- ✔ Roaming in circles, pacing, or erratic movements
- ✔ Reluctance to get up or lie down, climb stairs, or get into the car
- ✔ Trembling or tension
- ✔ Being quieter or more clingy than usual

✔ Retreating or withdrawing from his family and animal companions

✔ Lack of appetite

If you've done all you can to try to alleviate his pain but he still displays the symptoms of extreme discomfort, you need to figure out whether now is the time to let your dog go. How do you make that decision? Ask yourself some important questions.

✔ Why is he still here? For your benefit? Will you be lonely without him? If that's the only reason you're keeping your dog alive, you're putting your own needs ahead of your dog's.

✔ What is his quality of life? Is the expensive veterinary treatment you're putting him through merely adding days or weeks to his life? Or is it adding years — and if so, what kind of years? Happy, pain-free ones, or ones of misery? If you're only adding a couple days or weeks, think about the quality of life he's leading. Is he comfortable? Is he happy? Is he wanting to go outside and play, or hiding in a corner?

Overall, you need to consider whether your dog's bad days outweigh his good ones. Try to be objective in your assessment and be fair to your dog.

Although your vet can tell you there's not much more you can do to help your dog, only *you* can make the final decision. Your mixed breed has been your loving companion for many years. You've cared for him, shared wonderful moments together, and enjoyed each others' company. You don't want him to suffer — you'll be suffering alongside him, and he won't understand your sadness and grief, which will only make him even more depressed.

I've had to make this impossible decision more times than I can count. It never hurts less, and I'll never forget the dogs I've helped travel to the Rainbow Bridge. I still see them in my mind; in the rearview mirror of my vehicle, smiling at me as they look forward to adventure; the times we shared hiking, camping, and working. Every one of them is still special to me and will forever live within my soul.

You know and love your dog — and you'll know when the time is right to say goodbye.

Whether you're thinking about putting your dog to sleep, or you've recently done it, talking with friends and family helps. They can be a huge support, helping you weigh your options and cope with your grief. Your family and friends understand the loss of your dog better than anyone else. They've seen the relationship you shared. They'll understand your stories and sit there holding you as you cry.

In addition to your friends and family, there are books you can turn to, Web sites to go to. Here are just a few:

- ✔ *Pet Loss and Children: Establishing a Healthy Foundation,* **by Cheri Barton:** If you have children, this book will guide you in helping them, and yourself, through the loss of your beloved dog. I like how it involves the children in the recovery process through artistic expression and teaches how to recognize when to say goodbye.

- ✔ *Saying Good-Bye to the Pet You Love: A Complete Resource to Help You Heal,* **by Lorri A. Greene and Jacquelyn Landis:** This book helps you overcome grief by writing out your memories. It also mentions how taking a moment to remember your pet through a special memorial is helpful. This book also helps you recognize when the time is right to say goodbye.

- ✔ *Pet Loss: How to Prepare, Say Goodbye, Honor Your Pet's Life,* **by Lisa Shover:** This book covers everything you need to recognize when it's time to say goodbye, how to go about the process, how to help others as they grieve and how to create a memorial for your dog.

- ✔ **PetLoss.com (`www.petloss.com`):** This is a great Web site for counseling, support, and information regarding pet loss. This group also has a regular Monday-night candle vigil paying tribute and memorializing our lost loved ones.

- ✔ **The Association for Pet Loss and Bereavement (`www.aplb.org`):** This Web site is a great resource for anyone who needs help in preparing for the loss of a pet or who needs support in the grieving process. There are chat rooms and actual counselors available to speak to. Sometimes all you need is an ear to listen to your stories.

If you're really having trouble coping with the loss of your pet, seek the help of a professional grief counselor. You can talk to your family physician to get a referral of someone in your area.

Don't feel guilty about your decision to put your dog to sleep. You kept him from pain and suffering, and that's the most responsible thing a pet owner can do.

Part V
Having Fun with Your Dog

The 5th Wave   By Rich Tennant

"I don't think teaching the puppy how to help you cheat at cards was the training and bonding experience the vet had in mind."

In this part . . .

Your dog doesn't need a pedigree to have fun or participate in club activities. Many organizations are open to mixed-breed dogs, and others are specifically *for* mixed-breed dogs.

In this part, I list some of the clubs and activities that you and your mixed breed can participate in, including agility, obedience, and Rally-O.

Mixed breed dogs are all over the airwaves. In movies, on television programs, commercials, videos of all types and advertisements, dogs grab attention and nothing does so better than the unique attributes of a mixed-breed dog. If you want your dog to be a media hound, you have to prepare him for his time in the spotlight. In this part, I show you how.

You and your mixed breed can do all kinds of activities together. In this part, I open your eyes to the pleasures of camping, hiking, boating, swimming, and horseback riding with your dog at your side. If you like to travel, you can include your dog — sharing your travels will make the entire trip more enjoyable. In this part, I help you locate pet-friendly places to stay and tell you what to bring (besides your dog!).

Finally, if you have to travel without your dog, you have to find a safe place for him to stay (or someone to stay with him). I fill you in on your options.

Chapter 16

Not Just for Purebreds: Showing Off with Your Mixed Breed

In This Chapter

▶ Competing in performance trials

▶ Making your dog a star

Your dog doesn't have to be pedigreed to compete in shows or participate in fun activities. In this chapter, I introduce you to the world of obedience shows, agility trials, and Rally-O. I also let you know how you can get your mixed breed into commercials, TV, and movies. If you and your dog are looking to take "play" to the next level, this is the chapter for you!

Participating in a Mixed-Breed Dog Club

Just because your dog didn't come to you with a pedigree doesn't mean you can't participate in any number of performance exhibitions. Your dog's performance has nothing to do with her appearance and everything to do with the work you put into her.

Two of the largest clubs offering many show opportunities are the Mixed Breed Dog Clubs of America (www.mbdca.org) and the United Kennel Club (www.ukcdogs.com). The UKC is actually a club for purebred dogs, including rare breeds, but it allows mixed-breed dogs to compete in their performance activities. The clubs will inform you of trial dates, but you need to work with a professional dog trainer or local dog training club to learn how to teach your dog to perform in obedience trials.

Competing in obedience matches and dog shows

You and your dog can compete in obedience matches and/or trials at dog shows. The difference between a *match* and a *trial* is that the match is a practice run — a place where you can test your and your dog's skills prior to entering a trial and working toward an obedience certificate. In a match, you can repeat an exercise or guide your dog into performing correctly, and the judge will give you advice on how to get your dog to achieve a better performance. In a trial, you cannot do these things. You and your dog will be judged — period.

I recommend achieving good scores in a match before attempting to perform at a trial. That way you can iron out the kinks and keep the entire experience positive for your dog, because there's no need to stress over getting something wrong at the match.

There are three main levels in the obedience ring. Each level has its own series of behaviors for your dog to perform. Here's a list of the classes, from easiest to hardest:

✔ **Novice:** In the Novice class, you and your dog will try to complete the following behaviors:

- Heeling on and off-leash

- Figure-8, on leash, around two people standing 8 feet apart

- Stand and Stay with the judge touching the dog as you remain 6 feet in front of the dog, with the dog off-leash

- Stay from 30 feet away

- Recall from 30 feet away

- Finish after the Recall

- One-minute Sit/Stay side by side with up to 12 other dogs and handlers 30 feet away

- Three-minute down/stay side by side with up to 12 others dogs and handlers 30 feet away

✔ **Open:** In the Open class, you and your dog will try to complete the following behaviors:

- Off-leash heeling pattern

- Off-leash figure-8 around two people standing 8 feet apart

- Drop on Recall

- Retrieve on the flat

- Retrieve over a high jump (1½ times the height of your dog at the shoulders)

- Send over a broad jump (2 times the height of your dog at the shoulders)

- Three-minute sit/stay side by side with other dogs and the handler out of sight

- Five-minute down/stay side by side with other dogs and the handler out of sight

✔ **Utility:** In the Utility class, you and your dog will try to complete the following behaviors:

- Off-leash heeling pattern using only visual cues, no voice at all

- Stop and stand, using visual cues and move over 20 feet away, faced away from dog

- Call dog to heel position while standing still

- Directed Retrieve: Retrieving a specific item (usually white gloves) out of three identical items

- Scent discrimination: Retrieving both a leather and metal article, bearing your scent, from other identical articles

- Directed Go Out: Leaving your side, running to the opposite end of the ring, and turning and sitting until you direct the next exercise

- Directed Jump: As the dog remains across the ring, you direct the dog to one of two jumps — a bar jump or high jump — repeat the Go Out again, and direct the dog to the other jump (at the judges' prompt)

Also, in a match there are non-regular classes that are both fun and a stepping-stone between different levels:

✔ **Sub-Novice:** This is a starter class in which you can keep your leash on your dog so that if the dog becomes distracted while performing, she won't be able to run off.

✔ **Graduate Novice:** This is a tweener class between Novice and Open. It has exercises from both classes, preparing you for the challenges you'd see in Open, while still allowing you to work on perfecting some of the exercises done in the Novice class.

I've had lots of success with these non-regular classes — they gave me and my dog the confidence to continue to the next level.

There are three main obedience titles to strive for. To earn these titles you must qualify with a score of 170 out of a possible 200 at three different shows with three different judges. The titles are: Novice class–Companion Dog (CD); Open class–Companion Dog Excellent (CDX), and Utility Dog (UD). You can also work toward championships (Obedience Trail Champion [OTCH]), high in trials, and other awards though you can count on it taking *years* to reach these goals. Of course, that's years of fun (and hard work) for you and your dog!

Competing in agility

Agility is quickly becoming the most popular canine event in the United States and in some areas around the world. Dogs love performing, and people love to watch them. Any dog of any size or breed can compete, and some clubs allow mixed-breed dogs to compete.

Agility was modeled on equestrian stadium jumping, with a variety of obstacles that have both spectator appeal and the intention of displaying the dog's agile nature. In this sport, the dog must negotiate a number of obstacles, off leash, within an allotted time frame.

The courses consist of jumps, tunnels, a pause table, weave poles, an A-frame, a seesaw, a dog walk, and more — each challenging the dog in different ways. You must be adept at directing the dog from obstacle to obstacle without getting in the dog's path.

Agility is a timed speed event, but the dog must also perform with precision. She has to touch the contact obstacle (A-frame, seesaw, or dog walk) at specific points both getting on and off, not knock down the poles while jumping or weaving, and execute the obstacles in the right order.

You can find out more about agility competitions by contacting the following organizations:

- ✔ **United States Dog Agility Association (USDAA),** phone: 972-487-2200, Web: www.usdaa.com

- ✔ **Agility Association of Canada (AAC),** phone: 519-657-7636, Web: www.aac.ca

- ✔ **North American Dog Agility Council (NADAC),** phone: 208-689-3803, Web: www.nadac.com

- ✔ **Australian Shepherd Club of America (ASCA),** phone: 409-778-1082, Web: www.asca.org

✔ **American Kennel Club (AKC),** phone: 919-233-9767, e-mail: info@akc.org

✔ **United Kennel Club (UKC),** phone: 616-343-9020, Web: www.ukcdogs.com

✔ **Canine Performance Events (CPE),** Web: www.k9cpe.com

Competing in Rally-O

Rally-O (short for Rally Obedience) was derived from obedience trials, but it offers a more enjoyable means of competing with your dog because you're allowed to use praise as a means of reinforcement while you guide your dog through the stations throughout the course. It's gaining in popularity by leaps and bounds!

As in agility, Rally-O is a timed event. It includes 12 to 20 stations where you and your dog must perform different skills. There are three levels to achieve in Rally-O:

✔ **Novice:** This level is on-leash with exercises that demonstrate the dog's understanding of basic commands: Sit, Stay, Down, Come, and Heel.

✔ **Advanced:** This level is made up of a set of exercises where the dog performs off-leash and includes at least one jump.

✔ **Excellent:** This level is a difficult off-leash course that includes at least one jump and demonstrates more precise skill coordination than in the Advanced level.

The course is different at each show, with the layout posted at the ringside and handed out so you can learn the progression of the exercises. Often, you can also walk the courses prior to the start of class, because knowing where to turn and when to turn makes a big difference in your overall performance.

Signs are posted for each station, which give instructions that you and your dog must execute within 2 to 4 feet of the sign. After the judge tells you and your dog to go forward, you complete the course on your own without additional commands from the judge. Although you can use voice guidance and your hands to give signals to your dog, you can't use food or toys in the ring, and you can't place your hands on your dog or physically touch her.

This sport is great for dogs who are bored by the stop-and-go routines in the obedience ring. Many dog clubs now offer Rally-O at their obedience trials, giving you more competitions to participate in at a show.

You can find a complete description of Rally-O on the AKC Web site (`www.akc.org`) and at the Association of Pet Dog Trainers (APDT) Web site (`www.apdt.com`) at `www.akc.org/pdfs/rulebooks/RO2999.pdf`. You can find station signs for all three levels at `www.akc.org/pdfs/rulebooks/ROR999.pdf`.

Media Hound: Getting Your Dog on Camera

I've been providing animals for film and TV production work since 1983. It's one of the most enjoyable activities that I do with animals. Every production is a new challenge and preparing the animals is loads of fun! The dog's human guardians love the fact that their dogs will be seen on television, in print, or in the movies. Some of these dogs become quite popular and are used repeatedly for many different types of work. I had one client tell me, "It's like he was a kid who spent the day in a candy shop. He came home happy, tired, and full [of treats]."

Mixed-breed dogs are great for production work because each dog is unique in appearance. Though the more unique dogs aren't often chosen for *large* parts in feature films (because it sometimes takes more than one dog to do the part, so they need dogs who look exactly alike), mixed-breed dogs are popular for advertisements, TV shows, and TV commercials.

If you're thinking of allowing your mixed breed to work in the production world, your first step is to find an animal actors' agent. There are specific traits that agents look for, and you'll want to see if your dog has that special something that catches an agent's eye. You'll also need to know how to prepare your dog for the work and what to expect while she performs in front of the camera.

Even if an agent doesn't think your dog is special, *you* know she is, and that's all your dog cares about.

Knowing what animal agents look for

Agents are looking, first and foremost, for well-trained dogs. Any dog who can earn an obedience or agility title is always welcomed by an animal actors' agent. Your dog should be able to perform off-leash with all kinds of distractions going on around her — because a production can be a very distracting situation. A dog who can perform specific tricks on command (such as speak, hold something in her mouth, fetch, or wave), as well as a dog who doesn't mind wearing clothing, is ideal.

Agents also look for dogs who are photogenic — and cute and photogenic aren't necessarily the same thing. For example, few black dogs are chosen for production work because the camera can't see their facial expressions. Often, black-and-white, brown-and-white, tan, merle, or other color combinations are what the producers are looking for. Productions vary a lot, so dogs of all sizes are used at one time or another.

Another item of extreme importance to an animal actors' agent is the dog's overall appearance. A dog with a dry, flaky coat, dull eyes, or low or high weight cannot perform well, so she won't be chosen. Owners of canine actors have to keep their dogs in the peak of health and training at all times, because a healthy dog can better tolerate the long performance and on-set hours. A health dog shines inside and out.

If you want your dog to be an actor, you must allow the dog to be available at all times. Rarely will you be allowed on the set, unless you're a professional trainer. This means that you must trust the trainers who will work with your dog on-set — if you won't trust your dog in someone else's hands, you won't be happy with production work.

Preparing for work

Other than practicing your dog's obedience and special tricks, the only way of knowing how to prepare for a job is to talk with your dog's agent regarding the availability of layouts. A *storyboard* is a roughly drawn picture that helps the director and actors know where to stand and where the cameras will be. It gives the trainer an idea of the specific action required of the dog and from which direction the camera will be angled.

If you aren't a professional trainer, the agent will hire one to work with your dog. The trainer will either pick up your dog at your home, or make arrangements with you to bring her to the set. You'll be told whether you can remain with her at that time. During any given production day, the dog is spending more time relaxing than working. She'll be getting lots of food rewards while working, so she often isn't fed much for her normal meals.

If the dog is expected to retrieve something specific, you can practice this reaction ahead of time. If the dog is required to wear specific types of clothing, such as a hat and sunglasses, you can practice this as well. As is often the case, however, the animal actors' agent is told that certain behaviors will be required, but when the dog and trainer arrive on-set, the director has either changed his mind or embellished on the original action. This means that the dog must be well trained and easy to teach on the spot.

Sometimes, much to the dismay of the animal actors' agent and trainer, the director requests the dog to "be a dog." To a trainer, this is a nightmare directive. Many people don't understand that they won't get a specific action from a dog unless the dog is cued to perform it. In these situations, there's not much you can do to prepare other than working on basic behaviors and tricks, hoping that whatever will be expected is something your dog already understands.

What to expect when your dog performs in front of the camera

In order for a dog to give her best performance, the trainer must use positive reinforcement. This will make the entire experience enjoyable for your dog. After every couple of commands, your dog will be rewarded both verbally and with a treat or toy. What dog wouldn't love that?

A production is always a hurry-up-and-wait scenario. The dog is requested to arrive at a call time, often hours prior to the time she goes in front of the camera. So the dog gets to wait and wait and wait. During that time, she needs to remain quiet so that she has the energy to perform.

When she begins her performance, your dog will be in front of the camera for anywhere from 20 to 30 minutes. As a new scene is set up, she'll wait another hour or two for a possible second scene where she'll be in front of the camera for another 20 to 30 minutes. In all, there's more waiting than working.

Chapter 17

Traveling with Charley

. . . .

In This Chapter

▶ Preparing for your trip

▶ Driving or flying with your dog

▶ Leaving your dog at home

. . . .

> *There was some genuine worry about my traveling alone, open to attack, robbery, assault. It is well known that our roads are dangerous. And here I admit I had senseless qualms. It is some years since I have been alone, nameless, friendless, without any of the safety one gets from family, friends, and accomplices. There is no reality in the danger. It's just a very lonely, helpless feeling at first — a kind of desolate feeling. For this reason I took one companion on my journey — an old French gentleman poodle known as Charley.*
>
> —John Steinbeck, *Travels with Charley in Search of America*

Over the hills and through the woods, it's a travelin' we go! If only it were so easy. Traveling with a dog requires careful planning. You need to know what to pack, how to find hotels that accept dogs, and special considerations for flying with your dog — and in this chapter, I lay it all out for you. I also cover what to do if you have to leave your dog at home.

Deciding Whether to Bring Your Dog with You

When you're planning a trip and you own a dog, one of the first things that crosses your mind is whether you can take your dog with you. Although I'm sure you'd love to have your dog along for the ride, you have to ask yourself a few key questions to decide whether your mixed breed and this trip are a good fit:

✔ **Will you have time to spend with your dog?** If you're going on vacation, the answer will probably be yes — after all, you're on vacation to relax, right? But if you're going on a business trip, odds are your dog will end up having to spend a lot of time in the hotel room by himself. He'll be in a new place, and being alone there won't be as easy for him as it is at your house. Unless you'll be able to spend most of your time with your dog, you're better off leaving him at home.

✔ **Is your pet in good condition to travel?** If your dog is very young or very old, a road trip might be strenuous for him — he'll have to relieve himself more often, and you'll have to make lots of stops. Young pups need to run — unless you're driving a monster SUV with a doggy playground in the back, your pup will likely chew whatever is within reach (arm rests, seat covers, head rests, suitcase handles). Old dogs may have difficulty getting in and out of your vehicle.

A sick or injured dog should remain in a quiet environment, not be jostled about in a vehicle or extremely stressed by a ride in the cargo hold of an airplane.

✔ **Is there a pet-friendly place to stay at your destination?** Most hotel chains don't allow dogs in their establishments. You'll need to plan ahead and make reservations so that you don't end up driving around in the middle of the night searching for a place to stay.

✔ **If you're visiting family and/or friends, are they okay with the idea that your dog will be with you?** One of the best ways to make yourself unwelcome is to arrive at someone's house with your dog without first asking if they're cool with it. Believe me, after many years of having a relative come to my house with dogs who urinated on my carpeting or showed aggression to my animals, I can totally understand people who'd rather not welcome other people's pets into their homes — and I *love* dogs!

Finding Pet-Friendly Places to Stay

Most hotels, motels, and bed-and-breakfasts don't allow pets. And in the hotels that do, room availability may be limited — they typically set aside certain rooms for people with pets. Even so, you *can* find hotels and motels that accept dogs — you just need to spend a little more time looking than you would otherwise.

AAA publishes a great book, Traveling With Your Pet, that's updated yearly, listing all the pet-friendly places to stay in the United States. You don't have to be a AAA member to obtain this book at its Web site (`www.aaa.com`).

 You can also find information on pet-friendly hotels at `www.pets welcome.com`, `www.dogfriendly.com`, and `www.bringfido.com`. Both sites allow you to see hotels in any city, state, or province you're visiting. (As of this printing, `www.bringfido.com` is limited to just the United States, but the other two offer information on hotels in Canada as well.)

Packing for Your Trip

When you're traveling on your own, you may jot down a list of things you need to remember to pack. Well, you need to do the same for your dog when you're bringing him along. The good news: I've done much of the legwork for you. Here's a list of items to bring on your trip:

- **Food and water dishes:** The collapsible type are great when space is tight. Otherwise, lightweight plastic dishes work well.

- **A bottle of water from home:** If the trip is short, such as a day or two, a gallon of water should do. If longer, bring enough water for during the traveling and a bit for arrival to gently wean your dog onto whatever water is available at your destination. Water varies from location to location — a sudden change can upset your dog's stomach.

- **Food:** Place kibble in an airtight container to maintain freshness. If you're bringing canned food, be sure to bring a can opener if you'll need one. Be sure to bring enough food for the entire trip.

- **Your dog's bed:** If you don't want to bring a bulky bed, bring along a mat. You can find zippered mat beds that double as carrying cases for dog supplies. I usually use it for doggy toys, treats, leashes, and packaged food when I travel with my dogs.

- **Leash and collar with identification tags:** If your dog pulls on the leash when you walk him, bring a training device, such as a head halter or Easy Walk harness.

- **Treats and toys:** Interactive toys — such as treat-stuffed toys or those that are edible — are best. I've found that a plain, old shank bone, stuffed with ground up food is great. It's inexpensive and reusable.

- Grooming supplies
- Medications and supplements
- Bags for picking up droppings
- **Your dog's health records:** Regardless of where you travel or for how long, have a copy of your mixed breed's vaccination record and rabies certificate. This is especially important when crossing state lines or traveling in a foreign country.

If you're going to the beach, be sure to bring some means of shading your dog from the sun, such as a beach umbrella or a tent; an extra towel or two for your dog; and a keep-cool mat. These are special mats that can be soaked in cold water and will remain cool for hours — a great way to help your furry friend control his body temperature when it's very hot outside. You can carry it in a large cooler, along with your water bottles and soda.

If you're heading to the mountains, bring along a mobile first-aid kit (see Chapter 14). With exposure to wild animals and uneven terrain, your dog could get injured, and you want to be prepared. Bring along some insect repellent as well, such as Avon's Skin-So-Soft — it may help prevent topical parasites on your dog.

Keep the following contact info handy while you travel:

- **American Animal Hospital Association** (phone: 303-986-2800; Web: www.healthypet.com): Contact the association if you need to find a vet while you're on the road.
- **Dogpark.com:** This Web site can help you find a place to exercise your dog while you're on the road.

Traveling by Car

Traveling by car can be a fun and easy way to get to places with your mixed breed in tow. To make sure your trip is a fun one for you and your dog, be sure to acclimate your dog to car travel gradually. Begin with short trips to fun places — this makes the experience more rewarding.

An important part of traveling with your dog is keeping him safe on the trip, and that means containing him in some way so that he doesn't have free run of the car. If he can run all over the car, he may interfere with your ability to see or steer, or if you get in an accident or you have to brake suddenly, he could go flying.

You can contain your dog in a comfortable crate, strap him into a special body harness with a seat belt attachment, or let him hang out in a flat rear cargo area with a divider. The containment method you use depends largely on your dog's size and temperament. Here's the lowdown on each:

- ✔ **Crate:** The crate is best for anxious dogs or those who tend to chew or whine or bark in the car. Whether your dog is anxious or not, a crate is the safest place for him to be in your car. I recommend a metal crate because it's sturdy but provides ample air flow and gives your dog a view of everyone in the car and everything outside the windows. You can drape a reflecting blanket over it to keep the interior cooler on hot days.

  Never keep your dog in a hot car on a hot day with the windows closed or left open only a crack. Your dog will die of heat stroke and suffocation in an agonizing, cruel manner.

- ✔ **Seat restraints:** Many brands of dog seat restraints are available. Most come in the form of an upper-body harness with a clip that attaches either to the belt or to the actual seat belt insert clip. For a medium to large dog, use the type that clips directly into the seat belt clip insert. For smaller dogs, I recommend a booster seat with the seat belt attachment to a body harness. The booster seat lets your small dog look at the scenery while in a comfortable cushioned bed.

- ✔ **The rear cargo area:** If you have a station wagon or SUV, you can place your medium to large mixed breed in the back cargo area, with a metal divider keeping him from getting into the front seats. It's similar to a crate, though often larger. Your dog can see the passing scenery and remain secure behind the metal vehicle barrier. You will have to put up with nose smudges on the glass, though — a small price to pay from your dog's point of view!

  Don't leave your dog loose in the cargo area if he's destructive, has traveling anxiety of any sort, or likes to bark at everyone he sees while you drive. You'll be more distracted worrying about what he's doing back there than keeping your mind on the road. Also, don't put a small dog in the rear cargo area — he could go flying if you stop suddenly.

Flying with Your Dog

Some dog owners never let their dogs travel by plane; others have never had any problems and do it all the time. The main thing to consider: Unless your dog can fit under an airline seat, he'll have to ride in the checked baggage area or the cargo hold. Though the cargo hold is temperature-controlled while in flight (*not* while on the ground) and have an air-exchange system, it will still be more stressful for your mixed breed than remaining with you in the cabin.

Unless your dog can fit in his carrier under the seat, only certified service animals can remain in the cabin with their human companions.

If your dog has to remain in his air carrier for more than six hours straight, he may have trouble not being able to relieve himself. Imagine yourself having to do that — especially when stressed. It's tough. And, if you have flight layovers or you have multiple flights, you probably won't be able to visit with your dog. The airlines generally have people who check on your dog for you.

Some types of dogs should not travel by air — period. The U.S. Department of Agriculture (USDA) specifies that dogs under 8 weeks of age can't fly at all. If the dog is ill, injured, pregnant, or very old, they recommend that he doesn't travel by air. Also, dogs with very short noses such as Pugs and Boxers, as well as long-nosed dogs such as Collies, are prone to respiratory difficulties, and the UDSA suggests they only travel by air if they can do so in the passenger cabin. Some airlines won't accept short-nosed breeds at all if the temperature exceeds 70°F anywhere during the routing (between the terminals and airplane).

What to do before you leave

When you're flying with a dog, you'll need to make some preparations beyond the more-basic road-trip ones. In the following sections, I walk you through what you need to do.

Checking out the airlines' requirements

The first thing you need to do when considering an air trip with your dog is to determine the airline's regulations. Airlines change their regulations frequently, so check with your favorite airlines before buying your ticket.

Buying an airline-approved crate

The crate you use for your dog in your house probably isn't an air-line-approved crate, so the first thing to do when you start thinking about flying with your dog is to get one. You'll want a crate that's not only comfortable for your dog but that'll keep him safe throughout the flight.

The crate should have a hard shell, so that if something accidentally falls on it, your pet will be protected. If the crate (and your dog) are small enough to carry, it should have a strong handle. If your dog is too large to carry, make sure you can either push the crate on wheels or lift it onto a wheeled cart.

The crate should have plenty of ventilation and a leak-proof floor. Place an absorbent bed on the floor so that your mixed breed will be comfortable during the flight. The crate door should open easily, but also be secure enough to prevent your dog from escape or from it accidentally opening when it's jostled.

If you're able to bring your small dog into the passenger cabin, his crate must be able to fit under the seat in front of you, and the dog must stay within his crate. The under-seat space is approximately 23 by 13 by 9 inches. Beyond being able to fit in this space, there aren't any other restrictions on the kind of crate you use. Keep in mind, however, that your pet won't be allowed out of his crate during the trip, so he must be contained in a comfortable carrier with plenty of ventilation.

If you're traveling with more than one mixed breed, you can only have one per crate if either dog weighs more than 20 pounds.

Making sure your dog has proper identification and health certificates

Take your dog to your vet within ten days prior to your flight, have a complete physical examination, and request a copy of his vaccination record, rabies certificate, and a health certificate. If your mixed breed is traveling in the cargo hold, place his identification information (and yours) on the crate as well as any care instructions. When there are layovers or if you're traveling internationally, airline employees will be caring for your dog and should be given appropriate instructions.

Caring for your dog before and after the flight

Traveling by air can be stressful for both you and your mixed breed. So here are some tips for making it better for *both* of you:

✔ **Before the day of your flight, acclimate your dog to his air crate.** Make sure he likes it before you leave. (You can get your dog used to his crate by leaving it open at home and using it as his bed and eating area.)

✔ **Don't check in your dog until the very last minute.** Until then, allow him to be out and about with you, moving around and acclimating to the airport congestion and commotion. Stay upbeat and give him plenty of rewards.

✔ **Make sure his water and food bowls are securely fastened to the side of the crate so they don't spill in flight.**

✔ **Place a couple of his favorite toys in the crate, as well as some interactive chewies.** Just make sure that you don't leave him with anything he might choke on, such as rawhide.

✔ **After the flight, remove your dog from his travel crate (on a leash) as soon as you reach a safe area where he can stretch his legs and go potty.** Because he likely didn't do his business while traveling, and was very stressed during the trip, he'll be hopping from leg to leg by the time you arrive at your destination.

✔ **After he's emptied his bladder and bowels, offer him fresh water and food, and let him move around, play with some toys, and cuddle with you before you leave the airport.**

Leaving Your Dog Behind

You can't always take your mixed-breed dog with you when you travel. In this section, I cover your two main options for leaving your mixed breed behind.

Finding an in-home sitter

When you're looking for a reputable pet sitter, your best option is to ask your family and friends for referrals. If you can't find any good recommendations that way, try checking with either Pet Sitters International (phone: 336-983-9222; Web: www.petsit.com) or the National Association of Professional Pet Sitters (phone: 856-439-0324; Web: www.petsitters.org).

Here's a list of questions to ask a potential pet sitter:

✔ **Are you insured for commercial liability and bonded?** A sitter who is bonded and insured is serious about her services.

✔ **What do your services include?** Before you interview the potential pet sitter, make a list of all the things you'd want the pet sitter to do with your dog (walk him, hang out with him, play with him), and go down the list to be sure she'll do everything.

✔ **What does the sitter require of you?** Does the sitter require access to current veterinary information about your dog? (This is important in case of an emergency — she'll have to take your dog to a veterinarian and must have appropriate documentation.) Does she ask for a letter from you stating that she represents you in your absence?

✔ **What kind of animals does the sitter normally work with?** If the pet sitter normally only watches cats and fish, or if she's used to small dogs and you have a 100-pound mutt, it might not be a good fit.

✔ **How will the pet sitter handle emergencies?** What if the pet sitter gets in an accident and can't come to watch your dog? Does she have a backup plan for herself? And what if something happens to your dog while you're away? Will she take your dog to your vet, or will she go someplace else? Make sure you're comfortable with the answers.

✔ **Does the sitter fully understand your mixed-breed dogs' needs?** Always fully explain to the sitter your dogs' physical needs and overall behavior patterns. What times does he normally eat, sleep, play, and exercise? How does he behave while being walked? How much training has he had? What are his training commands? Explain the feeding process to the sitter — what your mixed-breed dog is fed, how much, where he eats, how he eats.

✔ **How much time will the pet sitter spend with your dog?** Many pet sitters charge by the 15-minute increment of time and allow you to choose how long you want them to stay.

Knowing what to look for in a kennel

As with a pet sitter, the best place to find a kennel is through a referral from someone you trust. If you can't get any recommendations, check with the American Boarding Kennels Association (phone: 719-667-1600; Web: www.abka.com).

Depending on where you live, you can find kennels that range from the most basic (the dogs stay in a fenced-in area with a concrete floor, and minimal access to the outdoors) to the most posh (dogs have their own human-size beds — just like a hotel). Some kennels offer many different levels of accommodations and care.

Before making a reservation, visit the kennel and take a tour. Check for cleanliness, employee knowledge, and the comfort of the animals (if they're making a lot of noise, pacing, or sitting in a dark corner, this may not be a good sign). Find out about the opportunities for your dog to receive attention, exercise, and grooming.

Here's a list of questions to ask any boarding kennel:

- ✔ **What's included in the fee?** Just feeding and cleaning, or also exercise and attention?

- ✔ **What vaccinations are required?** If the kennel requires no vaccinations, stay away! The kennel should require rabies, parvo, distemper, and other contagious-disease vaccinations, including bordetella (kennel cough).

- ✔ **How will emergencies be handled?** Is there a vet on call? Will your dog be taken to the vet he's used to seeing?

- ✔ **Where will your dog be housed?** A cage, run, or suite? What's in the room with him? His own toys and bed from home?

- ✔ **How often are the dogs fed and interacted with?**

- ✔ **How often are the dogs' sleep and other areas cleaned?**

When you drop your dog off at the kennel, leave your contact information along with a copy of your dog's health records, in case of emergencies. Also, let the staff know about his feeding routines, what he eats, how he eats, the type of exercise he prefers, the type of people he likes to interact with, and any commands he may know, as well as any psychological quirks, medical conditions, medication, or supplements.

Bring your dog's regular food with him to the kennel so that he isn't fed something that doesn't agree with his digestive system. Prepackage each meal and label it, so that there aren't any skipped supplements.

Part VI
The Part of Tens

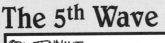

In this part ...

The Part of Tens is a part of every *For Dummies* book, and this one is no different! If you're in a hurry, and you want a whole lot of bang for your buck, this is the part for you. Here you find ten reasons to spay or neuter your dog, and ten events you and your mixed breed can enjoy together.

Chapter 18

Ten Reasons to Spay or Neuter Your Dog

● ●

In This Chapter

▶ Finding low-cost ways to spay or neuter your dog

▶ Understanding how spaying or neutering your pet can help the pet population

▶ Assessing the health risks of not spaying or neutering your dog

● ●

*W*hen you start thinking about spaying or neutering your dog, the first questions you should ask yourself are: Why did you get your mixed-breed dog? Because you wanted a companion, or because you specifically wanted to breed other animals? If you wanted a companion (the reason most people get dogs), you should sterilize your dog to improve the quality of your life and your dog's.

Dog breeding is not for everyone. Done *correctly* it is costly, time-consuming, and often heart-wrenching. Though many people deal with the aftermath of breeding accidents, or breed their dogs without thinking about the dogs' or puppies' welfare, you can be certain that a large percentage of pregnant female dogs and their puppies wind up either at animal shelters or suffer dreadful consequences.

Whether you have a designer dog that costs thousands, or a Heinz 57 you adopted, there is *no* reason for breeding your dog and many reasons not to. In this chapter, I give you ten of the many reasons why you should spay or neuter your pet.

It Doesn't Cost Much — and It May Be Free!

If you adopted your mixed-breed dog from a shelter, humane society, or rescue organization, you'll likely be able to get a huge discount when it's time to sterilize your dog. Just ask the people you got your dog from. The discounts can be anywhere from 10 to 60 percent!

Some veterinarians do spay and neutering clinics — often free to humane and rescue organizations. If you've adopted from those organizations, you may be able to get the service without charge. Information on free or low-charge spaying/neutering is often posted on bulletin boards at the volunteer veterinarians' hospitals; animal shelters are also aware of the locations and dates of the clinics, so check with them if you're unsure.

Many rescue groups already have sterilized their dogs before allowing them to be adopted, while humane societies require you to do it before they'll allow the dog to go home with you.

Some low-cost spay-and-neuter clinics are able to offer this service because they minimize the use of anesthetic monitoring, the use of intravenous fluids, and post-operative pain control. If you can afford this procedure through your normal vet, go that route instead — you'll decrease the risks and pain associated with surgery.

If you're choosing between getting your dog spayed/neutered at a low-cost clinic, and not spaying/neutering at all, always opt for spaying/neutering.

Breeding Is Time-Consuming and Expensive

If you're the owner of a female dog who got loose at the wrong time and came home pregnant, you've got a lot of expense ahead of you. Besides the time-consuming puppy and mommy care, you'll have to take the pups to the vet for worming and the first set of vaccinations when they're 5 weeks old, and again at 7 weeks. The costs of these vaccinations can range anywhere from $25 to $50 *per puppy per visit*. Did your dog have seven puppies? Do the math.

What if your dog becomes ill and can't feed her puppies? You'll have to hand-feed each one (more cost for formula and bottles for seven puppies for four weeks — *ka-ching!*) every two to four hours, 24 hours a day. That's more than a full-time job!

When the puppies reach 3 weeks of age, the mommy dog begins to wean them. She won't want to stick around and feed or clean them. Now it's up to you to make sure she does her time with them when she'd really rather not. You'll have to force her to do her job.

When the pups reach 4 weeks of age, it's completely up to you as the puppies are weaned. You'll have to feed them three times a day (more money for food), and clean up after them. Generally, a puppy pen needs cleaning three times a day, or the puppies are covered in a smelly mess.

Then there's the noise level. When they're hungry, puppies cry. When they play, they bark at each other. And they're not on *your* sleeping schedule — you're on *their* schedule, which means sometime around 2 or 3 in the morning, it's playtime!

Having puppies isn't all fun and games. Sure they're cute, and puppy breath can't be beat, but they're loads of work and cost a lot! Spaying your female dog will save you a lot of time and money.

You Reduce Your Dog's Risk of Cancer

The older your dog becomes, the higher the risk that she'll develop any number of cancers.

Male dogs are prone to testicular and prostate infection and cancer, while female dogs can get mammarian, ovarian, uterine, and cervical cancer. Not caught in time, these diseases are fatal. Even if caught in the early stages, cancer is extremely expensive to treat. You'll need to weigh the difference between the cost of sterilization ($75 to $150) and the cost of treating cancer (upwards of $2,000 for surgery, chemo, and/or radiation treatments). Plus, cancer causes all kinds of physical and psychological stress for you and your dog.

Cancer isn't the only health risk for an unsterilized pet. Unsterilized dogs are more prone to developing kidney and bladder infections. Female dogs are prone to uterine and pelvic infections, as well as frequent vaginitis.

Overall, the cost is too high — both materially and psychologically — *not* to spay or neuter your dog.

You Help Control the Number of Unwanted Dogs in the World

In the United States, a dog is euthanized every 4 seconds of every day. That's *millions* of dogs killed each year because people weren't responsible pet owners.

The average family of four would have to own eight dogs each in order for every dog in the United States to have a home. Are you willing to have eight dogs? Is your neighbor? How would that work in a high-rise apartment building in the city?

The rampant spread of disease is another reason that dogs are being euthanized at an alarming rate. The more feral dogs there are, without the benefit of vaccinations, the faster they will spread diseases such as rabies, parvovirus, distemper, and other highly contagious diseases, some of which are transferable to humans.

Also, homeless dogs can be dangerous to local wildlife and cats, as well as causing vehicular accidents. Some may even harm children. There are many known cases of wandering dog packs actually *killing* children and the elderly.

Your dog needs you to be a responsible guardian.

Your Dog Won't Be as Likely to Stray from Home

Female dogs in season seek male dogs. It's a hard-wired instinct. You open your front door, and out she goes — and she won't return for days, if at all. If she returns home, you'll have a pregnant dog to deal with.

Unneutered male dogs can smell a female dog in season from more than a mile away. They perform feats of spectacular escapism to reach that female. Plus, they become assertive and temperamental if they *aren't* allowed to reach the source of the scent. Do you want to lose your dog with the high probability of never seeing him again? Or knowing that he can become injured by fighting with other dogs over a female in season, or being hit by a car and dying on the side of the road because he had to get to that female dog across the busy highway? Is it really that important to keep your dog intact when the risks of permanently losing him are that high?

Your Dog Will Be on Her Best Behavior

Neutering or spaying does not change who your dog is, but it will enhance her behavior in a more positive way, making your relationship with her more harmonious. When your female dog is in heat or your male dog smells a female in heat, your mixed breed won't be the baby or best friend you've known.

Your Dog Will Be Easier to Housetrain

Neutered male dogs are less likely to spray the furniture in your home or otherwise mark territory indoors. They're more accepting of the fact that inside the home is *your* territory. When an intact male dog detects a female dog in heat, he'll likely break all the housetraining rules and behave as though he'd never learned them. The mess and stench will be tremendous. You'll be tempted to make your dog live outdoors instead of with you — and that means he'll no longer be a family member.

A neutered/spayed dog will be more likely to acquiesce to housetraining due to not having the desire to be in charge or behave in an instinctual manner. Your dog can't control her mood swings and needs.

Another important reason is the mess involved with a female dog in heat. She will be leaking blood for ten days during the first trimester of her heat. It's messy, smelly, and can stain your flooring, furniture, and bedding. Who wants to deal with that?

Reproduction Can Be Risky

Many things can go wrong with whelping puppies. There can be health and delivery risks for the mother. If she has a dead puppy in her womb, she can become seriously ill as the puppy decomposes or spreads any disease that might have killed the pup to the other puppies and to the mother. If one of the puppies doesn't exit the womb properly, causing the mother dog physical distress, she'll have to undergo a cesarean section to deliver the puppies. This will be very costly to you and physically stressful to her.

Some mother dogs don't want to be mothers. They won't clean up after their pups or feed them. Guess who will have to take over? Yep, that's right: you! Will you be willing to do this when she won't?

Your Dog Will Be a Better Watchdog

A neutered dog will want to protect his home territory instead of wanting to increase the size of his territory. Intact male dogs tend to mark every object they can when going for walks through the neighborhood. They want to increase the size of their territory and do so by leaving this "calling card." A neutered dog will be less likely to want to stop at every tree, fence post, and mailbox to leave his mark. He won't care about increasing his territory. He's quite happy with the one he has at home.

A dog who loves his home will tend to protect it better. You'll be alerted to the presence of strangers who enter the area instead of wondering why you never heard your dog bark when someone arrived because the dog was down the block investigating the source of an interesting smell.

So if you spend a lot of time home alone, keeping your dog home, too, will be very beneficial. He will want to stay home if he's not driven to roam by raging hormones.

Your Dog Isn't You

You love your mixed breed very much. You may even "identify" with her as a part of yourself — an extension or appendage. You think that *you* would hate to be unable to reproduce. It's the driving force of nature, of all living things.

You have to be realistic. Your dog is a dog, not a person, and not *you* in particular. You can prove your love and devotion to your dog by neutering or spaying, because you'll be improving your dog's quality of life as well as your dog's longevity.

Chapter 19

Ten Fun Activities You and Your Mixed Breed Can Enjoy Together

In This Chapter

▶ Showing off your mixed-breed dog

▶ Playing games

▶ Becoming a good citizen

▶ Having fun outdoors

▶ Helping others

There are loads of fun activities you can do with your mixed-breed dog — none of which require a pedigree! From competition to helping others, you can participate in many activities where both of you would have fun.

The more events you work for, and the more titles you earn with your dog, the better you and he work together. Never buy into the idea that your dog has accomplished all he can — there is *always* more to learn! You can also be certain that the more you teach him, the happier he'll be, because you're stimulating his brain and exercising his body.

If you want to help others, you can enlist your mixed breed as a helper. The first step is to prove that he's a good citizen. The next is to train him and prepare yourself as a therapy team going to schools, hospitals, and convalescent homes visiting those who can't have pets. The presence of an animal has great healing power. Just as your mixed breed keeps *your* heart whole, merely touching his coat or receiving a wet kiss from his lips has great benefits for another person. Your dog will love traveling to places with you, and the attention from everyone is a huge boost to his ego.

The things you can do and the places you can go together are endless. Take the time to peruse the possibilities in the great world of
mixed-breed dogs!

Competing with Your Dog at the Classic K-9 Show

The North American Dog Racing Association's Classic K-9 Show
(www.classick9.com) is open to dogs of all breeds or mixed combinations. It's a great venue to participate in many types of canine
sports to earn titles and prizes. These include high jumping and
timed agility.

The Web site is filled with information on how to join the organization as well as about competing. You can find an event schedule, so
you can check out a show in your area (or at least close). If you see
one in your area, go watch! Being a spectator is almost as fun as
competing — plus, it'll give you a sense of whether this is an activity you and your dog would enjoy!

Participating in United Kennel Club Events

The United Kennel Club (www.ukcdogs.com) is the largest all-breed
performance registry in the world. It registers dogs from across the
United States and in 25 other countries. More than 60 percent of its
licensed events are tests of natural abilities such as hunting, training, and instinct. They emphasize the dog's performance not
appearance.

The United Kennel Club is one of the few purebred dog clubs that
also allows mixed-breed dogs to compete. The club members
believe that this will improve the health and well-being of *all* dogs.

The UKC sanctions obedience trials, agility, dog sport, weight
pulling, and terrier races. All mixed-breed dogs are welcome to
compete in these performance classes. They are offered throughout the year all over North America.

Having Fun at Mixed Breed Dog Clubs of America Events

The Mixed Breed Dog Clubs of America (MBDCA; www.mbdca.org) is a registry for mixed breeds. It provides the same opportunities for competitions that the American Kennel Club does for purebred dogs. The MBDCA doesn't have the same conformation-type competition of the AKC (which judges dogs according to a breed standard, that includes all kinds of mostly appearance-related attributes). But the MBDCA does have performance events where you can earn similar titles to those put on AKC dogs, as well as a conformation competition where the standard is toward general soundness as well as a good temperament and manners (as opposed to appearance).

In obedience, your dog can earn titles in Novice (on- and off-leash obedience routines), Open (off-leash obedience routines), and Utility (advanced off-leash obedience routines), as well as the title of Obedience Trial Champion. The title initials are the same as the AKC initials, only with the letters MB in front of them, denoting that the dog is a mixed breed. For example, the title for Mixed Breed Companion Dog is MB-CD; for Mixed Breed Companion Dog Excellent, MB-CDX; for Mixed Breed Utility Dog, MB-UD; and for Mixed Breed Utility Dog Excellent, MB-UDX.

Training Your Dog to Dive

I'll never forget watching my first dock diving competition. I loved not only seeing those dogs racing down a dock and diving, but observing how much fun they and their handlers were having.

Dock diving is open to all dogs of any breed or mix. This event has become so popular that it's featured on ESPN, called the Big Air Games. Because of the sport's quick rise in popularity, the organization Dock Dogs was formed to oversee all the smaller organizations dedicated to this sport. Its Web site (www.dockdogs.com) features information on how to get started and a list of events throughout the country. Another great site for information on this sport is Sport Mutt (www.sportmutt.com).

In order to enjoy dock diving, you just need to have access to water with either a diving board or dock. Your dog must love the water. Dogs who have a high desire to retrieve are also naturals for this sport, because they'll want to chase down the ball as it soars over the water.

Currently, there aren't any training clubs where you can go to learn how to teach your dog to dock dive. But the sites mentioned earlier do explain how to train your dog and where to go for dock diving events.

Joining the Fun at the Australian Shepherd Club of America

Formed in 1957 to promote the Australian Shepherd Dog breed, it has opened its doors to allowing mixed-breed dogs to compete in ASCA-sanctioned shows and earn titles as well.

Before Australian Shepherds were recently accepted as a purebred by the American Kennel Club, they were only allowed to compete in open matches or at ASCA-sanctioned shows. Due to these restrictions, the group decided to allow other dogs not recognized by the AKC to also compete at its shows.

ASCA holds obedience and other performance events around the country. Visit the Web site (www.asca.org) to find an event near you.

Camping and Hiking: Finding Fun Outdoor Activities

What's better than exploring and enjoying the great outdoors with your mixed breed? At Dog Play (www.dogplay.com), you can find a useful list of camps and outdoor activities for dog enthusiasts. These camps offer accommodations, meals, scheduled activities and classes, a chance for dogs to play with other dogs, and opportunities for you to hike, bike, canoe, and explore. Whether you go with a special someone or by yourself, you'll meet many other dog enthusiasts who share your passion for mixed breeds.

Helping Your Dog Become a Good Citizen

The Canine Good Citizen (www.akc.org/events/cgc/index.cfm) is a great certificate to work toward with your dog. It proves your dog's temperament and control as well as social skills. Since its inception, it has become a popular goal for many dog owners.

There are even communities that require all dogs living within that community to be CGC-certified!

Though the AKC is a club for purebred dogs, it offers the CGC test to mixed breeds as well. You can often find CGC tests listed in the newspaper, or online at www.akc.org, where there are listings for each state.

To earn a CGC title, the dog must pass ten tests of social skill, temperament, and obedience. These tests include

- ✔ Accepting a friendly stranger

- ✔ Sitting politely for petting

- ✔ Being examined for overall health and well-being

- ✔ Going out for a walk (walking on a leash)

- ✔ Walking through a crowd

- ✔ Performing a Sit and Down on command, as well as staying for a short period of time

- ✔ Coming when called

- ✔ Observing your dog's reaction to new objects and the presence of strangers

- ✔ Observing your dog's reaction to the presence of other dogs

- ✔ Observing how your dog reacts when left alone for a short period of time

Help Your Dog Help Other People

If you're interested in training your dog to be a therapy dog (who goes to hospitals and convalescent centers to bring a smile to people's faces), the Delta Society (www.deltasociety.org) is the place to start. You can find out where to take a course in your area. (Courses are offered throughout the United States and internationally.)

Courses help you select and prepare animals for visits to nursing homes, schools, hospitals, and convalescent centers. They also cover how to recognize stress in your dog and provide information regarding animal health and safety. The Delta Society course also teaches you about the special needs of specific client groups, such as children, the elderly, or the physically challenged. This course also covers the legal codes related to the facilities you'll be visiting with your dog. Prior to passing its stringent testing, your dog must be well trained.

When your mixed breed is certified, you and your dog can visit hospitals, nursing homes, and schools bringing joy and healing to everyone. You'll need to make arrangements with each organization regarding appropriate scheduled visiting times and discuss the individuals you'll be working with. The Delta Society stresses preparedness and patient confidentiality, so this preparation will help you perform a better service.

Dancing with Your Mixed Breed

Yes, you can actually dance with your dog. This sport is known as *Canine Freestyle,* because dancing with dogs is not based on a specific pattern, but rather on your ability to choreograph your movements and your dog's movements in tandem, to music, incorporating obedience, natural canine movement, and fancy trick behaviors.

Several Freestyle clubs and organizations hold events all over the United States and some throughout the world. The two largest clubs are the Canine Freestyle Federation (www.canine-freestyle.org) and The World Canine Freestyle Organization (www.worldcaninefreestyle.org). It is now offered by the AKC as a point-earning event, and mixed breeds are allowed to compete with prior approval of the AKC.

Flying High with Flyball

Flyball is a relay race. At the starting signal the dogs are sent over a series of four jumps to a box where they must trigger the release of a ball or beanbag, take hold of it, and race back to their handlers over the four jumps, carrying the ball or beanbag all the way. The first team of four dogs and handlers to complete the course wins the race. Points are assigned according to the dogs' speed.

There's a reason this sport is paired with cheering: It's fun for your dog, fun for you and your team, and fun to watch. The sport is open to all dogs — purebred and mixed breed alike.

The North American Flyball Association (www.flyball.org) is the governing body for this sport. At www.flyballdogs.com, you can get information about how the game is run, what titles are available, where to find tournaments, and how to train.

Index

BUSINESS, CAREERS & PERSONAL FINANCE

Fundraising

0-7645-9847-3

Investing

0-7645-2431-3

Also available:

- Business Plans Kit For Dummies
  0-7645-9794-9
- Economics For Dummies
  0-7645-5726-2
- Grant Writing For Dummies
  0-7645-8416-2
- Home Buying For Dummies
  0-7645-5331-3
- Managing For Dummies
  0-7645-1771-6
- Marketing For Dummies
  0-7645-5600-2

- Personal Finance For Dummies
  0-7645-2590-5*
- Resumes For Dummies
  0-7645-5471-9
- Selling For Dummies 0-7645-5363-1
- Six Sigma For Dummies
  0-7645-6798-5
- Small Business Kit For Dummies
  0-7645-5984-2
- Starting an eBay Business For
  Dummies
  0-7645-6924-4
- Your Dream Career For Dummies
  0-7645-9795-7

HOME & BUSINESS COMPUTER BASICS

Laptops

0-470-05432-8

Windows Vista

0-471-75421-8

Also available:

- Cleaning Windows Vista
  For Dummies 0-471-78293-9
- Excel 2007 For Dummies
  0-470-03737-7
- Mac OS X Tiger For Dummies
  0-7645-7675-5
- MacBook For Dummies
  0-470-04859-X
- Macs For Dummies 0-470-04849-2
- Office 2007 For Dummies
  0-470-00923-3

- Outlook 2007 For Dummies
  0-470-03830-6
- PCs For Dummies 0-7645-8958-X
- Salesforce.com For Dummies
  0-470-04893-X
- Upgrading & Fixing Laptops For
  Dummies 0-7645-8959-8
- Word 2007 For Dummies
  0-470-03658-3
- Quicken 2007 For Dummies
  0-470-04600-7

FOOD, HOME, GARDEN, HOBBIES, MUSIC & PETS

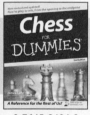

Chess

0-7645-8404-9

Guitar

0-7645-9904-6

Also available:

- Candy Making For Dummies
  0-7645-9734-5
- Card Games For Dummies
  0-7645-9910-0
- Crocheting For Dummies
  0-7645-4151-X
- Dog Training For Dummies
  0-7645-8418-9
- Healthy Carb Cookbook For
  Dummies 0-7645-8476-6

- Home Maintenance For Dummies
  0-7645-5215-5
- Horses For Dummies 0-7645-9797-3
- Jewelry Making & Beading
  For Dummies 0-7645-2571-9
- Orchids For Dummies 0-7645-6759-4
- Puppies For Dummies 0-7645-5255-4
- Rock Guitar For Dummies
  0-7645-5356-9
- Sewing For Dummies 0-7645-6847-7
- Singing For Dummies 0-7645-2475-5

INTERNET & DIGITAL MEDIA

eBay

0-470-04529-9

iPod & iTunes

0-470-04894-8

Also available:

- Blogging For Dummies
  0-471-77084-1
- Digital Photography For Dummies
  0-7645-9802-3
- Digital Photography All-in-One Desk
  Reference For Dummies
  0-470-03743-1
- Digital SLR Cameras and
  Photography For Dummies
  0-7645-9803-1
- eBay Business All-in-One Desk
  Reference For Dummies
  0-7645-8438-3

- HDTV For Dummies
  0-470-09673-X
- Home Entertainment PCs
  For Dummies 0-470-05523-5
- MySpace For Dummies
  0-470-09529-6
- Search Engine Optimization
  For Dummies 0-471-97998-8
- Skype For Dummies 0-470-04891-3
- The Internet For Dummies
  0-7645-8996-2
- Wiring Your Digital Home
  For Dummies 0-471-91830-X

* Separate Canadian edition also available

† Separate U.K. edition also available

 WILEY

SPORTS, FITNESS, PARENTING, RELIGION & SPIRITUALITY

0-471-76871-5

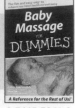

0-7645-7841-3

Also available:
- Catholicism For Dummies
  0-7645-5391-7
- Exercise Balls For Dummies
  0-7645-5623-1
- Fitness For Dummies 0-7645-7851-0
- Football For Dummies 0-7645-3936-1
- Judaism For Dummies 0-7645-5299-6
- Potty Training For Dummies
  0-7645-5417-4

- Buddhism For Dummies
  0-7645-5359-3
- Pregnancy For Dummies
  0-7645-4483-7 †
- Ten Minute Tone-Ups For Dummies
  0-7645-7207-5
- NASCAR For Dummies 0-7645-7681-
- Religion For Dummies 0-7645-5264-
- Soccer For Dummies 0-7645-5229-5
- Women in the Bible For Dummies
  0-7645-8475-8

TRAVEL

0-7645-7749-2

0-7645-6945-7

Also available:
- Alaska For Dummies 0-7645-7746-8
- Cruise Vacations For Dummies
  0-7645-6941-4
- England For Dummies 0-7645-4276-1
- Europe For Dummies 0-7645-7529-5
- Germany For Dummies
  0-7645-7823-5
- Hawaii For Dummies 0-7645-7402-7

- Italy For Dummies 0-7645-7386-1
- Las Vegas For Dummies
  0-7645-7382-9
- London For Dummies 0-7645-4277-
- Paris For Dummies 0-7645-7630-5
- RV Vacations For Dummies
  0-7645-4442-X
- Walt Disney World & Orlando
  For Dummies 0-7645-9660-8

GRAPHICS, DESIGN & WEB DEVELOPMENT

0-7645-8815-X

0-7645-9571-7

Also available:
- 3D Game Animation For Dummies
  0-7645-8789-7
- AutoCAD 2006 For Dummies
  0-7645-8925-3
- Building a Web Site For Dummies
  0-7645-7144-3
- Creating Web Pages For Dummies
  0-470-08030-2
- Creating Web Pages All-in-One Desk
  Reference For Dummies
  0-7645-4345-8
- Dreamweaver 8 For Dummies
  0-7645-9649-7

- InDesign CS2 For Dummies
  0-7645-9572-5
- Macromedia Flash 8 For Dummies
  0-7645-9691-8
- Photoshop CS2 and Digital
  Photography For Dummies
  0-7645-9580-6
- Photoshop Elements 4 For Dummies
  0-471-77483-9
- Syndicating Web Sites with RSS Feed
  For Dummies
  0-7645-8848-6
- Yahoo! SiteBuilder For Dummies
  0-7645-9800-7

NETWORKING, SECURITY, PROGRAMMING & DATABASES

0-7645-7728-X

0-471-74940-0

Also available:
- Access 2007 For Dummies
  0-470-04612-0
- ASP.NET 2 For Dummies
  0-7645-7907-X
- C# 2005 For Dummies
  0-7645-9704-3
- Hacking For Dummies
  0-470-05235-X
- Hacking Wireless Networks
  For Dummies
  0-7645-9730-2
- Java For Dummies
  0-470-08716-1

- Microsoft SQL Server 2005
  For Dummies 0-7645-7755-7
- Networking All-in-One Desk
  Reference For Dummies
  0-7645-9939-9
- Preventing Identity Theft For Dummie
  0-7645-7336-5
- Telecom For Dummies
  0-471-77085-X
- Visual Studio 2005 All-in-One Desk
  Reference For Dummies
  0-7645-9775-2
- XML For Dummies
  0-7645-8845-1

HEALTH & SELF-HELP

0-7645-8450-2   0-7645-4149-8

Also available:

- Bipolar Disorder For Dummies 0-7645-8451-0
- Chemotherapy and Radiation For Dummies 0-7645-7832-4
- Controlling Cholesterol For Dummies 0-7645-5440-9
- Diabetes For Dummies 0-7645-6820-5* †
- Divorce For Dummies 0-7645-8417-0 †
- Fibromyalgia For Dummies 0-7645-5441-7

- Low-Calorie Dieting For Dummies 0-7645-9905-4
- Meditation For Dummies 0-471-77774-9
- Osteoporosis For Dummies 0-7645-7621-6
- Overcoming Anxiety For Dummies 0-7645-5447-6
- Reiki For Dummies 0-7645-9907-0
- Stress Management For Dummies 0-7645-5144-2

EDUCATION, HISTORY, REFERENCE & TEST PREPARATION

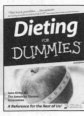

0-7645-8381-6   0-7645-9554-7

Also available:

- The ACT For Dummies 0-7645-9652-7
- Algebra For Dummies 0-7645-5325-9
- Algebra Workbook For Dummies 0-7645-8467-7
- Astronomy For Dummies 0-7645-8465-0
- Calculus For Dummies 0-7645-2498-4
- Chemistry For Dummies 0-7645-5430-1
- Forensics For Dummies 0-7645-5580-4

- Freemasons For Dummies 0-7645-9796-5
- French For Dummies 0-7645-5193-0
- Geometry For Dummies 0-7645-5324-0
- Organic Chemistry I For Dummies 0-7645-6902-3
- The SAT I For Dummies 0-7645-7193-1
- Spanish For Dummies 0-7645-5194-9
- Statistics For Dummies 0-7645-5423-9

Get smart @ dummies.com®

- Find a full list of Dummies titles
- Look into loads of FREE on-site articles
- Sign up for FREE eTips e-mailed to you weekly
- See what other products carry the Dummies name
- Shop directly from the Dummies bookstore
- Enter to win new prizes every month!

* Separate Canadian edition also available
† Separate U.K. edition also available

Available wherever books are sold. For more information or to order direct: U.S. customers visit www.dummies.com or call 1-877-762-2974.
U.K. customers visit www.wileyeurope.com or call 0800 243407. Canadian customers visit www.wiley.ca or call 1-800-567-4797.